The Jews and the Bible

STANFORD STUDIES IN JEWISH HISTORY AND CULTURE

EDITED BY *Aron Rodrigue and Steven J. Zipperstein*

The Jews and the Bible

Jean-Christophe Attias

TRANSLATED BY PATRICK CAMILLER

STANFORD UNIVERSITY PRESS
STANFORD, CALIFORNIA

Stanford University Press
Stanford, California

The Jews and the Bible was originally published in French in 2012 under the title Les Juifs et la Bible ©Librairie Arthème Fayard.

This work was published with the help of the Centre national du livre (CNL).

Printed in the United States of America on acid-free, archival-quality paper

Library of Congress Cataloging-in-Publication Data

Attias, Jean-Christophe, author.
  [Juifs et la Bible. English]
  The Jews and the Bible / Jean-Christophe Attias ; translated by Patrick Camiller.
      pages cm—(Stanford studies in Jewish history and culture)
  "Originally published in French in 2012 under the title Les juifs et la Bible."
  Includes bibliographical references and index.
  ISBN 978-0-8047-8907-3 (cloth : alk. paper)—
  ISBN 978-0-8047-9319-3 (pbk. : alk. paper)
    1. Bible. Old Testament—Criticism, interpretation, etc., Jewish—History.
  2. Judaism—Doctrines. 3. Jews—Identity. I. Title. II. Series: Stanford studies in Jewish history and culture.
  BS1186.A8713 2014
  221.6088'296—dc23
                                        2014023174
  ISBN 978-0-8047-9321-6 (electronic)

Typeset by Bruce Lundquist in 10.5/14 Galliard

Contents

Acknowledgments

The plan for this book began to take shape in 1999. I was busy with other things over the next twelve years, writing and publishing on a number of subjects, but the idea never left me. Nor did I ever abandon it.

Many encouraged me to see it through and helped me along the way. It is hard to mention all who, in one way or another, have been part of this adventure. First among them has been Esther Benbassa, my companion, professor of Modern Jewish History at the École pratique des hautes études (Sorbonne, Paris), and most often my initial reader.

The Alberto Benveniste Center for the study of Sephardi culture and history, part of the École pratique des hautes études, has accommodated and generously supported my work since its foundation in 2001, and I greatly appreciate the freedom and comfort it provides to its researchers.

I am also grateful to my students and others at the École for their patient attention over the years. I was able to try out on them at seminars some of the ideas I later developed in these pages.

Thanks also to the conference organizers and journal editors who gave me the opportunity to formulate those ideas in an early, often fragmentary and imperfect, form.

I also think with gratitude of the devoted staff who allowed me access to all the documentation I needed at libraries in France or during study trips abroad: the Library of the Alliance israélite universelle in Paris, the National and University Library in Jerusalem, the libraries of Columbia University and the Jewish Theological Seminary in New York, and many others.

Thanks are also due to Fayard, the publisher of the first, French edition of this work; to Stanford University Press, which has included this edition in the prestigious Stanford Studies in Jewish History and Culture series founded by Aron Rodrigue and Steven J. Zipperstein; and to the Centre national du Livre (Paris), which partly subsidized the costs of the translation.

Last but not least, I would like to express a debt of gratitude to my translator, Patrick Camiller. I have long appreciated—and now appreciate once again—the talent, sensitivity, and unfailing dedication that he places at the service of authors fortunate enough to work with him.

Note on Transcriptions and Biblical and Rabbinical Quotations

The transcription from Hebrew and Aramaic follows the norms of the *Encyclopedia Judaica*, with a few simplifications. Diacritic signs are not used. No distinction is made between *alef* and *ayin*. *He* and *het* are both transcribed as *h*. The *u* should always be read as "oo," and the *e* is always short.

Some words (such as those of certain feasts or bodies of work) and some personal names, however, appear in a form more commonly used in English, even when this departs from the general transcription norms used in this book.

As a general rule, biblical quotations follow the Jewish Publication Society's Tanakh Translation (1985, 1999) in *The Jewish Study Bible* (Oxford University Press, 2003, 2004). But in a few cases, where the context demands it, the text may differ from this translation. Except where indicated, all other translations from the Hebrew are by the author and translator.

Prologue

> In the beginning [*Be-reshit*],
> God created heaven and earth.
>
> Genesis 1.1

The Bible is the book of childhood—for each one of us, at whichever age we discover it. The Bible is the book of childhood because it presents itself as the book of beginnings, and we like to believe it is, or to pretend we do. It is precisely this illusion that Judaism tries hard to dispel.

Here, to begin with, is a first illustration.

The beginning, if ever there was one, is before. It is elsewhere. It is something else. The Bible "begins" with the second letter of the Hebrew alphabet—the initial *bet* of *Be-reshit*—not with the first, *alef*.[1] The "beginning" to which it refers is at best a relative beginning— only the start of the process of creating heaven and earth—not an absolute beginning. But is it even a relative beginning? Perhaps *reshit* simply means something else.

First interpretation: *reshit* is really the Torah*,[2] the Law given by God to Israel, which is the Bible itself but also much more and other than the Bible alone. In Proverbs 8.22, the Torah calls itself *reshit*: "The Lord created me at the beginning [*reshit*] of His course / As the first of His works of old." [3] It is by and for the Torah, the only really absolute beginning, that God created this world. The Torah, which was the model for it,[4] and is also its end.

Second interpretation: *reshit* is also Israel. As it is said in Jeremiah 2.3: "Israel was holy to the Lord, the firstfruits [*reshit*] of His harvest." This world was created for Israel, and in this, as in everything else, the end— Israel—is the true beginning.

Besides, the Bible should have begun, not with Genesis 1.1, but with another verse: "This month shall mark for you the beginning[5] of the

months . . ." (Exod. 12.2). Why? Because this verse from Exodus introduces the first of the commandments given to Israel as a people, the
sacrifice of the paschal lamb.[6]

Question: in that case, why begin the Bible with the account of
the creation of the world? To integrate Israel's history into a universal
narrative: the history of the world and of the human race? Perhaps
not. Perhaps the exact opposite. Maybe God just wanted to remind
the nations that, being the omnipotent creator of this world, he was
free to dispose of it as he wished, and that through a free, sovereign,
and legitimate act of will, he would take the Land, always destined for
Israel, from the peoples who occupied it "in the beginning."[7]

This suddenly makes the Bible different from what it was for us
as children: the book of the history of absolute beginnings. It simply
ceases to be history and becomes revealed Law. It places the beginning
at a different time and place from the ones we imagined. And it tears
us away from abstract universality to speak of the particular mission of
a single people. A singular mission, indeed, though with an ultimately
universal scope. According to the third-century Jewish teacher Resh
Lakish, if Israel had refused the Torah (when God presented it on
Sinai) that would have sufficed for the world He created "in the beginning" to return to outright chaos.[8]

The subject of this work is the special link that the Jews formed with
the Bible. It was an unstable, ambiguous link—and if there is another
illusion we need to shake off in these pages, it is the one that makes
us think of the Bible as the "founding book" of Judaism. It is not the
book of the beginnings, nor is it the book of the foundations. In any
case, much more than the Bible itself, it is the unstable, ambiguous
link they have formed with it that has made Jews and Judaism what
they are.

So, the reader should not be taken in by the deceptive—biblical,
one might say—simplicity of the title of this work, *The Jews and the
Bible*. The "and" joining the two terms hides a dense undergrowth
packed with lures and traps. We shall see the Jews define themselves
in various times and places *with* the Bible, *without* the Bible, *against*

the Bible. With the Bible, but not with it alone. Without the Bible, but never completely without it. Against the Bible, but at the same time always "right up against it." We shall see the Bible itself escape any unambiguous definition. One book, or a disparate library? Text or object? Divine revelation or national myth? Literature or legislative code? Space of dialogue or field of battle? Pretext for all regressions or springboard for all changes? For the Jews, over the past two thousand years or more, the Bible has been all that and much else besides; the various metamorphoses of the Jews themselves are there to be read in the Bible and in the sundry relationships they have constructed with it. Not that the metamorphoses of their opponents or rivals have been less numerous: indeed, the Bible has also been brandished *against* the Jews to convince them of their error, to convert them, to demonstrate the supposed baseness or mediocrity of their nature.

This gives us full measure of the task lurking behind that little "and." To dare take it on, it was necessary to be unthinking, foolhardy, even presumptuous. No doubt such a subject called for a *summa*: a vast, ambitious historical fresco, a kind of grand "Book on the Book." But was that reasonable? Was it within the powers of one individual? Would it indeed be useful? Perhaps an essay would have been more appropriate: an essay that, to be sure of affecting its contemporaries, would have centered on some of the burning issues of the day. I am not unaware of those burning issues: they will be touched upon here and there in these pages. But I did not want to make them my chief focus.

Whatever radical secularists say, the Bible is not only a war cry, a firebrand, a weapon in the hands of fundamentalists of every ilk. In fact, the Bible is nothing in and of itself. No one can claim to be restoring its "original" meaning. Its "literal" meaning does not exist: only "a-theologians" in a hurry think that it does, and only fundamentalists try to make us believe it. Like the Koran, the Bible has never been anything other than what its readers make of it. And after all, in more than two millennia of tireless interpretation, the Jews have made of it a thousand other things than, for example, the absolute reference for a violent ultranationalism obsessively attached to the least West Bank hillock. I was not going to begin with that—even to win over my readers.

Neither a *summa* nor an essay, then. I chose a different option: a freer, more sinuous, more meditative path that sets out to inform, instruct, and enlighten. But it will also leave some things out and question others, sometimes disturb, even go astray from, shattering truths that are taken for granted, and enable others to be recovered. It will strengthen and deepen, sometimes also abolish, the sense of familiar strangeness that the Bible inevitably arouses in all of us, whether we are Jews or non-Jews, whether we believe in Heaven or not.

✳

Abraham breathed his last . . . and was gathered to his kin.

Genesis 25.8

The Bible, I said, is the book of childhood. It was the book of my childhood too. And the book of my father. So the present work is also, more than indirectly, a homage to my childhood—and to my father. In my childhood, apart from the Bible, and apart from my father, I had almost nothing to attach me to Judaism. Of course, I knew very early on that there was some connection between the Old Testament and the New, or some hiatus where (since my mother was not Jewish) I myself was situated. To my child's eyes, however, the link between the Bible and my father was clear—especially as it was he who, having decided to brush up his own knowledge of Hebrew, taught me the basics of it when I was around ten, so that I became vaguely capable of deciphering and stumbling through my first verses without really understanding them.

I, a child, discovered Judaism in the Bible, and I then spent the rest of my life discovering, understanding, and finally teaching that Judaism was something other than what I, as a child, had discovered in the Bible. That discrepancy—between what we think the Bible tells us about Judaism and what Judaism actually tells us about the Bible—is precisely the ground explored in this book.

I do not know what the Bible meant to my father during his childhood in prewar Algeria. He never told me, and I never asked him. What I do know, though, or anyway guess, is what it meant to him in the final years of his life.

For my father devoted those years to a curious activity, which he admitted to me only grudgingly, as though it were a secret garden, to be kept truly secret. On large blank sheets of paper, which he carefully filed in plastic folders, he first copied out almost the entire text of the Hebrew Bible, in a fine, rounded cursive script, word by word, letter by letter, without omitting a single vowel sign. Then, feeling that this was not enough, he enlisted the help of all the existing versions in French for his most ambitious task yet: to translate the text into his native language. But that, it is clear, was still not sufficient. Drawing on the Jewish library he had amassed over the years, he set out to produce a commentary of his own, at least on certain passages.

This huge enterprise left behind an impressive pile of folders, which I looked at almost incredulously and skimmed rather than actually read. In any event, my father did not finish anything: neither the copy nor the translation nor the commentary. His labors, performed outside any constituted "Jewish community," were addressed mainly to himself, in the little village where he lived with my mother and was the lone Jew.

I did not ask my father what all this really meant to him. But his incomplete translation, his fragments of commentary, never had value except for himself. His copy has importance only as the single tangible trace left by his own hand. It was a peculiar pastime that accompanied my father in the years up to his death. Peculiar? Perhaps not. It may simply be that, after a long life spent far from the Jews and Judaism, this was the means he had found to reestablish the link, to reinsert himself into a genealogy, perhaps mythical and strangely disembodied, but a genealogy all the same. His end had brought him back to a kind of beginning.

A few hundred kilometers away, his son was teaching Judaism in Paris, home to one of the largest Jewish communities in Europe—teaching Judaism and beginning to plan this book.

The Jews and the Bible

One   An Elusive Book?

Bible. Secularized, in everyday language, the word has become a common noun; a "bible," in lower case, is then no more than a (usually thick) work that explores a subject or a wide yet definite field of interest, enjoying a special authority for its readers. A bargain-hunter's bible, an amateur gardener's bible, a gun collector's bible, a Chinese cookery bible—the possibilities are endless. These are profane uses of the term, of course, but they already give us some idea of what ordinary mortals make of the model: *the* Bible. With a capital B.

The Bible is a thick work too—except when printed on the famous "bible paper," a super-lightweight grade, which seems to emphasize by contrast the richness of a content that defies compression. And it enjoys a special authority, at least in the eyes of the faithful who adhere to its teachings and seek in it their spiritual sustenance. The Bible, the actual one, is indisputably all of that, and it is not hard to recognize in the original what led to and justified the metaphorical uses made of its name.

Still, even the least sophisticated of its potential readers are well aware, or should be, that the resemblance stops there. The Bible is obviously more than that. Having just opened it or leafed through it a little, or even read a fair number of its pages, one has some difficulty identifying the "subject" or the "wide yet definite field of interest" that the Bible encompasses. Indeed, without a special shelf on "religious literature," it would be far from easy to decide where it should go in one's bookcase.

Its place is not with novels, nor does it bear an author's name; all kinds of literature are represented within it. Prose and poetry, narrative and law, feats of arms and love stories: almost nothing is missing. But that is not a defect for its readers, since the very profusion of genres maintains the illusion of a total book. A unique book. A book par excellence—does not the word "bible" simply mean "book?"—and one like no other.

But there is more. Does not its antiquity, even at a rough estimate, confer on the Bible every appearance of a "book of origins"? Whether welcomed or deplored, is it not the case that this international bestseller, translated into every language and found in countless hotel drawers around the world, is the founding text of "Western" or "Judeo-Christian" civilization, whose military, economic, cultural, and symbolic imperium has established itself over the centuries and in a way still stretches over almost the entire globe? Is this not why even readers with no religious belief continue to feel considerable respect for it, mingled with a degree of fear?

None of these assumptions stands up to scrutiny, however. First of all, the Bible is not the oldest book of our shared humanity. To be sure, with its various Hebrew and Aramaic strata, it does bring together nine centuries of literary output, starting with a few archaic hymns (e.g., the Song of Deborah in Judges 5), but closing rather late, in the second century BCE, with the Book of Daniel. In the scale of human history, that makes it a compendium of only relative antiquity.

Nor is it so voluminous. It consists of selections made by particular individuals, which doubtless add up to little in comparison with all that the vagaries of history and the omissions and injustices of later generations have eliminated. Ancient Hebrew literature was much richer and more diverse than what we find in the pages of our Bibles. The very language of the surviving body of text—a grand total of 300,000 words—is rather poor: the biblical vocabulary contains 8,000 words, including 2,100 hapax legomena (that is, terms that appear only once, whose meaning is therefore not always perfectly clear). It is thought that 68 percent of the Hebrew words in use in biblical times are absent from the Bible.[1] Had all the author-compilers of the Hebrew Bible been keen to use the entire vocabulary at their disposal, their book would have been much larger and said many more things. Such was evidently not their intention, and economical literature may, of course, be great literature.

If the Bible is not the vast, ancient, magnificent book one likes to imagine, is it at least the founding book of a civilization that is, perhaps a little hastily, defined in a single sweep as "Western" or "Judeo-Christian"?

To be blunt, that may be no less true of Homer—or, more generally, of what might be called the Greco-Latin humanities. The Bible is at most, together with them, one of the foundations of this civilization. Moreover, its relations with them down the ages have ranged, according to the context and milieu, from open conflict to virtual osmosis. And when, from the Renaissance on, it gradually became subject to the same critical and editorial procedures that scholars applied to the pagan literature of antiquity, its text ended up losing in authority what it gained in philological correctness.

"Western civilization" and "Judeo-Christian civilization" are anyway difficult to define and do not overlap exactly. We know how much these civilizations owe to their contacts with the Muslim world, notwithstanding occasional attempts to question or deny this.[2] Furthermore, the Bible has not played the same role for Catholics and for Protestants; it has been the catalyst of deep divisions and violent conflicts, a terrain of struggle no less than of confluence or shared identity. In the contemporary epoch, its status has largely depended on national idiosyncrasies. To take a single example, no one would dream of comparing its central place in North America to the scant respect that secular France has shown for it in recent times.

So, what are we left with? The Bible as the founding text of two of the great monotheisms: Judaism and Christianity? That is not sure either. And it is precisely this zone of uncertainty that the present work explores.

A Strangely Plural Singular

The word itself, deceptive and paradoxical, will be enough to get us started. For it is doubtful whether the Bible is actually one *book*. The singular number creates an illusion and obscures a complex history. "Bible" does, it is true, come from the singular Latin feminine noun *biblia*, but that is only the medieval latinization of a Greek neuter plural: *ta biblia*, "the record books." The Bible is not one book but primarily and historically a collection of books, a library.

In Western Christendom it became a *book*, and *one* book, only in the course of the High Middle Ages. This passage from plural to singular is recorded in historical time, and it was probably not determined a priori, from all eternity, by the intrinsic or "original" nature of the texts that eventually made up the Bible. In fact, it may tell us less about the idea that its readers formed of a unity underlying the collection than it does about the changing perception of it "as a book" in the most material sense of the word: "a book that will be owned, carried around and studied, not simply a sacred text whose magnificence accompanies the liturgy."[3]

In Judaism, this unification process was never fully completed, and although the Bible has been read and interpreted "as a book,"[4] even an absolute book, for nearly two millennia, Jews have never lost sight of its heterogeneity and plural composition. Indeed, this awareness has been deliberately nurtured. This is already apparent in the varying harmonics of the words denoting the scriptural corpus in rabbinical language.

Words for the Bible

The Bible is commonly referred to as *that which is read*: in Hebrew, *ha-Mikra*, literally, "the Reading." The term serves to designate both the scriptural text as a whole and one of its minimum components; a simple verse may also be called *mikra*. Based on a Semitic root (*kr'*), also found in the Arabic *Kur'an* (Koran), the word evokes—especially in the language of the Bible itself—the notion of a "call" or "summons," as in the expression *mikra kodesh* ("holy convocation" or "religious gathering"). In fact, in rabbinical Judaism, the ritual reading of certain biblical books or fragments forms the core of the great collective celebrations of Shabbat* and the festivals; it periodically brings together the community of believers and crystallizes it regardless of age or gender.[5]

Another word for the Bible in the rabbinical tradition is *ha-Katuv*: "that which is written." This term, which acquires its full meaning only in relation to *that which is not written*, but like the teachings of the Oral Tradition may be vested with comparable authority, serves, within the rabbinical literature, to designate and introduce a biblical *quotation* in support of an idea, teaching, or religious prescription. Similarly, the term *ketuvim* (the plural of *katuv*) is used for a part—

only one part, not the entirety—of the canon of the Jewish Bible: the "Hagiographa" or "*Ketuvim*."

It can hardly be denied that, bearing in mind their ambiguous uses, neither *mikra* nor *katuv* can be reasonably presented as an equivalent of our "Bible." It is clearly not a question here of "Bible," or even of "book" in the usual sense of the word.

Other terms come closer, of course, but care needs to be taken with them too. Thus, the Hebrew singular *sefer*, ordinarily and correctly translated as "book," is not a particularly apt term for the Bible as a whole, rather than for that part, admittedly considered essential, which is known as the Book of Law, the Five Books of Moses, or the Pentateuch. It refers to these especially when the Pentateuch is presented in the form of the Sefer Torah*, the Scroll of the Law,[6] as it is read aloud during synagogue services. For "the Bible," the preferred term is the plural *ha-sefarim* ("the books") or, more precisely, *sifrei ha-kodesh* ("the holy books") or *kitvei ha-kodesh* ("the holy writings"). Hebrew seems more resistant than Latin, or English, to a slipping from the plural (*ta biblia*) to the singular (*biblia*).

Another common Hebrew term for the Bible is *TaNaKh*, a simple acronym, devoid of meaning in itself, constructed from the initial letters of the three words referring to the tripartite structure of Scripture: *Torah*, *Nevi'im*, and *Ketuvim* (the Law, Prophets, and Writings). Here, the very designation of the whole seems to have the primary function of recalling its composite character. The Book, if Book there is, is not one but at least three. And these three books, each in turn a collection of books, but ultimately part of the single biblical canon, do not at all have the same status in the eyes of rabbis, nor are they vested with the same authority. The highlighted plurality and diversity of the documents making up the Bible here go together with their arrangement in a hierarchy.

In this context, the Pentateuch enjoys absolute preeminence. In antiquity, it rather than the Bible was the common ground for all the Jewish sects, tendencies and "heresies," however tense and conflictual their relations with one another.[7] In the Jewish literature in Greek, from the end of the second century BCE on, the Pentateuch alone is called *hē biblos*, "the Book."[8] And for Philo of Alexandria (13 BCE to 54 CE), the leading representative of Hellenistic Jewish culture,[9] who read it in Greek translation, the Pentateuch or the Law of Moses was always the only "Scripture." Although he sometimes mentions other books, all his commentaries bear on it—apparently because he thought it the only one worthwhile.[10]

Rabbis never challenged this preeminence, even after a much larger canon of holy books was finalized. The Sefer Torah, the Scroll of the Law read at services, must unfailingly contain all five books of the Pentateuch—Genesis, Exodus, Leviticus, Numbers, and Deuteronomy—none of which may be copied separately.[11] On the other hand, according to a talmudic* teaching, "the Pentateuch, Prophets, and the Hagiographa must be written in separate books,"[12] and in the twelfth century, long after the codex form had been adopted for nonliturgical uses (which favored the grouping of biblical books in a single volume),[13] the philosopher, physician, and halakhist* Moses ben Maimon, or Maimonides (1138–1204; also referred to by the acronym for Rabbi Moshe ben Maimon: RaMBaM),[14] still seems to have recommended that the Bible be copied in three different volumes.[15]

The privileged position of the Pentateuch is not the only sign that a sense of the disparateness, or even fragmentariness, of the biblical corpus was deliberately maintained. The Pentateuch is itself made up of five distinct books. And, just as the word *TaNaKh*, denoting the Bible as a whole, stubbornly reminds us of its composite character, there is a traditional formula for the Pentateuch that displays the same exemplary ambiguity: *hamishah humshei Torah*, literally "the five fifths of the Law." What should we understand by this? That the Pentateuch is both five and one, that it is one only on the condition that it is five, and that these five fifths together inextricably constitute the Law. And they constitute the *whole* Law, since it is contained in its entirety in those five books. This inevitably raises the question of the status of the other books of the Jewish biblical corpus: the books of the prophets and the Hagiographa. Are they not the Law?

A Heterogeneous and Hierarchical Corpus

The canonization of the Hebrew Bible—that is, the establishment of a biblical corpus of sacred writings, to the exclusion of all others, by rabbinical Judaism—was a lengthy and complex process. The Torah, the core of Mosaic Revelation, was the first to receive this consecration. In the form that we know it today, the Pentateuch made its appearance between the Exile (586 BCE)[16] and the beginning of the Hellenistic period,[17] and was probably finalized in the last third of the fourth century BCE. The importance of the Law in Judean society after the return from Babylon (538 BCE)[18]—some writers have spoken of a "nomocracy"—gave a powerful stimulus to the crystallization and stabilization of the text.[19] Critics generally find there a high degree of coherence, arguing that the initially disparate materials comprising it were manifestly edited in such a way that they became a book.[20]

This does not mean that contradictions, duplication, and inconsistencies simply disappeared—far from it. For the editing work did not result in—and probably never aimed at—an absolutely perfect fusion of the different textual traditions, or an elimination of the diversity of style and inspiration reflected in them. More generally, the literary characterization of the whole remains a matter of debate.

In terms of material, the Pentateuch is divided almost equally between legislative and narrative texts. It tells of the history of the world, especially of the people of Israel, from the creation of heaven and earth down to the death of Moses. But one also finds there an impressive number of legal requirements and religious practices, in an order of exposition that (at least for today's reader) is not always transparent. In this respect, the Book of Leviticus—the third of the five books— introduces a clear and excessively long break in the narrative structure of the Pentateuch, which ancient and modern commentators have had some difficulty in explaining.[21]

It has been suggested that the Pentateuch may at first have been a narrative, to which legal sections were then added to the point where they became essential; or else that it was originally a book of law that was then endowed with a narrative framework over the centuries.[22] In Hebrew, however, the very word *Torah*—whose first testified use to designate the Pentateuch dates from the second century BCE— evidently refers to something other and more than a history, but also to something other and more than a law.[23] This ambiguous literary status allowed the Christian tradition to interpret the Pentateuch as an ancient history of Israel, whereas Judaism saw it first of all as the Book of the Law.

Whatever the ambiguity of its literary status, it appears that the Pentateuch is the (direct or indirect) result of Persia's promulgation of a "law of the Jews," valid for all of them living in the satrapy of Syria, in line with the well-attested policy of officially sanctioning local laws.[24] This would explain the nonprophetic, even anti-eschatological, tone of this document—the fact that it contains virtually nothing that might have been interpreted as a challenge to Persian power, and does not include traditions relating to Israel's territorial conquests or testifying to its ambition to establish a sovereign state. All this may be found in another segment of the canon, with less authority, agreed upon at a later date.[25]

In any event, even after the context of its emergence as a legal document had disappeared, Judaism—and rabbinical Judaism in particular—never ceased to recognize the precedence of the Pentateuch within the biblical canon; this has given it unequaled authority up to the present day, and maintained the essential principle of the heterogeneity of the canon itself, the *TaNaKh*. The canonization of the *TaNaKh*—crucially beginning with that of the Pentateuch (Torah) in the Persian period—actually extended over several centuries, encompassing the books of the prophets (*Nevi'im*) only in the late Persian and early Hellenistic periods, and the Hagiographa (*Ketuvim*) only around the time of the destruction of the Second Temple (70 CE).[26]

This process of canonization presupposed, entailed, and perpetuated a distance from the prophetic tradition itself. To finalize the canon is to indicate that no other "inspired" book (or none that claims to be such) can be added to it. But to confer an absolute, definitive authority on Moses and his prophecy in the Pentateuch is to assert that no subsequent prophet—even if included in the canon—may be regarded as his equal. Although, in certain teachings of the mishnic* and talmudic era, a proof derived from the books of the prophets or the Hagiographa still counted as a proof derived from the "Torah," it tended to become an absolute rule that no law could be inferred from assertions that drew on post-Mosaic books of the Bible.[27]

The Torah was given to Moses in its entirety on Mount Sinai. All later revelation imputed to the post-Mosaic prophets was in fact *already* handed down to Moses there.[28] No one may argue against an explicit teaching of the Mosaic Torah from a teaching in the books of the prophets. Limited to a role of reminding and admonishing, the latter update and confirm a Law that precedes and governs them, and any Jewish exegete worthy of the name is duty bound to dispel in favor of the Mosaic Torah any apparent contradiction (and all such contradictions can only be apparent) between the teachings of the greatest of the prophets and those of his successors—one almost dares to say, of his epigones. Is it not written, at the very end of the Pentateuch, that "never again did there arise in the land of Israel a prophet like Moses—whom the Lord singled out, face to face" (Deut. 34.10)?

If the books of the prophets have an ambiguous status in the biblical canon (they are inspired but do no more than confirm the revelation that precedes them), what can be said of the Hagiographa? It is well known that this third set of texts was not considered finally closed until sometime in the second century CE. The canonicity of Song of Songs, Proverbs, and Ecclesiastes, three works traditionally attributed to King Solomon and associated with the three ages of his life (youth, maturity, and old age), was thus the object of protracted debates. So too was that of the Book of Esther.

Could such texts really be thought of as divinely inspired? To take just a couple of examples, a hurried or uninitiated reader cannot fail to be astonished that the canon includes a near-licentious love song such as Song of Songs and a narrative like the Book of Esther, with its indecent episodes, its pretty Jewish heroine who is willing to marry out and who decides only after some hesitation to risk her life for her people, and—a curious detail—the apparently total absence of God from it. Philo, for one, never quotes Song of Songs,[29] and only a purely allegorical exegesis was finally able to "save" it in the first to second century,[30] when Rabbi Akiba explained its profane loves as an allegory for the relations between God and his people.[31] The Book of Esther, however, still needed to be "redeemed" by a reading that placed it "in the best possible light."[32]

In this case, however, at least according to certain masters quoted in the Talmud*, it is not just the general tone of the narrative but a *juridical* point that might present a problem. For how is possible to reconcile the absolute principle that no prophet after Moses can introduce a substantive innovation with the fact that Esther and Mordecai established a new festival, Purim*, to commemorate the rescue of the

Jews from Persia, long after the giving of the Law at Sinai? Fortunately, it would not be too difficult for an ad hoc exegesis to find allusions to its establishment elsewhere than in the Book of Esther—most
notably in the Pentateuch. And some rabbis did not hesitate to settle
the question more generally by asserting that "this scroll [of Esther]
was revealed to Moses at Sinai."[33]

The Torah thus ensures against possible challenge the canonical status of the Book of Esther—yet another sign of the heterogeneity of
the canon and the privileged place of the Pentateuch in the hierarchy
of its components. One can imagine that the books of the prophets or
the Hagiographa will one day be annulled, says Rabbi Yohanan, but
never the five books of Moses![34]

Figures and Books

If further illustration is needed of this consistent Jewish awareness of
the composite character of the Bible—a "book" that is perhaps quite
simply not one, and in a sense should not become one—a final traditional term for the corpus perhaps speaks more eloquently than all the
others: the Jewish Bible is commonly known in Hebrew as "the twenty-
four books." Here the plural is once more de rigueur. The figure clearly
has a limiting function: no twenty-fifth book may be admitted, on pain
of introducing (according to an ancient rabbinical teaching) a harmful
confusion.[35] But twenty-four there are: the five books of the Pentateuch; the eight books of the prophets—the three "major" prophets,[36]
plus Joshua and Judges (which makes five), Samuel 1 and 2 together
(making six), Kings 1 and 2 together (seven),[37] and the twelve "minor"
prophets[38] together (eight); and the Hagiographa in eleven books,
treating Chronicles 1 and 2 as a single book, and Ezra and Nehemiah
likewise. So, "twenty-four books" to make "one" Jewish Bible.

Twenty-four? Unless, as the Jewish soldier and historian Josephus
(Yosef ben Matityahu, or Flavius Josephus; 38–c. 100 CE)[39] thought,
it is only twenty-two, like the number of letters in the Hebrew alphabet. "We have only twenty-two books," not "an innumerable multitude," Josephus contended; they "contain the justly credited records
of all the past times."[40] His list comprised the five books of Moses,
the thirteen in which "the prophets who came after Moses told the

history of their time," and four collections of "hymns to God" and "moral precepts." There are two possible explanations for the apparent lack of two books: either Song of Songs and Ecclesiastes had not yet, in Josephus's time, been included in the Jewish canon; or, more likely, Josephus ran the Book of Ruth together with Judges,[41] and Lamentations with the Book of Jeremiah. This would mean that, in his approach to and structuring of the biblical corpus, he relied at least partly on the Judeo-Greek rather than Hebrew tradition.

Bibles, Canons, and Languages

Here arises another dimension of uncertainty about the status of the Bible, both as a "book" and as a "Jewish book." For, apart from the fact that it is a singularly plural book, and that it is not the "whole" Bible in the eyes of Christian readers (who add a "New" or "Second" Testament), the Hebrew Bible that we know—which anyway can only approximately be described as "Hebrew," since it contains more than one passage in Aramaic[42]—did not always hold undivided sway over the Jewish world itself. Its twenty-four books, and their arrangement in three separate sequences, with a hierarchy of authority, did not at once command everyone's unreserved recognition. It finally prevailed only at the expense of other options, after a long process of selecting and fixing the texts that composed it.

Although the ancient Jewish world could agree on the idea of a set of divinely inspired books somehow set apart from all others, their list, number, and even content fluctuated for a long time. In the age of Jesus there was quite simply no Bible in the sense we understand today; indeed, it would seem that sentences altogether unknown in our Bibles were commonly quoted then as "Scripture."[43] The existence of the Samaritan* Pentateuch, the discoveries of Qumran, and the Greek so-called Septuagint translation prove that a variety of textual traditions coexisted with one another until the end of the Second Temple period (70 CE).

For the Samaritans*—who considered themselves direct descendants of the tribes issuing from Joseph (that is, Ephraim and Manasseh), and who held that it was not in Jerusalem but on Mount Gerizim, to the south of Sichem in Samaria, that God chose to establish his name and to have himself worshipped[44]—Moses was the prophet par excellence (Joshua being the only other biblical prophet they held in great esteem), and the Pentateuch was the only holy book. Moreover, the version of the Pentateuch that had authority in their eyes differed in certain ways from the one in our Bibles today. All allusions to Jerusalem as the center of worship were changed to Sichem and Mount Gerizim. And the Decalogue*, which for the Samaritans actually numbered nine commandments, was supplemented by a tenth that asserted the primacy of Mount Gerizim.

At Qumran, northwest of the Dead Sea, in the Judean Desert, the Essene* segment of ancient Judaism—which disappeared after the great defeat of 70 CE—gave up many of its secrets between 1947 and 1956, when a dozen more or less complete scrolls were found, along with a large collection of mostly fragmentary texts. The trove included numerous copies of biblical books (including an almost intact Isaiah), which are the oldest biblical manuscripts available to us today, as well as fragments of the Apocrypha and Pseudepigrapha. But there were also original writings not known from any other place, which cannot be related to any known biblical tradition, yet were vested with eminent, probably equivalent, authority for the community that read and studied them.[45]

As to the Greek Septuagint—a title referring to the seventy, or more precisely seventy-two, Jewish scholars who, according to an ancient tradition, translated the Pentateuch—it was the Holy Scripture of Greek-speaking Jewish communities from the middle of the third century BCE to the early centuries CE. Quite close to the Hebrew corpus that would eventually be established, it nevertheless differs from it, not only in language, but also in content and in its way of numbering and ordering the books. It demonstrates, if that was necessary, that a "Bible" is not only the mathematical sum of the books included in it. The logic of classification is here decisive, as are the interactions between the whole and the parts or among the parts themselves.

The Septuagint, a translation of the Hebrew Bible, is therefore something both more and other than that. It also contains translations of texts originally written in Hebrew or Aramaic but not included in the Hebrew canon, as well as original texts written directly in Greek.

Begun in the middle of the third century BCE, the process of its production stretched over several hundreds of years. For this reason it is
far from presenting the features of a stylistic and linguistic unity, and
the translators' methods seem to have ranged all the way from the dri-
est literalism to the freest paraphrase. It is not certain that the body of
text that has come down to us should be regarded as more than a near-
fortuitous aggregation of documents with diverse origins. Nor is it easy
to specify what might be legitimately considered "the" canon of the
Septuagint, whose establishment was in fact largely contemporaneous
with the emergence of the Hebrew Bible as a collection of sacred texts.

With the exception of a few fragments, all the manuscript copies are
of Christian origin. In any event, the overall structure of the Judeo-
Greek corpus appears to have clearly followed a different logic from
that of the Hebrew corpus. The Hagiographa do not appear in it as
a distinct set of texts, and, although the Torah has pride of place by
virtue of its age and preeminence, a four-part structure—Pentateuch,
historical books, poetical and didactic writings, prophetic books—is
preferred to the tripartite organization of the Hebrew Bible.

This type of arrangement combines literary with chronological
criteria. In contrast to the "concentricity" of the Hebrew corpus, in
which the Torah is the core of Revelation, the books of the prophets update and confirm it, and the Hagiographa function as a "complement,"
the Septuagint favors a more "linear," even historical, conception.[46] But
this "historicization" of the corpus—evident in Josephus, whose Bible
is tripartite, but who mentions "annals" in reference to it and makes all
the prophets historians—is most certainly not neutral. We are talking of
a qualitatively "different" Bible. It is a different *Jewish* Bible, to be sure,
but Christians would have no difficulty taking it over as part of a larger
whole and seeing it as "a *history* leading up to fulfilment of the prophecies, particularly those of the coming of the Christ, which is the subject
of the New Testament."[47]

This appropriation of the Septuagint, making it the biblical reference text for all Christian authors in the early centuries, partly explains
the defiance and hostility that it eventually aroused in the Jewish world,
as well as its general replacement with new translations from the third
century on. The very text of the Septuagint became an issue of dispute,
as Christians either invoked the Greek against the original Hebrew

or accused Jews of falsification or mutilation.[48] With the exception of Byzantium, where debate continued, for example, over whether reading the Bible in Greek was enough to fulfil one's weekly liturgical obligations,[49] the Jewish tradition of Greek translation of Scripture, exemplified by the Septuagint, underwent a near-total eclipse; other translations or paraphrases took over (in Aramaic, and later in Arabic), and above all nothing would ever again compete for Jews with the authority of the Hebrew original.

Content, structure, destiny: the Judeo-Greek Bible is clearly distinct at these three levels. There remain two key questions. How and why did the Jews nevertheless come to translate the Bible into Greek? How did it happen that, at least for a time, Jews vested this translation with almost as much authority as the original? If we read certain Judeo-Greek sources carefully, these two issues appear closely linked.

The translation of the five books of Mosaic Law around 285 BCE was among the great achievements of Alexandria, a major cultural center of the ancient Jewish diaspora. Its purpose was probably to meet the needs relating to liturgy and cultural identity of a Jewish community that did not have a command of Hebrew. But it also testifies to a wish on the part of Jews to make this monument of Jewish wisdom accessible to a non-Jewish public, while doubtless satisfying the intellectual curiosity of local elites.

Moreover, since the authorities in Alexandria permitted the various communities to live in accordance with their own laws, they would have found it useful to know more about those that governed the life of the Jewish community. According to the "Letter of Aristaeus," an apology for Judaism written for pagan readers, probably in the first half or the beginning of the second century BCE, this translation was the result of a state commission under the ruler of Egypt, either Ptolemy I Soter (325–285 BCE) or his son, Ptolemy II Philadelphus (285–246 BCE). The story told of this undertaking has all the features of a mythical account. That precisely is its value.

In response to a request from Alexandria, the High Priest of Jerusalem sent there seventy-two scholars (six per tribe), "men who had not only acquired proficiency in Jewish literature, but had studied most carefully that of the Greeks as well." They set to work, "comparing their several results and making them agree" on every point, and so it was that they completed their task on seventy-two days and seventy-two nights exactly, "just as if this had been arranged of set purpose."

It is only one short step from "set purpose" to celestial guarantee. And the rest of the story helped not a little to endow the translation with a dignity close to that of the original. Just as, in the Bible itself, Ezra is said to have solemnly read the Hebrew text of the Mosaic Law to the whole Judean community upon its return from captivity,[50] the translation is now read aloud to an enthusiastic gathering of all the Jews of Alexandria. And just as, under the provisions of the Mosaic Law, nothing may be added or subtracted from what God has ordained,[51] a curse is pronounced "upon any one who should make any alteration either by adding anything or changing in any way whatever any of the words which had been written or making any omission. This was a very wise precaution to ensure that the book might be preserved for all the future time unchanged." The translation, like its original, is untouchable, because it too, like its original, is perfect.[52]

Philo gives an even more impressive version of this mythicized episode. The translators, gathered in a part of the island of Pharos (just off the coast at Alexandria and connected to the city by a long mole), take the books and raise them at arm's length, asking God that they shall not fall short of their purpose. And God grants their prayer. "As if under the influence of divine inspiration," they eliminate the entire distance that would seem fated to separate the two languages and produce a work so perfect that no one would dream of calling these "hierophants and prophets merely translators," these "men who were able to follow the pure thought of Moses with transparent expressions." By dignifying the translators in this way, Philo makes the translation itself a divinely inspired text and brings it a little closer to its eminent model. Indeed, he tells us that the anniversary of the publication of this immortal work is marked by an "annual festival" and a "general assembly" at the site of the miracle: the island of Pharos—rather as if each year the Jewish people celebrated on Mount Sinai itself the festival commemorating the giving of the Law (Shavuot*, the Festival of Weeks).

These are eloquent parallels. They speak volumes about the status of the Septuagint translation (at least of the Pentateuch) for its Judeo-Greek readers. On one point, it even seems to exceed the status of the original. Whereas, at the foot of Mount Sinai, there is only one people, Israel, to greet the Divine Law through Moses, its transmission through the translators on Pharos becomes universal. "Formerly," Philo writes, "our laws were written in Hebrew (Chaldean) and remained unchanged for a long time, with no change in language, so that their beauty had not yet been revealed to other men." Now that they are translated into Greek, they are no longer "reserved for just one part of humanity" but are available to the whole of the hellenized world. It is therefore not surprising that "not only Jews but all manner of other peoples" travel to the annual festivities on the island of Pharos.[53]

As told by Philo, the Alexandrine Jewish publishing enterprise heralds and permits the universal (especially Christian) appropriation of a particular text, which, in being translated, ceases to be particular. The ambivalence of the rabbinical tradition about the value of this enterprise becomes all the more comprehensible. For any translation means promotion, but it is also a degradation. Whatever people say, any sharing involves dispossession. And however one defines the corpus this time—the precise list of books and the order of their arrangement matter little here—the Bible appears to its Jewish readers as a highly ambiguous good: special to them and in principle inalienable, yet inexorably alienated all the same.

To divulge the Book is to begin losing it. And to begin losing it is to begin losing oneself. If we are to believe the fourth-century Palestinian Jewish master Rabbi Yehuda bar Shalom: "The Holy One, blessed be He, foresaw that the nations of the world would one day translate the Bible, that they would read it in Greek, and that they would say: 'We are Israel'"—and so He rejected Moses's request to convey the Mishnah* [that is, the Oral Tradition] in writing.[54] What this apologist does not say, although it is the heart of the problem, is that the first to translate the Torah were not the nations of the world but the Jews themselves. No wonder the ancient rabbinical sources did not unanimously hail the publication of the Alexandrian Greek Bible as a happy event!

The Talmud has its own version of the story of the seventy-two translators.[55] Shut up in seventy-two cells, working separately with no knowledge that the same task was asked of each of them, they received divine inspiration and miraculously produced the identical translation, even emending in the same way fifteen passages that, if rendered literally, might have caused confusion or seemed to confirm ideas opposed to the correct doctrine. The miracle is still there, as is the divine inspiration, but they manifest themselves especially in an alteration of the text—unanimous and justifiable, indeed, inspired by God himself, but an alteration all the same.

Elsewhere, the day of this translation is presented as "difficult" for Israel—as difficult as "the one on which the [Golden] Calf was made," because "the Torah could not be translated completely." [56] Here, too, emendation is seen as inevitable, but it is clearly an imperfection, and an imperfection is an evil. The translation is to the Torah what the Golden Calf is to God: an unworthy substitute, a betrayal. The date when it was completed—an event that, according to Jewish tradition, was followed by three days of darkness over the world—is far from being an occasion for rejoicing; some think it should be commemorated by a day of fasting and mourning, to expiate the sin committed when the Torah was divulged in the language of the Gentiles.[57]

Too readily evoked as the founding book of Judeo-Christian civilization, the Bible appears here clearly in a more ambiguous light. At the very moment when it becomes "common property," the Bible becomes an item that divides. And above all it divides Jews against one another, since they have made it a good without an owner—abandoning it, to their own great dismay, to the firstcomer.

This being so—and it is not the least paradox—a relative mistrust of the Septuagint Bible eventually surfaced in Latin Christendom, too, for both similar and different reasons. In the view of Saint Augustine, toward the end of the fourth century, the Hebrew Bible and the Septuagint still derived from the same divine source; both had the same degree of holiness, because both were divinely inspired. The observable differences between the two texts actually served a divine purpose. Although Isaiah and his translator expressed themselves differently in certain key passages, each was as much a prophet as the other. Here Augustine still clearly displays a traditional "Philonian" way of perceiving the Septuagint.

Saint Jerome, his contemporary, broke with this model by turning his back on the old translation used for centuries by Latin-speaking Christian communities—a translation based on the Greek text—and producing a new Latin translation of his own, based on the Hebrew original. In his view, the changes introduced by the Septuagint were no more than the fruit of the translators' own judgment; they were fallible men, neither prophets nor, as Philo would have said, "hierophants." Having lived before Jesus, and lacking any prophetic foreknowledge of his coming, they inevitably erred in their understanding of Scripture. Jerome himself was not a prophet either, but as he was living after Christ's death and resurrection, he could produce a translation that was simply a history, in which that event functioned as the ultimate hermeneutic key.[58]

On one point at least, Jerome's approach coincided with the rabbinical tradition: the age of prophecy was over. For the Jewish masters, it had ended at the beginning of the Second Temple period, with the deaths of Haggai, Zechariah, and Malachi.[59] But the closure of the canon of the Hebrew Bible had to do precisely with that event. It was the record of past prophetic speech and the sign of the end of that speech. With the Bible, the prophet disappears; all that remains is a text that its readers now have to keep alive. The "Bible"—that is, the biblical revolution—consists in this exclusive worship of a *text*, much more than in the elusive *book* with rather imprecise contours that one likes to see in it. This privileging of the text, however, is not without its ambiguities.

Prophets, Texts, and Books

In fact, prophecy is speech before it is text. It is spoken by the prophet, and heard by his audience, before it is written down to be read. In a sense, this original primacy of oral-aural communication never disappears completely. Even after a prophecy was fully enclosed in a written text that was itself part of a closed canon, the ancient rabbis continued to memorize it as a *heard* text much more than a *read* or *seen* text. This explains the remarkable agility of their exegetic parallels, which, being often based on phonetic rather than physical closeness, took no account of different spellings imperceptible to the ear, and simply overlooked the constraints of the page, column, or book as a unit of reference.[60]

On the other hand, although prophecy was still primarily speech, it was already text—even written text. The God of the Bible speaks. It is through the power of His word that He creates the world. It is by making His voice heard that He communicates with His people.[61] His very commandments are primarily words, things spoken.[62] And the people listens to and does what God tells it to do.[63] But God does not only speak; He writes and He dictates. Similarly, His prophet does not only hear and repeat; he transcribes, reads, and has things read. The first two Tablets of Testimony that the Eternal One gives to Moses are stone tablets "inscribed with the finger of God" (Exod. 32.18). Broken in the episode of the Golden Calf, they are replaced with others, which seem to have been fashioned (and perhaps written) by Moses.[64] On more than one occasion, God orders His prophet to write—or to transcribe—"in the book" what He says and commands.[65] And the prophet solemnly reads this book to the people.[66] Indeed, it is not only the aurally transmitted word but the read word and the reading of the book that ground the Covenant.

So, even before the prophetic word—the spoken, transmitted, heard, transcribed, and read word—solidifies into a canon (the Bible), it is not only speech but *text*. But for a long time the prophet keeps control over it, and although he is certainly not its source—the text ultimately emanates from God—he remains its privileged, or even exclusive, conduit. This continues until the text finally emancipates itself from the prophet and acquires the function traditionally ascribed to him.

From the Prophetic Word to Magisterium of the Written Text

In 622 BCE, in the eighteenth year of the reign of Josiah, king of Judah, renovation work brought to light a "book" in the Jerusalem Temple. This discovery is presented in 2 Kings 22 and 23 as the origin of an extensive religious reform. The king read aloud this Book of the Covenant in the Temple, addressing "all the men of Judah and all the inhabitants of Jerusalem" (2 Kings 23.2). The book and its sudden unearthing thus triggered a profound movement calling for a return to God and the Law. It, and it alone, played the role that the prophet normally could and should have fulfilled. The prophet—in this case a woman, Huldah—intervened only at a later stage. She was consulted about the meaning of the discovery. And when the book was read in public, everyone gathered there—prophets included!—formed the audience.

Not long afterwards, in the fourth year of the reign of one of Josiah's sons, Jehoiakim, who "did what was displeasing to the Lord" (2 Kings 23.37), another event only appeared to restore the roles imparted to prophet and text respectively. God told his prophet Jeremiah to take a parchment scroll and to "write upon it all the words" he had spoken so far "concerning Israel and Judah and all the nations" (Jer. 36.2). It was as if God considered that a *text* (book or scroll) suitable for public reading in the Jerusalem Temple was more likely than mere *speech*, or the living presence of the prophet himself, to touch the heart of a faithless people and to get it back on the straight and narrow. And in fact it was Baruch who, at Jeremiah's dictation, committed to the scroll what the Lord had addressed to the prophet, then went to the Sanctuary and solemnly read it aloud "to all the people."

God is absent here. So is the prophet. A third person, Baruch, writes the scroll "at his dictation." The same third person reads it in public. And the reading produces a great effect—except on King Jehoiakim, who has it read to him again later, in the privacy of his palace, not by Baruch this time but by another, Jehudi. There, the narrator tells us, "every time Jehudi read three or four columns, [the king] would cut it up with a scribe's knife and throw it into the fire in the brazier, until the entire scroll was consumed by the fire in the brazier" (Jer. 36.23). The impiety of the rebellious monarch expresses itself for now in the physical destruction of the text dictated by the prophet, rather than in his persecution or murder, the reduction of his speech to silence.[67]

The Bible gives other indications of this gradual effacing of the prophet by the written text. Thus Ezekiel, the prophet of the Exile, is not simply the one who hears the divine word and passes it on to his people. A hand reaches out to him, "holding a written scroll." It is unrolled before him, and he sees that it is inscribed on both the front and the back with "written lamentations, dirges, and woes." God orders him to eat it, to feed his stomach, and fill his belly with it, to digest it therefore, and only then to go and speak to the House of Israel. Ezekiel does this meticulously, and in his mouth the book "tasted as sweet as honey."[68]

Later comes Zechariah, one of the three (together with Haggai and Malachi) whose deaths were taken by the ancient rabbis to mark the end of the age of prophecy. Zechariah, for his part, raises his eyes and sees a "scroll" fly in the air. To the angel who converses with him and asks what he actually sees, the prophet replies: "A flying scroll, twenty cubits long and ten cubits wide." Perhaps this is already the Torah scroll, or simply the written text of the curse that will strike anyone who has stolen or given false testimony.[69] The autonomy and power of the written text stand out all the more because the prophet is reduced to no more than a spectator as the angel explains it to him. While the text tends to supplant the spoken word, the prophet gradually gives way to the exegete.

The solemn public reading of the Law of Moses, organized in Judea by Ezra at the time of the return from captivity, appears in this light as not really a turning point but one moment in an evolution that began before the fall of the kingdom of Judah, asserted itself during the Exile, and continued after the Return. The Torah, as a written text, is intended for the whole people: for "the men and the women and those who could understand" (Neh. 8.3). It must be read to them, taught to them, interpreted for them. Thus, even before the biblical corpus has been fully constituted, even before some of its final parts have been composed, the text has become the key element of the dialogue between God and His people.[70]

It is naturally at the center of the new Judean society, which appears so "bookish" or at least, and more precisely, so "text-centric," that some historians present it as almost "abnormal." Study and interpretation of the Divine Law—of God's *written* word—are essential once any transgression is regarded as the cause of past destruction, and once the ways of the Lord are expressed in this text rather than in the order of the world.[71] This cardinal importance of the text or of "what is written," *ha-katuv*,[72] is undoubtedly more foundational or more revolutionary for Jewish religious history than are the official closure of a canon and the emergence of a "Book" (the Bible). Anyway it predates them, explains them, and extends well beyond them. It does not even depend on the establishment of a definitive text: it requires or demands that, of course, but in actual practice it can and even should do without it.

Settling the Text Without Fixing the Word

The establishment of a uniform, authoritative text, especially of the Pentateuch, naturally began before the destruction of the Second

Temple. And the immense aggadic* and halakhic* output of the Sages (Pharisees* and early rabbis) presupposed the more or less shared acceptance of a single version. As we have seen, however,[73] the Septuagint translation, the Samaritan Pentateuch, and the discoveries at Qumran show the diversity of the texts circulating at the time. At Qumran, for example, there is no "authorized version," nor any strict definitive rules governing the production of a Sefer Torah. The catastrophe of 70 CE, which shook ancient Jewish society to its foundations, and the debates with all kinds of (mainly Christian) sectarians changed the situation on the ground, making more urgent, and therefore speeding up, the process of fixing the text. The fact remains that, at the time of the Sages, the idea of the absolute sanctity of the text down to its minute details coexisted in practice with fluctuations that were difficult to absorb.

Today as yesterday, every believing Jew holds it as a virtual dogma that the biblical text in our hands is a flawless whole; any challenge to that affects the credibility of Judaism itself. The view of contemporary biblical criticism that the books making up the Bible could be a late compilation, sometimes clumsy, sometimes faulty, of documents with various origins and dates, and that in general these cannot be thought of as genuine complete works by the authors to whom they have been traditionally attributed, arouses among the Orthodox something more than defiance or anger: absolutely categorical rejection.

After all, how can the slightest doubt about the authenticity of the text or the reliability of its transmission be reconciled with the halakhic rule that a Sefer Torah missing a single letter is unfit for liturgical use, or with the solemn warning of Rabbi Ishmael (first half of the second century): "If by accident you omit or add one letter, you destroy the entire world"?[74] And yet, even within a Judaism that might be described as Orthodox , the establishment and transmission of the text of the Hebrew Bible proves to have been a much more uncertain affair.[75] In reality, that text was definitively fixed only after the invention of printing, with the publication of the second edition of the "rabbinical Bible,"[76] by the Christian printer Daniel Bomberg in 1524–25.[77] Until then, despite a huge effort of correction and editing over a number of centuries, disparities and mismatches had never ceased to occur.

Originally, the Hebrew text of the Bible had been exclusively consonantal, and that is still the case with the Sefer Torah used in synagogues for liturgical purposes. The absence of vocalic signs left a not inconsiderable margin of freedom in the reading, pronunciation, and therefore interpretation of the text. Similarly, the ancient Hebrew notations lacked punctuation. Scrolls like those found at Qumran do have breaks between words, but they do not mark divisions between sentences, verses, or chapters.

Other notation systems, especially ones containing vowels, appeared only gradually at quite a late date, in Babylonia, at Tiberias, and in southern Palestine—perhaps in reaction to the danger that the Arab conquest of Palestine in the early seventh century seemed to pose to survival and mastery of the Hebrew language, or more likely in the context of the birth and development of a sectarian current, Karaism,[78] that preached a return to Scripture. The Tiberias system was the one that eventually prevailed, in the tenth century.

The text available for us to read today in printed editions of the Hebrew Bible is thus the fruit of cumulative labors stretching over a number of centuries, performed not only by scribes, or *soferim* (who, since the Second Temple period, had played an essential role in establishing and transmitting the sacred texts), but above all by generations of masoretes (or masters of the *masorah* = tradition) up to the tenth century. Indeed, the term "masoretic" is commonly used to denote this reference text.

A manuscript typical of this tradition is the so-called Aleppo Codex, although it actually only arrived in the city after which it is named around 1478. It was completed around 930 in Tiberias, in the Holy Land, by Solomon ben Buya'a for the consonantal text, and Aaron (ben Moses) ben Asher for the vocalization.[79] In all probability, this is the manuscript that Moses Maimonides praised as a model in his code of Jewish law.[80] Paradoxically, however, modern editions of the Hebrew Bible are not based on this manuscript (today incomplete and kept in Jerusalem), which for centuries was very difficult to access, but rather on the so-called Leningrad manuscript, produced in Cairo in 1008, which, though very close to the Aleppo model, differs from it at certain points and is sometimes less precise or consistent.[81]

The masoretes not only introduced vowel signs to clear up uncertainties inherent in the reading of a text that was at first exclusively consonantal, they also divided the text into sections at two levels: new paragraph for a new subject; and a simple space in the middle of the line to mark smaller subunits. This system is obviously not neutral: it presupposes or reflects real exegetical choices. Nor is this all. There is another division into basic units or "verses," the end of each being marked by a particular sign (the *silluk*).[82]

This being the case, the division of the various books into chapters—which is so familiar to us that we might think it "natural"—is actually of Christian rather than Jewish origin, and it became established at quite a late date.[83] More important, at least from a liturgical point of view, was the division of the Pentateuch into pericopes (*parashiot* or *sidrot*): 154 or 167 in the defunct triennial cycle of readings formerly practiced in Palestine; 54 (or 53) in the annual cycle practiced in Babylonia that became the norm.

The verses themselves were given cantillation signs (*te'amim*), which also involved an exegetical decision: their function was not only to guide the chanting of the text at synagogue services, but also to mark the emphasis within a word, and to signal the type of syntactic relationship (disjunctive or conjunctive) between words. However, in the Tiberias tradition of accentuation-punctuation-cantillation (there were two others, as there were for vowel sounds), the system used in Job, Proverbs, and Psalms is different from that in the other books of the Bible.

Although, thanks to all the work of systematization and unification, Jewish communities around the world eventually had the same signs accompanying the scriptural text, they still continued to read and chant it in accordance with distinct traditions of pronunciation (of certain letters and vowels) and cantillation. These varied so much that the biblical text read aloud by Jews in Poland or Lithuania would have been quite unintelligible to a Jew in Morocco or Egypt!

The main contribution of the masoretes to a fixed biblical text was the production of a critical apparatus, the *masorah*. Intended above all to guide the pen of scribes, it was also a guide to how the text should be read. For the *written* text is not necessarily what must be *read*. In a great number of cases (between 848 and 1,566, depending on the tradition), the *masorah* invites the person reading the text to set aside its written form (*ketiv*) and to read one or several different words (*kere*). Curiously, in many manuscripts and editions, the *kere* (the word that should be read) appears in the *masorah* without a vocalization, whereas the *ketiv* (the word that should not be read) appears in the biblical text with the vowels of the *kere*. In some cases, the reader is asked to say a word that is not written in the text (*kere ve-la ketiv*), or not to say a word that is written there (*ketiv ve-la kere*).

The origin of the *kere* is still being debated. Were they at first corrective additions to the written text? Or variants observed in certain manuscript traditions? Or simply unwritten traditions of reading? Whichever one accepts, the masoretic effort did not put a final end to the textual uncertainties—indeed, it registered them and strangely perpetuated their traces; the effort only partly attained its objective.

The disparities persisted. Moreover, although the medieval Sephardi* world excelled in the quality of its masoretic activity, the situation seems to have been less clear in Ashkenazi* regions. More symptomatic still are the important differences that could exist within the same manuscript between the biblical text actually copied by the scribe and the *masorah* placed in the margins.

The last paradox is a veritable irony of history. When printing finally fixed the biblical text among the Jews, after centuries of ceaseless work of correction, the debate erupted in a different form and with different implications in the Christian world. Doubts were raised about the reliability of the masoretic text. Questions relating to poetics, but also to the paternity and unity of the various books, became central. A new biblical scholarship took shape, establishing an unprecedented distance between the "Book" and its readers.

Beginning in the late Middle Ages and early Renaissance, then carried forward by the Reformation, this process continued in changing forms as historical doubts and philological criticism became more systematic and radical. The theory of biblical sources, initiated by Julius Wellhausen (1844–1918),[84] grew more complex and sophisticated in the work of his successors, eventually resulting in ever more advanced attempts "to subdivide the text into superimposed layers, strata, and editings":[85] that is, to disarticulate—some would say cut up—the existing corpus. Once again, its unity seemed disturbingly fragile.[86]

✳

Uncertain text? Elusive book? So is the Bible, so singular and so plural, nothing but a "loose anthology,"[87] hazy in content and with a curiously variable geometry? Everyone speaks of the Bible, but does it really exist? And is everyone thinking of the same "Book" when they utter the word? Heterogeneous literary genres, diverse languages and canons, composite texture and unreliability of the documents, internal contradictions: everything seems to be ganging up against what is regularly presented to us as one of the pillars of Jewish, Christian, or "Judeo-Christian" civilization.

Philo's Bible is not that of the masoretes, nor is the Bible of the Jews that of the Christians. The Catholic Bible is not the same as the Protestant one. Yet they are all the Bible—a locus of sharing *and* confrontation within and between confessions. To be sure, any canon both reflects and induces a particular reading of the whole and of each of its parts. A word, a sentence, a narrative, a book are read differently according to whether they form part of this or that wider whole, or according to the place they occupy within it. The five books of Moses evidently have a different meaning if they open a (Jewish) canon that excludes the New Testament or a (Christian) canon that includes it. In the first case, the Torah is principally the Law: it lays it down, with an authority that is entire and definitive. In the second, the Pentateuch is but the first chapter of a sacred history that finds completion and clarity in Jesus.

Every canon produces meaning, in a way that is unique to it. Every canonization establishes a unity that tends to attenuate, without completely dispelling, the inconsistencies and discrepancies. And every canonization does this in a way that is unique to it. Yet, however diverse the canons witnessed in history, none of them has really been arbitrary.

The Hebrew Bible—to speak only of that—does not exist through the retroactive force of a violent, authoritarian act of canonization that disregarded the original nature of its components. The remaining discrepancies of form, content, and inspiration are testimony to the contrary. Without subjecting this huge corpus to rigid criteria of absolute coherence, generation upon generation of authors, author-editors, and editor-compilers have striven, if not to ensure a smooth and continuous reading, then at least to make the points of convergence resonate clearly. As Robert Alter and Frank Kermode rightly point out, "the Hebrew Bible, because it so frequently articulates its meanings by recasting texts within its own corpus, is already moving toward being an integrated work, for all its anthological diversity."[88] Its constituent parts maintain a constant and genuine dialogue with one another, and it is possible to detect in each the seeds of canonicity.

The very power of the Bible may have to do precisely with the irreducible ambiguity of its identity. No doubt the choice of language, the selection of books for the canon, the order in which they are placed, and the type and degree of the authority associated with them configure a new Bible each time. And all these Bibles are at once reflection and product of a complex, high-contrast history stretching over many centuries. On the one hand, all the orthodoxies speak repeatedly of stability, solidity, and unity; on the other hand, the reality is a flexibility and evanescence that have never been totally overcome. The paradoxical combination of these two dimensions is probably the price paid for the Bible, for all Bibles, to play their role in full.

In Judaism, this "upstream" ambivalence is reduplicated "downstream." For, curiously enough, just as relative uncertainty about the identity of the "Jewish Bible" (and any other Bible) did not weaken but tended to establish and strengthen its power, it would appear that, in real life and liturgical practice, that Bible is all the more present as a reference, the more it tends to unravel as a corpus. It is as if its eclipse and endless fragmentation were the very preconditions of its ubiquitous presence.

Two Bible Object, Bible in Pieces

Before being a book, the Bible is an object. And if we accept with René-Samuel Sirat, the former chief rabbi of France, that it "accompanies the Jew from birth to death, and from death to eternity,"[1] it does this first of all as an object—much more than as a text that is truly readable and actually read.

There is no better illustration of this paradox than the type of holiness with which, over a period of centuries, the Jews of Aleppo surrounded the famous "Crown of Aleppo" codex, or *Keter Aram Tsova*.[2] For scholars, as we have seen, this book is an exemplary witness to the medieval masoretic tradition.[3] When Maimonides consulted it in Cairo, it was already held up as a model of trustworthy editing. But in Aleppo itself, where it arrived only in the second half of the fifteenth century and was jealously guarded for more than five hundred years, it acquired a dignity and function of a very different nature.[4] For the Aleppo Jews, their codex could have been written only by the hand of Ezra himself—who, according to local tradition, was buried not far from their city. Although it was a codex, not a scroll, and although its text was accented and vocalized, they regarded it as a perfect reconstitution of the Torah*, more sacred even than the Scrolls of the Law, or *sifrei Torah*, reserved for liturgical use.[5] Yet very few ever had an opportunity to set eyes on it, let alone to read it.

Along with three other precious books, the codex resided in a small vaulted chapel in the Great Synagogue of Aleppo. This chapel, oriented toward Jerusalem and situated in the wing built in the sixteenth century to receive Jewish immigrants from Spain, Portugal, and Italy, was known as the "Cave of Elijah," since an old tradition had it that there was once an apparition of the prophet there.[6] Far from being placed on view, the four codices were locked in a double metal safe to protect them from fire; two eminent notables held the two keys in safekeeping, and it is said that the safe could be opened only in their presence and under the supervision of the Jewish council of sages. Access to the codex was indeed always tightly controlled: few people had the privilege to consult it, still less to copy or (in later times) photograph it. These precautions and mistrust had to do with old beliefs that anyone who tried to steal, sell, or pawn the codex would bring down a curse not only on himself but on the whole Jewish community of Aleppo.

Sealed up so that it could not be seen or read, the Codex of Aleppo nevertheless played a central role in the life of the city's Jews. Men and women—especially women, who in traditional Jewish society had less access to the book—visited the "Cave of Elijah" throughout the year, but above all on the eve of Yom Kippur*. They prayed there for an end to sterility or an illness, or for a successful childbirth. A lamp was constantly burning, and anyone could light a candle there before telling of their woes in front of the Ark containing the codices.

It is not impossible that the traditions concerning the holiness of the "Crown of Aleppo" appeared quite recently, dating essentially from the second half of the nineteenth century. They may even have simply resulted from a kind of transference, when the "Crown" took over the status and function initially ascribed to the "Cave of Elijah" that housed it. Such hypotheses do not, however, invalidate the idea of the original centrality of the Bible as object—in fact they reinforce it. It may be that two powers meet up in the Aleppo codex: the magical power of the cave's hidden occupant, the benevolent prophet of popular oral tradition; and the sacred power of God, the hidden inspirer of the message transcribed in the pages of the book. Just as one did not have to meet Elijah in person to hope for a miracle or an effective intercession, it was not necessary to see or read the biblical text contained in the "Crown." It was enough to *be there*, in the cave of the prophet, close to the Book of God in its outermost materiality, even if the Book itself remained inaccessible.

Before this Object, the Bible, is a book, and long before it is a text, it makes itself available in a multitude of different objects. The "Crown of Aleppo," as paradigmatic as it is exceptional, is only one among many others that are certainly more modest but play a similar role—

objects that people see and touch, kiss and clutch to their heart, carry, exhibit, and sometimes conceal. Without yet being books, and despite their sometimes humble appearance, these objects are already more than just objects: they are almost persons whom one clothes or un-clothes, with whom one dances and becomes betrothed, and whom one solemnly takes into the earth when the end comes. The Bible is incarnated and personified in this mass of objects, which augment its presence in the daily life of the believer, while consecrating its inescapable dismemberment.

The Bible in Boxes

If the presence of these "Bible objects" in the lives of believers were represented as a series of concentric circles, then the innermost circle would be the body of the Jewish man himself. I say Jewish *man*, because for centuries traditional Jewish society and Orthodox (or orthopraxic) Judaism excluded women from the practice I am about to describe, for reasons of ritual purity and by virtue of a hierarchical, differentialist construction of gender.

Tefillin

On every day that is not a holiday, during morning prayers, the ob-servant adult[7] Jew places his skin—his upper brow at the hairline and his left arm[8]—directly in contact with small Bible objects with a high symbolic potential that are known as tefillin, a word often inaccurately translated as "phylacteries." The intimacy of this physical contact does not detract from its public character: the tefillin are worn by a man praying either alone at home or as part of the synagogue community. Besides, the practice is one of those that mark the religious coming of age of a young male Jew; it initiates his full participation in the ritual life of the collective.[9]

The tefillin are Bible objects par excellence, both in their redundancy and in their selectiveness. Fitted with black leather straps that allow them to be attached to the body, these two small cube-shaped black boxes contain four extracts from the Pentateuch[10] handwritten in Hebrew on parchment. Each of the passages dwells on themes, principles, events, and practices that may be considered essential to Judaism—oneness of God, divine reward and punishment, consecration of the firstborn, exodus from Egypt, feast of Passover*. But each also refers to the "sign upon [his] arm" and the "symbol on [his] forehead" that the believer is apparently obliged to "attach" and to "wear."[11]

I say *apparently* because the rabbinical Judaic reading of these four texts that establishes and/or justifies the practice of wearing the tefillin is not altogether compelling. True, there is evidence of the custom since antiquity, but it was not adopted throughout the Jewish world. The Samaritans* and the Karaites[12] ignored it. In fact, a purely allegorical interpretation of the texts was always possible and, it would seem, should not be dismissed out of hand.[13] Do they not simply urge the believer, in figurative language, to keep in his heart and mind certain teachings of divine origin and certain events bearing the mark of divine intervention?

Furthermore, the unique way in which rabbinical Judaism chose to implement what it saw as a divine command can certainly not be derived directly from these biblical texts. The form, dimensions, and color of the tefillin, production techniques (including the calligraphy of the copied texts), materials used (leather, parchment made from the skin of a ritually pure animal, ink, and so on), specification of the precise texts and of how they should be inserted into the boxes,[14] type of straps and knots (for fastening to the forehead and arm), the moments when the tefillin can and must be worn or not worn, the order and manner in which they should be attached and removed: all this derives from teachings and prescriptions in the Oral Tradition; none of it has a scriptural origin.[15]

So, the movement linking scriptural text with Bible object is redundant and circular. It is a circularity, though, which as in other cases cannot dispense with a mediation; the Oral Tradition establishes and authenticates the self-confirming movement through which a text refers to an object and is embodied in it, and through which the object refers in its turn to the text, both materially containing it and ritually making it come true.

The circular movement is selective, because it can take place only through one of several possible readings of the text. Of course, it is selective also in the sense that the tefillin do not contain the whole Bible, or even the whole Torah, but only a few fragments that are themselves partly redundant. Nevertheless, the selectivity is relative, since every- thing or nearly everything comes together in them by virtue of their source and what they represent: the Written Torah, the Oral Torah, and the concreteness of an actual practice.

In these conditions, it is not surprising that rabbinical Judaism makes so much of the tefillin: the wearing of them is supposed to en- courage humility and fear of Heaven, and to express the submission of all human faculties to the service of God; their holiness is comparable to that of the Sefer Torah; God in person is said to wear them.[16] If one of them falls, even by accident, the person responsible must force him- self to fast throughout the day. But the tefillin—portable pieces of the Bible that each morning leave a fleeting trace of their straps on the skin of the arm, forearm, and fingers—seem to me to stand above all in a relationship of exemplary intimacy with the believer who wears them.

He may certainly lend his tefillin to a passing believer who does not have any with him; he may even use someone else's in case of necessity. Nevertheless, every Jewish man cultivates a special personal bond with his own tefillin. He handles them with care and verifies their integrity with an expert at least once every seven years. He kisses them before putting them on, and kisses them again before putting them back in the embroidered pouch that will protect them for the rest of the day.

Yet—this is not the least of the paradoxes—he never sees their con- tent. Should he happen to read the texts in question, it will definitely not be from the fragments of parchment inside these little boxes. And then he will do so in a liturgical context most often independent of their wearing: a weekly reading of the Torah (if the pericope includes one or other of the texts, on the basis of a printed Pentateuch or—if he is called forward—the Sefer Torah), a recitation of the Shema* at the morning service (when the tefillin are worn), but also during the evening service or before retiring for the night (when they are not worn), and so on.

Mezuzah

Beyond this first circular encounter between the body of the believer and his tefillin, a wider but no less essential circle, involving a different combination of private and public, manifests itself in the mezuzah.

This term originally denoted a gatepost, but it came to refer to the small parchment scroll ritually attached to the right doorpost of Jewish houses and containing two calligraphic extracts from the Pentateuch.[17] Once again, the principle of redundancy and circularity applies in full, since the two passages include the injunction: "Inscribe them [the duties prescribed by God] on the doorposts of your house and on your gates."[18]

Many details differentiate this practice from the wearing of the tefillin. The individual is no longer the only support or actor; rather, the mezuzah marks a territory generally common to more than one member of the collective. In essence, it is the space of the family, but by extension (though not as a strict requirement) mezuzot are also fixed to the gates of Jewish public places such as synagogues, community centers, and schools, or even, as in Israel, to official buildings and the gateways to the Old City in Jerusalem. The attachment of this small Bible-object thus "judaizes" certain segments of the space in question, in both the topographical and social sense of the word. And it does so by displaying the Jewishness of those segments in a way that is visible to all, Jew and non-Jew alike.

For an ordinary believer, the mezuzah Bible object is more "transparent" and in a way more "familiar" than the tefillin. Doubtless only a professional scribe is qualified to execute the calligraphic work and to check (twice every seven years) the Hebrew text on the small fragment of manuscript. But the believer who attaches the text to his doorpost actually sees it; he is often the one who rolls it up and places it inside its little container.

Originally, the mezuzah was inserted into a small recess in the doorway. So that the calligraphic word *Shaddai*[19] on the back of the parchment should be visible, glass (or nowadays plastic) containers are not uncommon, and a small opening has traditionally been made if they are of an opaque material such as wood, metal, or stone. More usually, this name of God is simply reproduced on the container itself, which, unlike the tefillin box—whose shape and appearance are strictly regulated—may take a wide variety of forms; Jewish artists and silversmiths have long expressed their talent and imagination in such work.

This familiarity with the mezuzah Bible object is not reserved, as in the case of the tefillin, for adult males. Everyone sees it, and everyone can physically display their reverence, either by directly applying their lips as they enter the house or by touching it with their right index and middle fingers before raising them to their mouth. Women and children do just the same. Nor is it rare to see a Jewish parent lift a child to the height of the object, either to familiarize him or her with this mark of respect, or because the child spontaneously wishes to imitate adults.

The mezuzah thus serves to mark both the collective identity of the household and the Jewish identity of each of its members. However, the attachment shown to it—an aspect common to all the Bible objects mentioned in these pages—is largely independent of the content of the calligraphic text inside it. Many of those who kiss it have never read this text, or else—as with the tefillin texts—they have done so in a liturgical context, without necessarily understanding what they read; even those who have real knowledge of it surely do not have all the words in mind when they devoutly touch their mezuzot with their right hands.

Nor is this all. The attachment may also be largely independent of the initial function of the mezuzah, which is to recall God's commandments. In principle, the mezuzah, like the tefillin, helps to engrave duties to God on "the heart" of the believer—the same duties that he must inculcate into his children, speaking about them at home or on a journey, at bedtime and first thing in the morning.[20] But is all that really in the thoughts of every Jew who comes across a mezuzah, or who, even if not especially practicing, still attaches one to his doorpost (perhaps a door inside the house, in a concern for discretion hardly in line with Orthodox practice), or who is careful to pack his mezuzah when he moves home or is forced to leave in difficult circumstances? Nothing is less certain. The mezuzah is definitely not an amulet, but in the Middle Ages some endowed it with magical powers of protection and inscribed it with, not only the prescribed verses from the Bible, but also angels' names and seals thought likely to make the house safer. And is not *Shaddai*, that name of God present in every mezuzah, also taken to be short for Sh*omer* d*altot* Y*israel*, "protector of the gates of Israel"?

Even more powerfully than in the case of the tefillin, this reduction of dismembered Scripture to a minimal material expression that fits in the palm on one hand—its "degradation" into a magical little object fixed to each doorway—reflects the inevitable ambiguity of a ritual reality in which the strong material presence of the *object* seems to drive the *text* itself into the limbo of a virtual absence.

The Bible in Scrolls

The third and last circle in the geography of the Bible's presence/ absence in the life of the believer is no less paradoxical, even if the objects it involves are of a partly different nature. There is a change of format here. We are still talking of parchments, but they are of a respectable size, because the text they contain is much longer. The format change is also due to a change in use: the text has to be *read* or chanted in public, in a precise ritual framework. In one case, it must even be shown—literally exhibited before the community.

When the entire Jewish library, including the Bible itself, had existed for centuries in the form of codices, the two books in question here—both extracted from the canon—continued to appear to the eyes of believers in the form of scrolls if they were to be used for liturgical purposes (and not simply for study or the pleasure of reading them).

Describing Jewish "ceremonies and customs" to Christians, Leon of Modena (1571–1648) had reason to stress: "This Pentateuch [he is speaking of the Sefer Torah] is not in the form of the books that people use today, but in the volume or scroll form, as in olden days." The "strangeness" of this custom, due only to the passing of centuries and the general triumph of the codex (that is, the book in bound sheets), is here combined with another strangeness. For it is a question of manuscripts and parchments—"vellum skins sewn not with thread but with the nerves of a clean animal"—at a time when paper and printing had finally swept all before them.[21]

These exotic props, and the resolute attachment to ancient production processes that technical advances have not threatened, may seem quite external to the texts and their content. But, apart from the fact that the purposes are essentially liturgical, they serve to enhance the sacred aura that, in the eyes of believers, surrounds these two rather special Bible objects: the Scroll of Esther and the Torah Scroll. Note, however, that this remark applies much more to the Torah than to Esther.

Esther

As already mentioned, Esther is one of the texts whose place in the canon of the Jewish Scriptures was for a long time problematic, and its authority is by no means on a par with that of the Five Books of Moses.[22] In fact, it stands at the other extreme of the biblical canon. Whereas the Torah is designated by the nobler, more austere term *sefer*, Esther is a simple megillah, a "scroll." Moreover, it is one "scroll" among others, since the word is traditionally used for five biblical texts: Song of Songs, Ruth, Lamentations, Ecclesiastes, and Esther,[23] which are solemnly read aloud at Passover (Pesach*), Shavuot* (the Feast of Weeks), the Ninth of the Month of Av*, Sukkot* (the Feast of Booths), and Purim*. Whereas the reading of the Torah is spaced out through the year, that of the Scrolls takes place all at once, on a single day of festival or mourning. The fact remains, however, that Esther is the megillah par excellence; this word is used alone, with no further specification, only to refer to the Book of Esther; and, above all, Esther is the only one of the five texts to be ritually read aloud from a true parchment scroll.

Of course, this singularity of the Scroll of Esther does not cancel the distance between it and the Sefer Torah. As regards format, its dimensions are much more modest. From the sixteenth century on, and especially in the seventeenth and eighteenth centuries, the custom of illuminating the megillah spread in Italy, in Holland, and then else-where in Europe and beyond: that is, illustrating it, often very richly, with scenes from the narrative episodes. It was not, and still is not, uncommon for individuals to have copies of their own. Believers have a relationship of closeness and familiarity with their megillah that is certainly not the norm with the Sefer Torah.

Purim, a very popular festival, during which children are kings, gives rise to joyful outbursts when it is permissible to get drunk, and when the spirit of derision and subversion is by no means banned. And the two readings of the megillah (at the evening service, then the next morn-ing) take place in a semi-carnival atmosphere that reflects this gaiety. Any mention of the names of Haman, the persecutor, and his sons is drowned out with the noise of rattles or hammering on the ground.

The Sefer Torah

The Sefer Torah and its ritual reading come in for incomparably stricter treatment. The Five Books of Moses, in the shape of a single, rather heavy scroll, are at the center of worship in the synagogue. The text is copied by hand, "with extreme care and precision,"[24] in a special ink and characters, on a parchment made from specified pieces of ritually pure animal skin. The two ends of the parchment are attached to two rods called *atsei hayyim* ("trees of life"), the rolling and unrolling of which enable it to progress in the course of the reading.

The holiness of the object and the legitimacy of its liturgical use do not stem only from the general nature, meaning, or ostensibly divine origin of the texts it contains. They are due just as much to the halakhic* rules governing its production, to its material integrity—not one letter must be missing—and to the spiritual integrity of the expert responsible for its production. "A Torah scroll, tefillin, and mezuzot written by a heretic, informer, idolatrous pagan, slave, woman, minor, Samaritan, or apostate Jew are unfit for use," the Babylonian Talmud states.[25] Only those who submit to the commands of the Law because the Law requires it of them, and who do this with the right intention, are capable of producing truly holy objects of worship.[26]

But in addition to its divine origin and material integrity, as well as the spiritual purity of its crafter, there is perhaps another source of the Sefer Torah's sacred character: more than any of the Bible objects mentioned so far, it produces community. First of all, the whole community is associated with its production. Women themselves are not excluded from the process: it is they, as Leon of Modena points out, who fashion the cloak that envelops the scroll, "a work of linen or silk that is ordinarily the masterpiece of the finest that women know how to make and that they devote to this purpose."[27]

To own a Sefer Torah is held to be a command for every male Jew, whether he writes it himself, has someone else write it for him, or purchases it. Often, though, the command and the accomplishment of a Sefer Torah are an enterprise involving all the members of a community, in accordance with the talmudic* principle that he who corrects even a single letter in a Sefer acquires a merit comparable to that of him who writes it out in full.

This conjunction of individual and community is part and parcel of the Sefer Torah. Along with the wearing of the tefillin,[28] the solemn call to the reading of the Torah before the assembled believers marks the religious coming of age of the young male Jew and his integration into the adult community under the Law.[29] The book ordered by an individual always serves the community, and every Saturday morning its ritual reading by seven individuals chosen from its midst (who are supposed to represent the three components of the priestlike Jewish people)[30] manifests, strengthens, and re-creates the community bond. If the rigors of history force a community into exile or flight, it is always eager to take its sacred scrolls with it or somehow to smuggle them out.[31]

Any desecration of this Bible object is therefore perceived as an unpardonable assault, not only on the holiness of the book and the word of God recorded within it, but also on the very being, individual and collective, of those who read or simply keep and revere it. Hence the despair of that rabbi from Lodz who, to save his life, was forced by the Nazis to spit on a Torah scroll: when the saliva dried up in his mouth, his tormentor spat into it so that he could continue to spit on the Book. Hence the horror of that Jew from the Praga district of Warsaw who told a local rabbi that, since he and his family were reduced to living in filth, he had no choice but to leave with him the Torah scroll he kept at home: "Please, rabbi, take this, my most sacred possession, and guard it as the apple of your eye. Nothing is left to us but this Torah."[32] How can we fail to read the "us" in "nothing is left to us" as referring beyond the individual and his family to the whole persecuted community of European Jewry?

There are most surely reasons why, at the other end of the chain of woes marking the historical and religious trajectory of the Jewish people, an ancient rabbinical narrative associated Titus's desecration of the Jerusalem Temple in 70 CE—a paradigmatic moment of collective ruin—with another terrifying sacrilege. It is as if he wished to render the horror absolute: "The evil Titus forced his way into the Holy of Holies,[33] holding an unsheathed sword in his hand; he cut through the veil [parokhet],[34] took two prostitutes, unrolled a Sefer Torah beneath them, and possessed them on the altar."[35]

One of the finest illustrations of this emblematic status of the Sefer Torah is the talmudic*[36] account of the agony that the Roman authorities inflicted on one of the Ten Martyrs of the Empire,[37] Rabbi Haninah ben Teradion. In defiance of the Roman prohibition, he was caught teaching the Torah to a large audience, "with a Sefer Torah

Here the Sefer, and more generally the Torah, are of an evident femininity: the daughter of a divine king, the object of a people's love (the people of Israel), a crowned princess to whom each of its men may one day—at Simbat Torah—be personally "betrothed."

Simbat Torah, literally "the joy of the Torah," is celebrated at the end of the autumn ceremonies that begin with the New Year (Rosh Hashanah*) and Yom Kippur, and continue with Sukkot and its concluding *Shemini Atzeret*.

Simbat Torah became a celebration clearly distinct from *Shemini Atzeret* at a fairly late date; its particular practices only gradually won acceptance, once the annual cycle of Torah readings established in Babylonia had more or less supplanted the triennial cycle formerly prevalent in the Holy Land. It is the day that closes the Pentateuch reading cycle of one year and opens that of the next.

At Simbat Torah, as a mark of special consideration, the community calls upon one believer to read solemnly, from a first scroll, the final verses of Deuteronomy; he is honored with the title *hatan Torah*, literally "betrothed of the Torah." A second scroll is then opened, and another member of the congregation is allocated to read the first verses of Genesis; he is honored with the title *hatan Be-reshit*, "betrothed of Genesis."

These annually recurring betrothals involve many more than two privileged individuals: in fact, all (male) members of the community are called upon to read the Torah, and the final chapters of Deuteronomy are repeated as many times as are necessary for everyone to read a minimum of three verses. Minors are entitled to have a special ritual reading addressed to them. Thus, the whole community manifests the pact with the Book, and the betrothals give rise to collective rejoicing that naturally centers on the scrolls of the Law. These are all removed from the Ark and carried seven times in procession around the reading table. When the context permits it, the singing and dancing usually extends beyond the synagogue walls into the public space outside.

Each week, and at every solemn festival (Simbat Torah, in particular), the community forcefully displays, in emotion, joy, and veneration, the indissoluble link joining it to the Sefer. This bond demonstrably establishes it as a community. It is through the almost exclusive worship of this object, the quasi-personification of a revealed Word, that the community expresses and celebrates its collective existence.

But although the Sefer imposes itself precisely as an object, or even as a person, none of this yet makes it a "book." For in the pious devotion of ordinary people—and ordinary people always form the majority—the epiphanic appearance of the object, which should be only a *means*, undoubtedly counts for more than its *end*: the public reading. As soon as the scroll is laid on the table ready to be read, as soon as the reading begins, the tension and rapt attention begin to flag again. Or, as Heine described it:

> As passages from the laws of Moses were being read from the Books of Moses, the devotion somewhat lulled. Many made themselves comfortable and sat down, whispering perhaps business affairs with a friend, or went out into the court to get a little fresh air. Small boys took the liberty of visiting their mothers in the women's apartment; and here worship was still more loosely observed, as there was gossiping, cluttering together, or laughing, while, as will always happen, the young quizzed the elder, while the latter blamed the light-headedness of the girls and the general degeneracy of the age.[56]

The Bible in Pieces

Heine's *The Rabbi of Bacharach* (1840), an unfinished work of his youth, situates the above scene in the Great Synagogue of Frankfurt-am-Main, in the late Middle Ages. The poet's imagination certainly fed on observations he made in his own time, but there can be little doubt that the well-meaning irony he shows here would be no less in place at many a synagogue service today.

True, it is a great honor to be called forward to the Sefer, one that can be sold to the highest bidder and even become the object of rivalry or intense conflict among the congregation.[57] True, each important moment in the life of a believer—birth, coming of age, marriage, recovery from illness, mourning—is an occasion for going up to the Torah. True, if we are to believe the *Zohar**, anyone intending to read the Sefer should do it as if he were just then receiving the Torah on Mount Sinai; he should be clearly aware of the theurgic repercussions of the reading, since a chariot has been assigned to each of the fifty-three pericopes of the Pentateuch, each chariot bears the recited words to the Holy One, Blessed Be He, and these words end up adorning the divine throne in a process of unification of the higher spheres.[58]

Nevertheless, it is undeniable that, as soon as the *object* is no longer the main focus of attention, as soon as the *read text* takes pride of place, some of the solemnity of the occasion often shatters.

Readings

In a traditional or Orthodox setting, the women who have so far been able to follow with emotion the ritual opening of the Ark and the carrying of the scroll—at least from the balcony, or from behind the grille or curtain separating them from the men—are kept away from the reading. None is called to the *bimah*. As for the underage children, they often wander between the men's and women's rows. Seven believers, all adult males, "go up to the Torah."

As the pericope is solemnly read aloud, the others follow it, not always comprehendingly, from the vocalized and punctuated text in the little printed volume they have in their hands; it generally contains the book of the Pentateuch from which the pericope of the day has been extracted, together with an Aramaic paraphrase (the targum*) and the classical medieval commentary in rabbinical Hebrew by Rashi.[59] Those who cannot even decipher the text and read it in a drone without understanding the words have to make do with half-listening to it.

Only the most literate and experienced members of the congregation remain alert, ready to correct in a flash any mistakes that the cantor makes in reciting or cantillating the text. All he has in front of him is a manuscript, without the reading aids provided by vowel signs and *te'amim*. He follows it with the help of the *yad* (literally "hand"), the ritual pointer that enables him to avoid touching the parchment with his finger. He will usually have rehearsed during the week, but he can still make a mistake, and sometimes an assistant stands next to him and indicates the *te'amim* he may have missed or forgotten.

The believer called up to the Torah rarely reads the allotted passage of the pericope himself. Besides, he often does not grasp one word or another in what the cantor reads for him. And once he has touched the beginning of the passage with the corner of his prayer shawl (which he then raises to his lips), he is usually content to utter—before and after the reading—the customary blessings, written out in Latin script for the least educated members of the congregation.

In this precise case, as well as more generally in the recitation of daily prayers, the mystical efficacy of the reading does not depend upon correct understanding (or "cognitive comprehension")[60] of the text in question. A curious mix of closeness and distance, a familiar strangeness, one might say, creates, establishes, and preserves the sacred, while also making dealings with it possible. Here, *not to understand* the words of the language in which the divine Word is expressed—a language both close (in its sonority and melody, often since childhood) and mysterious (because nonvernacular)—is also paradoxically, but no less surely, a way of participating in the worship of that Word.

Whatever the degree of Jewish literacy and culture in the community, there is a remarkable variation or blatant, inevitable inequality—in terms of age, gender, knowledge, and social belonging—concerning the extent and modes of access to the Sefer object, the words written on it, and a fortiori the meaning of the words. Moreover, this is coupled with a deliberate material and textual splintering of the Bible: as material support or as mere accessory of the daily or festive liturgy.

Only the Pentateuch is there in its entirety, copied in the Sefer, an object for that very reason hard to manage. Only a fragment is read aloud on each occasion—the pericope of such and such a Monday or Thursday, such and such a Shabbat or festival or day of fasting—and each believer "called to the Torah" reads only a fragment of that fragment. To be sure, the synagogue ritual incorporates the other two major divisions of the scriptural canon into its cycle of ritual readings: the *Nevi'im* (Prophets) and the *Ketuvim* (Writings). But it does so in a modest, measured manner, almost parsimoniously. Except in the case of Esther, as we have seen, the codex used is always vocalized and punctuated—lower on the scale of holiness. The books of the prophets are only ever read in snippets (a choice of a few dozen extracts in all), in the form of the *haftarah* (literally, "conclusion"), *after* the reading of the Torah.

This complementary and highly selective reading is sometimes explained by reference to a decree banning the study or public recitation of the Torah that the Seleucid king Antiochus IV Epiphanes promulgated in the second century BCE, on the eve of the Maccabean revolt. Starting out as a substitute—it is argued—the reading eventually came to take its place alongside that of the Pentateuch.[61] With the recitation of the "Five Scrolls," it allows the believer to be put in solemn periodical contact with the three sections of the Jewish biblical corpus, though always in a fragmented, uneven, and hierarchical fashion.

Nor is this all. In certain periods and milieux, this limited, fragmentary liturgical use of the corpus became the only occasion when the believer had real contact with the Bible. In Ashkenazi regions, which overvalued the Oral Tradition and its chief incarnation, the Talmud*, a deliberate intention to *reduce* the Bible to a simple liturgical text made itself felt from the eleventh to the thirteenth century on—which meant, of course, that the Bible became marginalized as an object of study.[62] In Islamic countries, too, the manuscript "Bible" usually found in most families consisted only of the Pentateuch and the *haftarot*: that is, what was needed for the synagogue.[63]

Generally speaking, the forms and meaning of Jewish liturgical appropriation of the Bible exhibit a profound ambiguity. To take another example, Psalms is very present in the life of believers,[64] yet only a half of the 150 psalms in the Bible are actually recited in the course of daily, monthly, and annual ceremonies, or at key moments in individual lives. And they have found their way into those only gradually over the centuries, partly in response to a demand expressed by believers themselves.

Supererogatory reading of all five books of the Psalter is certainly a widespread practice, whether on the part of especially devout individuals (cultured or not) or of "societies" specifically formed for that purpose. But it is not immaterial that the prayer said after a recitation of each of the five books of Psalms establishes a correspondence between them and the five books of Moses, and hence, indirectly, between the merit earned from scrupulously reading the former—their songs, verses, words, and letters, their vowel points, *te'amim*, and the holy Names of God they contain—and the merit from reading and studying the latter. The Psalter here plays the role of Torah substitute, at once humbler, closer (it is a little book which, unlike the Bible, easily slips into one's pocket), and (almost) as efficacious.

The *siddur*, the prayer book that accompanies the believer in his liturgical life, is equally characterized by a real ambiguity. Although a great number of versions are in use, reflecting Jewish cultural diversity and various traditions of worship,[65] its architecture is more or less constant. But whereas the material of Karaite rituals is essentially biblical,[66] Rabbanite ritual combines and interweaves texts belonging to many different linguistic and literary layers: biblical literature, of course, but also normative texts, benedictions, and prayers from mishnic* and talmudic* epochs, liturgical poems (*piyyutim*) of various origins.

Here the Bible is the object of both extensive and selective use. In addition to Psalms, certain other texts are especially valued: Hannah's prayer,[67] the story of Isaac's sacrifice,[68] instructions for daily burnt offerings,[69] the ordering of aromatic incense,[70] consecration of the first-born,[71] the Canticle of the Sea,[72] the Shema, and so on. However, the logic behind the choice and order of these texts should not be sought in the Bible itself. It corresponds, first, to the exigencies of the synagogue liturgy, to the themes and prescriptions it is meant to underline and perpetuate, especially practices such as sacrifices that have been suspended since the destruction of the Jerusalem Temple. Moreover, many passages in the daily liturgy that look distinctly biblical are in reality patchwork strings assembled and rearranged from the whole scriptural corpus, with no account taken of their original context.[73]

Finally, and equally remarkably, some biblical texts that may appear fundamental to the modern reader were marginalized from Jewish ritual for what may be described as circumstantial reasons. First example: chapter 12 of Exodus, which establishes Passover and narrates the flight of the Hebrews from Egypt, is absent from the Haggadah (literally, "narrative"), the text read at the family celebration of the seder (literally, "order"),[74] whose main function is to allow those present to discharge the (originally biblical)[75] obligation of recounting and explaining this seminal event to new generations. No doubt because early Christianity took over Exodus 12 (to give it an allegorical interpretation), the rabbis preferred a midrashic exegesis of an incomparably denser and more concise biblical passage, Deuteronomy 26.5–8, which mentions neither Moses nor the paschal offering.[76]

Second (equally eloquent) example: the ambiguous liturgical status of the Decalogue. Since this text appears at two different places in the Pentateuch,[77] it is read twice during the annual cycle of public Torah reading, and even a third time at the festival of Shavuot. Its reading takes place in an atmosphere of particular solemnity: the congregation stand to listen to the ten commandments, whereas normally they remain seated during the Sefer reading. But the fact remains that the Decalogue is excluded from the daily ritual. "In law," Rabbis Matna and Samuel bar Nahman state, "the ten commandments should be read every day [in the framework of prayers]. So why are they not read? So that heretics [*minim*— that is, members of sects close to Christianity] cannot claim that they [those ten commandments] were the only ones given to Moses."[78]

Apart from clearly identifiable quotations from Scripture, and in spite of real recollections, the Hebrew of the *siddur* is not a "biblical" Hebrew. It is as if the masters of liturgy were committed to emancipating their production from that model (without disowning it) and ensuring the free development of distinctively rabbinical prayer. In fact, there is nothing "biblical" in the two emblematic texts of the daily prayers: kaddish* is essentially in Aramaic; and the *amidah*—which is first recited individually in silence by each believer, then repeated aloud by the cantor—develops its string of nineteen benedictions without embellishing them with scriptural quotations.[79] Note that kaddish and *amidah* are recited *standing*, whereas the Shema, a set of three fundamental biblical texts, is read *seated*.[80]

A little of the Bible, then, but not too much: such seems to be the guiding principle of the liturgy. However, what the congregation is supposed to hear and read, sometimes without understanding it, is not *the* Bible, a forgotten book, a dissolved corpus, but rather a *bespoke Bible* strangely put together through a complex process of concealment, cuts, and collages—highly malleable material (among other material) intertwined in a multilayer construction.

The Torah itself is in shreds, cut up into fifty-three pericopes. To be sure, these are read in the actual order of their succession in the text, but their reading never leads into the "sequel" (Joshua and the conquest of the Holy Land); once the final verse of Deuteronomy is reached, the inescapable logic of a partial, circular reading leads back to the first verse of Genesis.

So, are these the only (paradoxical) routes to Scripture available to the ordinary member of the synagogue congregation? Is there not a time and place at which all this falls into shape again, making clear sense and finally displaying its coherence, its fundamental unity? That time and place does exist: it is the time and place of *interpretation*. For, despite everything, the wish to make others *understand*—not only see and hear—has really and truly been there since the beginning.

Sermons

When Ezra and his adjuncts, in a founding gesture, proceeded to the first solemn reading "of the book, of God's Torah," they did so "distinctly" (*meforash*), "giving the sense" (*ve-sum sekhel*) "so that the people understood the reading" (*va-yavinu ba-mikra*). The verse (Neh. 8.8) that makes these points is somewhat obscure, but rabbinical tradition sees it as alluding to the institution of the targum: that is, "translation" into the vernacular language of the time—Aramaic—for an audience that, in Babylonia and then Palestine, had gradually become incapable of understanding the Hebrew original.[81]

The targum—which, far from being a literal reconstitution of the translated text, initially enriched it with aggadic material such as one finds in the midrashim* and the Talmud—is probably at the root of the homiletic tradition now thousands of years old. Varying in form and nature with the cultural-historical circumstances, marked by the author's own inclinations, and responding (or refusing to respond) to the expectations of the audience, the sermon is addressed to men, women, and children, the learned, the uneducated, and the poor in spirit, the cultured and the illiterate—to all who gather at least once a week, on the holy day of Shabbat, to behold the Sefer, to hear the divine word inscribed within it, and to listen to the lesson, often a practical moral one urging them to improve their ways, that the preacher intends the people to draw from it.

Whereas the reading of the Torah has been subject to strict and precise rules, the sermon, though an integral part of Jewish religious worship, has remained rather hazy in its status. The moment when it should be delivered has varied over the centuries—after the Torah reading, before it as an introduction, or even much earlier in the Saturday morning service—as has the nature of its intended link with the pericope of the week.

Its prime purpose is not necessarily to elucidate the biblical text read that day. Thus, a sixteenth-century Italian rabbi, Mordekhai Dato, mainly justified his practice of the sermon as a means of ensuring "that words of the Oral Law would be uttered after the recitation of the three-fold Written Law [encompassing] Torah, Prophets, and Writings."[82]

Clearly, the place of the sermon in the Sabbath ritual allowed it to benefit from the aura attached to Holy Scripture and the Sefer, whose removal from the Ark and solemn reading was the climax of the morn-ing liturgy. And by virtue of an old and scrupulously respected tradi-tion, Jewish sermons (like Christian ones) certainly began with a verse from the Bible.

In the thirteenth and fourteenth centuries, this opening quotation might well come from one of the books of Writings (rather than the Pentateuch), most often Proverbs, and the application of this verse to the pericope of the day came only halfway through, the discussion of the pericope being effectively reserved for the second part of the sermon. Later, in the fifteenth century, Joseph Ibn Shem-Tov did not hesitate to open his sermons in the period following Passover with a passage from the *Chapters of the Fathers*[83] read in the synagogue on that Sabbath, even if this meant barely skimming the pericope of the day.

In fact, even when it began with a biblical verse, the sermon might well have only a tenuous link with it. According to Isaac Aboab, for example, who was writing around 1492, the point of it was twofold: to indicate that the preacher's remonstrations with the public did not reflect his personal humor but had an actual basis in the Torah; and to illustrate the greatness of the Torah by showing that "ideas seemingly new are already present in it by allusion."[84]

In the end, it was only after the expulsion of the Jews from Spain in 1492 that the Sephardi sermon acquired a normal structure, open-ing with a biblical verse from the pericope of the day, immediately followed by a rabbinical *maamar* (literally, "saying"), midrashic com-mentary, or aggadic* narrative, whose link with the verse was not im-mediately obvious.

As we can see, the sermon was not meant to comment on the *whole* biblical pericope of the day; there was a clear wish to show the organic unity, not so much of the biblical text itself, as of the Torah in the broader, rabbinical sense, which includes the Written Law and the Oral Law. Once again, therefore, the biblical text appears as no more than one element—essential but not isolable—of a greater whole that alone gives it meaning and justifies it.

Whereas the ritual of the Sefer reading apparently maximized the grandeur and holiness of the written text of the Law—whose meaning remained nevertheless closed to many—the preacher's sermon, in a language accessible to all, inserted the text into a broader horizon that might seem in a way to have undermined it. At the same time, the sermon updated the text and brought it closer to the audience, making it a tool for their repentance and a guide for their daily lives.

But there is more. At least in a tendency that seems to have caught on in the late fifteenth century, this movement of reductive integration and didactic updating went together with a movement that ran partly in the opposite direction but was nevertheless complementary: that is, a deliberate, indefinite, almost infinite atomization of the biblical text itself. The verse opening the Sephardi sermon was thus subjected to a technique that either disaggregated it—successive explanations being given of the first two words, then the first four, then the first six, until the whole verse had been covered—or made it the stuff of an antithetical treatment, or offered, in repetitive mode, a series of different exegeses.

The principle underlying these interpretive games is clear: to show that even a minimal biblical text has endless semantic possibilities, that in Scripture, word groupings with no apparent meaning do actually have one, and that the smallest Torah fragment is capable of relating to the preoccupations of the moment.

Application of this principle naturally went beyond the Sephardi world. Take, for example, Jacob ben Wolf Kranz (1741–1804), the celebrated preacher better known as "the Maggid of Dubno," after the Ukrainian town where he officiated for eighteen years. Did he not have the reputation—which allowed him to be distinguished from imposters—of being able to take any Torah verse and liturgical text *at random* and, with the help of a *mashal* (a parable or allegorical story), to improvise a sermon explaining the intimate link between the two?[85]

There is thus a striking contrast between, on the one hand, the

highly rigorous attention to the material integrity of the Sefer, the respect, fervor, and veneration that the object itself inspires, and, on the
other hand, the liberty taken by the preacher in his sermon to dismem-
ber and reconstruct *ad indefinitum* the Word that has just been read.
To quote a text—for example, a biblical verse or fragment of a verse at
the beginning of a sermon—is a way of paying it homage, of bowing
before it, recognizing its authority, celebrating its power. But it is also
to demonstrate the power that one has—or would like to have—over
the text, if only by cutting it up and authoritatively extracting a tiny
sliver. Here, to serve the text already means to make it do service.

Quotations

What is true of the sermon, or of the liturgy itself and its patchwork
of verses, applies more generally to almost the whole of postbiblical
Jewish literary production.

With the one noteworthy exception of the Mishnah*—where the
Bible plays only a subordinate role, and which expresses a Judaism
that, instead of seeking its proofs in Scripture or constructing itself as
a commentary on it, presents itself as integrating the totality of Revelation (written and oral) into an autonomous rhetorical and logical
system[86]—classical and medieval rabbinical literature is saturated with
scriptural quotations.

Thus, whereas Maimonides, in his monumental code of Jewish Law,
the Mishneh Torah, deliberately chooses to refrain from mentioning
his rabbinical sources, he quotes frequently from the Bible—no doubt
to show, especially against the Karaites, that rabbinical Judaism is well
and truly derived from Scripture, that its theology and legal prescriptions have their roots in it.[87] In so doing, Maimonides, like so many
others before and after him, illustrates the profoundly dynamic character of the relationship of Judaism to the Bible—a relationship that
does not stop with the manifest sense of the text but postulates an
infinite polysemy, in the conviction that, abstracted from its literary
or historical context, disaggregated and put back together in line with
new circumstances and purposes, the text nevertheless continues to
impart meaning *here and now*. The only limit to this freedom in using
the text is the coherence of the Judaism that offers itself to be read and

heard, and it is precisely the scriptural quotation that helps to create this impression of coherence in the reader or listener.

"The painter," Jacob Neusner nicely puts it, "cannot paint without the oils. But the colors do not make the painting. The painter does."[88] No Judaism without the Bible, yet it is Jews, not the Bible, that make Judaism. One is talking of Judaism as the art and craft of scriptural quotation. For what are the tefillin, the mezuzah, the Sefer Torah? A choice of texts, of short or very long quotations, never the whole Bible. They are quotations embodied in distinct objects, which are themselves variously embedded in the life of the believer, showing on his skin in the morning, installed at the edges of his private space, appearing in glory at the heart of his community each Saturday morning. What then is the liturgy itself? Quotations. The sermon? Quotations. In each case, the quotation is a fragment twice over: a tiny sliver of a whole (the Bible) that is never present, but which it represents; and an element inserted into a new fabric (service, prayer, homily) that subsumes and transcends it.

"She is a tree of life to those who grasp her / And whoever holds on to her is happy." This verse from Proverbs (3.18) exalts the Wisdom (*hokhmah*) that the rabbis traditionally identified with the Torah. It is recited, along with others, during the ceremony of the ritual reading of the Torah, either at the point when the Sefer is removed from the Ark or when it is returned to it. As we have seen, the two wooden rollers around which the Sefer parchment is unrolled are themselves called *atzei hayyim*, "trees of life," and their decorative finials of precious metal like fruits, *rimmonim* (pomegranates) or *tappuhim* (apples).

This identification, both allegorical and near-material, of the Torah with a "tree of life," consisting "like a tree" of "branches and leaves, bark, sap and roots,"[89] is rich in theological and mystical implications. Here, however, I shall confine myself to what this verse from Proverbs mainly seems to be saying: that, for the person who grasps it, the Torah is a "tree of life," not only in the sense that it enlivens those who grasp it (and fills them with happiness), but also in the sense that *someone must grasp it* for it to become a truly living tree.

Anyone knows it who, once in his life, has been in a position to read even a brief passage of the Torah to his community from such a magnificently handwritten parchment—an object of absolute material perfection. Yet it is imperfect because incomplete: it lacks any aid to reading, such as vowels, punctuation, or cantillation. This imperfection is itself the ultimate perfection. "If the Torah had been vocalized," says an anonymous thirteenth-century Kabbalist, "it would have had limit and measure, as matter does when it acquires a shape, and it would not have been possible to interpret it except through a vocalization frozen onto each of its words."[90] The graphic imperfection or incompleteness of the Torah—which can be read in any number of ways—is the indirect sign of an infinite wealth of meanings: "For when the consonants are without vowels, they support a number of interpretations and may be divided in several ways . . . ; man can detect in them a multiplicity of wondrous and sublime meanings."[91]

In a liturgical context, of course, the Sefer reader does not have the exegetic scope of which the preacher will shortly make free use: he must comply strictly with the prescriptions of the *masorah*. If he happens to mispronounce a word or to miss a note, there will always be someone in attendance to correct him forthwith. But he is still aware of the real power he has over the text—a power that inevitably fills him with trepidation. He knows that "vowels are the *soul* of letters,"[92] and that he is the one who, by drawing on the memory he has acquired of them (sometimes at the cost of painful effort and long rehearsals), by raising his voice and reading or intoning a Word suddenly come to life, awakens a dormant text and restores its "soul" to a book that, when unread, was as if dead. He knows that, although he and his community are alive because of the precious life that the Torah breathes into them, he is still the one who, at this moment, makes the sap rise in the "tree of life" that is the Torah.

Thus, it is not simply that the Bible makes the Jew and brings him to life; the Jew also makes the Bible and brings it to life. And it is this Bible—the one that the Jew makes—that "accompanies the Jew from birth to death, and from death to eternity."[93] This "accompanying" is a form of companionship, the terms of which are fixed as much, indeed more, by the Jew than by the Bible. At the very moment when he seems lost in adoration of the *objects* embodying God's Word, including the Sefer (in principle, the "perfect example of the immutable book"),[94] the Jew is far from just passively worshiping images and simulacra ("paper and ink");[95] he preserves and exercises a strange, decisive power over that Word—an endless power to break up the Word and put it together again, a power of life and death over it.

The relationship of ambiguous symmetry between the people and its Book is thus unstable, dynamic, and fragile. In it, the people turns out to be much less the people of a book than the Book is the book of a people. And as we shall see, in spite of all the assignations, the people obstinately refuses to be reduced to this Book and hesitates to make it the key locus of its identity.

Three The Improbable Locus of an Identity

Take the Bible from the Jews, and they will no longer be Jewish. But if they are left only the Bible, will they still be Jews? All the ambiguity of the relationship between Jews and the Bible appears to be contained in this dilemma: the relationship essential to the Jews' identity is not sufficient to ground it. On closer examination, moreover, this seemingly nuanced, or anyway carefully balanced, judgment turns out to be a little too simple. Evidently more needs to be said. For a start, the "identity" problematic is itself inherently modern—or at least it has not been posed in the same way throughout the millennia of the Jews' historical trajectory as a collective, or of Judaism as a doctrine and culture. And the "identity" at issue is no less improbable than the "locus" where it is claimed to be established.

The Bible and Jewishness

Until almost the contemporary age, the great Jewish masters were not mainly concerned with preserving the "Jewishness" of Jews, their "identity;" indeed, the very notion of "identity" was probably quite alien to them. The preservation of *Judaism* as revealed Law, as the rule of individual and collective life, as authoritative teaching handed down from generation to generation, was their chief preoccupation. In their eyes, the stability of this complex construction—of which the Bible is only one component—was constantly under threat from the corrosive effects of exile, dispersal, and subjection to the nations, as well as from the seductive competition of other systems of thought and religious traditions with incomparably greater power resources. What they sought

57

to ensure was less that Jews "feel Jewish" deep down inside than that they behave as Jews and collectively take responsibility, in concrete terms, for the mission that God has assigned to them in this world.

Ancient and Medieval Foundations

This was doubtless the thinking of Isaac Abravanel (1437–1508), in the introduction to his commentary on Jeremiah, when he rejected the idea of some previous Jewish exegetes that the transmission of the sacred text may not have been altogether flawless. The Torah* was the only thing left to the Jews in exile, and any questioning of its integrity exposed them to grave perils. "Nothing stable will remain on which to support ourselves," he wrote.[1] However, he certainly did not believe that the Bible's only or main function was to guarantee the Jewishness of Jews; it was not a simple "cultural reference" grounding the identity of his fellow believers.

If the Bible had been no more than a "cultural reference," the idea that the text in our hands might not conform exactly to the text at the moment of its composition would not have represented a challenge to its status. But if the Torah was a divinely inspired legislative text, its very authority would be shaken by doubts about the reliability of the document from which it could be read. So, beyond the Bible itself, the whole edifice of Judaism was at stake, rather than that of a "Jewishness" that was anyway impossible to pin down. In rabbinical Judaism, this issue of flawless transmission of the Law went far beyond the text of the Bible alone. Any questioning of the authentic continuity of the *Oral* Tradition was equally fraught with dangers; that too, one might say, would leave us with "nothing stable on which to support ourselves."

This being so, the Jews of late antiquity or the Middle Ages undeniably saw themselves as, and claimed to be, the only legitimate continuators and direct inheritors of the people whose birth and early centuries of existence are narrated in the Bible. The situation called for this type of self-affirmation all the more because certain non-Jews (in this case, Christians) openly presented themselves as the *verus Israel*—the "true Israel," Israel in the spirit rather than the flesh.

Born out of the appropriation of a genealogy with its associated blessings, Christianity imposed this partly reactive posture on the Jews.

Faced with Jesus's claim in the Gospel of John that "the Father who sent me testifies on my behalf,"[2] or with Paul's identification of the "offspring" of Abraham[3]—and the promises made to him—with the person of Christ alone, Jews could only insist that *they* were "the descendants of Abraham,"[4] that their "Father" was "Abraham,"[5] and ultimately God himself.[6]

For Jewish apologetic discourse, therefore, along with the authenticity and reliable transmission of God's Revelation to the Jews, one of the unchallengeable foundations of what it meant to be a Jew was the continuity of a *history*, embodied in the Jews alone, that had its roots in the biblical narrative (for us half-mythical, half-historical, but for our predecessors absolutely historical). Thus, the Jews saw themselves as the true descendants and sole legatees of a biblical founding ancestor, Abraham, and ultimately as the faithful disciples of a founding master, Moses, a no less biblical figure and even the biblical "author" par excellence.

From this, however, no one can honestly conclude that the Bible occupies a central position as a *book*, nor this time as revealed Law or a "family novel," in the premodern—and even modern—traditions that conceive of "Jewishness" from the point of view of ordinary believers. Nor should one mechanically conclude that this "Jewishness" is a definitely biblical identity.

Of course, at every seder when the Haggadah is recited around the family table—to take just one example—every Jew was, and is, ritually exhorted to think of himself or herself as having been liberated in person from Egyptian servitude. But this "making present" of the biblical past as an identity is no less ambiguous for all that. As we have seen,[7] the story of the departure from Egypt told at the seder evening is not the same as the scriptural narrative in Exodus; apart from anything else, it does not mention Moses, the main hero of the episode. Here, therefore, the "locus" of the identity is clearly not the book or text but a narrative schema—a myth, one might say—whose links with the book and the text are in the end rather loose.

The Israeli writer A. B. Yehoshua hits the nail on the head when he says that, regardless of place, language, or national culture, *all* Jewish identity is ultimately based on foundational narratives, or "metanarratives."[8] These cannot be changed but only interpreted. Above all, they only partly depend upon the texts or books where they first offered themselves to be read. Many of these narratives are certainly of biblical origin: for example, Isaac's sacrifice, the Exodus, or the saving of the Jews by Queen Esther. But others that equally play a role in founding Jewish identity do not stem from the Bible: for example, the miracle of Hanukkah*, or the Ninth of the Month of Av* (commemorating the destruction of the Temple).

Finally, nothing indicates that the "identity" question—at least in the sense in which we usually understand it today—was really central in the ordinary experience of premodern Jews. The fact of belonging to one's community was then inescapably bound up with one's birth; individuals had no legal existence outside it. Born Jewish, a Jew was spontaneously recognized as such by Jews and non-Jews alike, and he was required to live in accordance with the norms of his community, the compulsory interface linking him legally and fiscally with the surrounding society. The definition of "inner identity" was a decidedly secondary matter. Jewishness was thus much more a condition, from which Jews could escape only by conversion to the dominant religion. And the individual's relationship with the Bible as a book played an altogether subordinate role in defining that condition.

The "judaization" process involved in conversion to Judaism further illustrates this relative indifference to the biblical referent. It has traditionally been the theme of debates about its very possibility, about the nature of the change it effects in the convert, and about the degree of integration into the community that he can hope to achieve from it. Remarkably, however, the theme of attachment or allegiance to Scripture as such has been far from central to such debates.

In the famous talmudic account of the conflict between Hillel and Shammai (second half of first century BCE to early first century CE)[9] over criteria for the acceptance or rejection of three would-be converts,[10] it is not at all the Bible per se but rather the candidates' relationship to the Torah in its entirety—the Written and Oral Torah inextricably associated with each other—that is at the center of debates. Similarly, Scripture hardly features at all in a passage from the talmudic tractate[11] that codifies the procedure for acceptance of a proselyte and the dialogue to be held between him and the community he wishes to join. The main things about which he should be informed are the (currently unenviable) fate of the Jewish people in the Diaspora, his religious and social obligations if he decides to take the leap, and the grave sanctions he would face in the event of transgression. To become a Jew, there is no need to show you are a devout biblical scholar; on the contrary, what counts is to show that you have acquired a humble awareness of the commitments you will be assuming, and of the difficult *condition* you will be sharing.

Finally, the main disputes over the principle of integrating the Other through conversion into the community of the faithful focused precisely on questions with a genealogical tinge not unlike those in the debates with Christianity mentioned above. How to integrate a convert into the genealogy of Israel when he is completely alien to it in blood and even threatens to introduce a degree of confusion harmful to Israel itself? How, despite everything, can he be made at least the symbolic descendant of the father of the nation (Abraham)? And how can he acquire indisputable rights to the special heritage of the people he is joining: that is, to the Torah it was given in the desert through the intermediary of Moses?[12] Once again, it must be said that the Bible as such remains strangely out of the picture.

Modern Ambiguities

In the end, the question of Jewish "identity" (as we now usually understand it) and the question of its "biblical" foundation only emerged as concomitants of particular historical contexts. It is thus worthy of note that the Bible regularly served to underpin and express the processes of identity *reconstruction* accompanying "returns to Judaism."

Any such movement was experienced as a "return to the sources," and the Bible was usually the first "source" to present itself to the minds of those executing the return. But was that because it really constituted the "prime source" of the Judaism that was the goal of the return? Or was it because those executing the return had no idea that Judaism was anything but simply biblical, and because, of all the "Jewish" sources, the Old Testament has remained the most easily accessible, being a cultural reference shared by *others* (especially Christians)?

This ambiguous status of the Bible—its familiar strangeness or strange familiarity, we might say—naturally marks it out as a bridge from one world to another. This being so, anyone who remains on the bridge (the Bible) after beginning to leave one world (the non-Jewish) has not yet truly entered the other world (the Jewish). To return to Judaism via the Bible makes you at best a "Judaizer," certainly not a Jew.

The most telling example of this biblical ambiguity, its reference as both mark of identity and path to rejudaization, is the itinerary of the Marranos*—or at least some Marranos—who returned to Judaism at the beginning of the modern age. For them, the Old Testament was the easiest "Jewish" printed book to obtain, not only in the Spain and Portugal of the Inquisition, but also, at least for a time, outside the Iberian Peninsula. "To judaize" then meant making "heretical" (non-Christian, anti-Christian, supposedly Jewish) use of the Old Testament.

Such was the case, from 1596 on, with those "secret gatherings" of Portuguese merchants in Saint Jean de Luz that "read out passages relating to Judaism from a French Bible, and then had to speak about them." Shortly afterwards, around the turn of the century, the same people were reciting a Bible in Castilian, published by the Spanish Calvinist Cipriano de Valera in Amsterdam in 1602—which obviously also included a New Testament. Everyone bowed most deeply "whenever the reader uttered the word Jehovah."[13]

For many Marranos, the rejudaization process went smoothly enough right up to the full and rigorous adoption of rabbinical norms, which meant that the Bible became once more what it was supposed to be: just one component of a larger whole, which alone gave it meaning and framed the reading of it. Others, however, somehow stopped at the first (scriptural) stage of the return to Judaism, never reentering the bosom of Jewish Orthodoxy.

Rather as Nicolas Antoine (1602–32) left Catholicism for Protestantism, then invented his Judaism "by working alone on his Hebrew Bible,"[14] the former Marrano Uriel da Costa—reading only a literal translation—cultivated a kind of integral scripturalism that led him to reject, first Christianity, then rabbinical Judaism itself! "The Pharisees*," he wrote, meaning the rabbis, "are such that out of duty or folly they take it upon themselves to change words, to distort, twist, and misinterpret Scripture, in order to strengthen and confirm their confused reveries by these deceitful means."[15] And far from just reproaching the rabbis for their whimsical exegeses, da Costa went so far as to suspect them of manipulating the scriptural text and introducing "unauthentic" books into the biblical canon.[16] Here the Bible is evidently not a bridge to Judaism: it even blocks access to it. Representing a deviation for both Jews and Christians, the biblical scholarship of a Uriel da Costa therefore never made him into a Jew—indeed, it prevented him from becoming one.

As the case of the Marranos shows, adherence to the biblical referent is not by itself a conclusive indicator of Jewish identity. It may be the equivocal expression of a still awkward, unfulfilled wish to move beyond indecision, the first stage in a move toward Judaism that may never be completed. At best it is the *point d'appui* of a fragile consciousness—perhaps, above all, the consciousness of a fragility, the Bible appearing either as the foundation stone of a Judaism still to be reconstructed or as basically all that remains of a Judaism that the vicissitudes of history have largely emptied of its traditional content.

The theme of the biblical foundation of Jewish identity only really takes hold in historical contexts where that identity is in an advanced state of dissolution, where Scripture serves as a final anchorage for those whom the assimilationist current threatens to carry away, or where the Jewish teachers of the day brandish it themselves to ward off the devastating effects of that current. It is therefore hardly surprising that the contemporary period, unlike those that went before it, has witnessed a massive Jewish reinvolvement in the Bible—as if, in a sociohistorical environment of massive upheavals, it alone could still serve as compass and rallying point for a fragmented Jewish world with no clear sense of direction.

Over the decades, emancipation, integration, and acculturation have distorted—and most often distended—the link that roots Jews in their community. Their affiliation is now only voluntary: it no longer insinuates itself between them and the state. A Jew becomes just one citizen among others; no trade or responsibility is closed anymore; it is possible to believe or not to believe, family traditions are gradually unravelling, exogamous marriage is free to compromise the continuity of the genealogical chain, and the Jewish religious spectrum has widened considerably to include currents that are often at loggerheads with one another. The question of "Jewish identity" and its possible definitions then becomes vital. And the Bible is again called upon, though always ambiguously, to play a key role.

Contemporary Problems

For the German poet Heinrich Heine, who converted to Lutheranism in 1825, the Bible was a "portable fatherland";[17] it partly replaced the lost Jewish home. For the French Orientalist James Darmesteter (1849–94), the theorist of Franco-Judaism—a kind of Jewish coopting of the values of Republican France, identified with the values of the prophetic tradition—Jewish Scripture purely and simply supplanted the notion of the Jewish people: "Israel," he declared, "has not been what it is, nor done what it has done, nor lasted through all the forces of destruction, by virtue of a mysterious racial virtue, but only by virtue of a book: it is what the Bible has made of it . . . and we should speak not of a mission of the Jewish people but of a mission of the Jewish book."[18]

More surprisingly, a century later at the beginning of the 1990s, the editors of a modern Hebrew commentary on Scripture—Israeli biblical scholars and distinguished academics, religious though not ultra-Orthodox, who knew well the exigencies of a critical approach—still presented the Bible as the "spiritual and cultural heritage" enjoying the broadest consensus within the Jewish people. They saw in it the source of "Jewish identity," of the way in which Jews perceive their "existence" and their "vocation" as "individuals" and a "national collective." As the "foundation" of Jewish culture, Scripture was the "common denominator" of all "parties" in Israeli society, as well as the factor uniting "all Jews in all the countries of their dispersion."[19]

Probably the influence of Zionism can be felt here, given that it too made novel and intensive use of the biblical reference,[20] but the discourse in question went well beyond that particular ideological and political horizon. Around the end of the twentieth century, the Bible was still being presented, even in Israel, as the principal (or exclusive?) anchorage point of Jewish identity.

Thus if, over a period of more than two centuries at various places in the Diaspora, the Bible was regularly invoked as the final recourse against dissolution, or the main common denominator in the face of fragmentation, it is hardly surprising that it also served in France of the 1970s as the primary and compulsory point of entry for many of those executing a (chiefly cultural) return to Judaism.[21] In this case, however, as in every other, the Bible never ceased to have an ambiguous status, even in the eyes of those who exalted its power to crystallize Jewish identity. There were at least two reasons for this.

First, no one can be unaware that this textual heritage does not belong exclusively to Judaism; we are talking of a shared legacy. Although "the grains of Judaism are sown in the Bible,"[22] Jews themselves also perceive it as the grain sown by Judaism in the soil of world culture. Moreover, this sharing serves the aims of contemporary Jewish apologetics, which underlines the universal cultural merits of Judaism.

"The Bible is our sole *raison d'être*," said Solomon Schechter (1847–1915), an eminent scholar and thinker of American *conservative* Judaism, in a speech he gave in 1903. It is "our patent of nobility granted to us by the Almighty God." But it is also "our great claim to the gratitude of mankind," since through it "we gave to the world the word of God."[23] Even when a Zionist thinker like Eliezer Schweid (b. 1929) tried to clarify the place of the Bible in the Israeli (secular) educational system, he could not but recall—in line with Franz Rosenzweig (1886–1929)[24]—that the Bible is the most important book in the history of Western as well as Jewish culture, and that, although it symbolizes the unified existence of the Jewish people throughout its history, it is also the key to the continuity of Western culture.[25] Lastly, although the North American Jewish thinker Abraham Heschel (1907–72) saw the Jewish people as the specific "community in whom the Bible lives on," he still presented the return to the Bible as the solution to a global crisis—not only of Jewish modernity but also of non-Jewish modernity.[26]

Second, two conditions seem necessary for the Bible to play in full its role as the mainstay of Jewish identity:

(a) The return must be to the *Hebrew* Bible,[27] since the Bible is truly Jewish only insofar as it is read in Hebrew. Hermann Cohen (1842–1918) called Hebrew precisely "the language of *our* Bible," not wishing to see it become "a secular tongue in everyday use."[28]

(b) The return to the Bible can never be more than a first stage of rejudaization, because it is always important to go beyond it.[29] For Leo Strauss (1899–1973), "the rock bottom of any Jewish culture" is not only the Bible but also "the Talmud* and the Midrash*"—and beyond those we have to remember that "the substance of Judaism" is "not culture, but divine revelation."[30] Similarly, for André Neher (1914–88), "Scripture," "the Oral" (the Talmud), and "lived experience" (the *Zohar**, Kabbalah*) together form Judaism, which therefore can be opened only with a "three-notched key."[31]

✳

In the end, therefore, whichever the period or the type of Jew one has in mind—great masters of the medieval tradition, ordinary believers of premodern communities, Marranos finding their way back to Judaism, or contemporary dejudaized individuals in search of spiritual renewal—the Bible never seems to have been able to provide the stable and definitive foundation that Jewish identity may have needed. But this cannot be attributed entirely either to the peculiarities of rabbinical Judaism—for which the Hebrew Bible is only one source among others—or to Scripture's having become common property.

The Bible is not and cannot be simply a *frontier*, because it is itself a *territory*—one that is sometimes disputed, being both a meeting point and a locus of confrontation with the (internal as well as external) Other. Above all, it is a territory whose definition or characterization often depends less on the Jew than on the one who gazes at him. If the Bible seems to "make the Jew," this is only because in one way or another, the non-Jew—pagan, Christian, or Muslim—has decided that it should be so.

The reduction of Jewish identity to its biblical source has never had, and can never have, the status of self-evident fact. Nor is the Bible ever just what Jews spontaneously ask it to be for them.

The Greeks, the Arabs, and Us

In the pagan world of late antiquity, the identification of Jews with the Bible was primarily a weapon for their detractors to belittle them. The contempt in which certain anti-Christian polemicists held Holy Scripture naturally went together with contempt for its authors and editors, while the high regard that Jews (and Christians) had for their literary heritage was seen and presented as an evident sign of their mediocrity.

Pagan Denigration, Christian Responses

Celsus in the second century, for example, did not spare the Jews when he aimed his arrows against the new religion born out of the teaching of Jesus and his disciples.[32] This was only fair: did not Christians draw their "insane doctrine" from the "barbarian source" that the Jews had handed down to them? Huddled in their remote corner of Palestine, ignorant that Hesiod and other incomparably more inspired poets had already sung of such things, they concocted a crude history that utterly defied belief and was better suited to amuse little children than to occupy the public limelight. Jews and Christians themselves, Celsus claims, blushed at the laughable fictions they had brought into the world. And their absurd allegorical reading of them was certainly not likely to save the reputation of that monumental piece of bad literature, which could never compete with the depth and majesty of the poetry and philosophy produced by the Greco-Roman world.

Faced with such denigration, Christianity did not simply respond in kind. Lactantius, an early fourth-century Christian apologist, accepted that the Bible might be scorned "by people who do not wish to hear or read anything unless it is perfectly polished and well said, and whose minds can settle only on things that tickle their ears with caressing sounds."[33] Saint Augustine himself, at the end of the fourth century, recognized that when he first applied himself to the Scriptures they had "compared poorly with the polished prose of Cicero."[34] As to Origen, the author of a celebrated eight-book *Contra Celsum* in the third century, he readily accepted, before Lactantius and Augustine, that "the Jewish prophets and the disciples of Jesus refrained from the art of literary composition." But he saw this as a novelty that conferred an evident advantage: it placed them within reach of "the human crowds" they aimed to influence.[35]

However conscious it was of the distance between the pagan and biblical legacies, Christianity initially refused to choose one to the complete exclusion of the other. Indeed, it sought to coopt pagan literature, detecting in Aeschylus, Euripides, Homer, and especially Ovid and Virgil various insights that left the way open for a Christian interpretation of the classics.

It was not a major problem that the Bible departed somewhat from the aesthetic canons of the ancient world. Its holiness lay less in its form than its message. It had the privilege of absolute seniority, was the least corrupt of the existing literatures, and was safe from any contradiction. For it was the word of the living God Himself. It was thus much more than mere literature: its literal sense was still true, while alone containing a spiritual meaning; it accorded aesthetic pleasure and moral edification in perfect harmony with each other. Still, it was also literature and had to be approached as such. To deny its literary merit would have been to capitulate to its pagan detractors, and only an interpreter familiar with the ways of secular belles lettres was capable of penetrating all its secrets.[36]

This middle position involved a delicate balance. It was not without dangers, since a Christian reader with an overdeveloped aesthetic sense could always end up preferring Virgil to Scripture. In any case, the debate within Christendom was settled once and for all in favor of the Bible by the English monk and historian Bede (672–735), for whom Scripture was superior to any other literary production, not only because of its absolute authority and divine origin, but also because of the quality of its rhetoric.[37]

Greek Reverence, Rabbinical Countertendencies

Even before the emergence of Christianity, Hellenistic Judaism had adopted a position that was in many ways similar. In fact, the history of the Bible as literature really began in Alexandria—in a distinctive context, to be sure, even though hellenized Egypt was certainly not immune from anti-Jewish prejudices.[38] Ever since Alexander's conquest of Judea, in the last part of the fourth century BCE, the Greeks had shown a certain deference for Jewish wisdom and its antiquity. The Bible sometimes reminded them of the great founding texts of Greek culture, and Moses could pass for a kind of Jewish Homer.

The allegorical reading of Scripture characteristic of the Alexandrian Jewish tradition, whose most masterly representative was Philo,[39] crystallized in this context and was essentially a Greek way of giving meaning to a Jewish classic.[40] But the fact remains that the Christians were the only true continuators of that tradition. The Pharisee* teachers in the Holy Land and their successors did not read the Bible in Greek like Philo or the Christians. And even if their hermeneutic practice resembles that of their non-Jewish contemporaries, they seem to have adopted an attitude to the critiques of Scripture emanating from pagan milieux markedly different from those of the Christians or their Alexandrian Jewish predecessors.

For the hellenized Jew Flavius Josephus, the holy writings were still excellent books of history. Although he thought that Jews "must yield to the Grecian writers as to language and eloquence of composition,"[41] he considered that, from a strictly historiographic point of view, they were quite exceptional and completely trustworthy, "because everyone [among the Jews] is not permitted of his own accord to be a writer, nor is there any disagreement in what is written."[42]

As to the rabbis, they neither bothered with such subtleties nor adopted such an apologetic posture. In their eyes, it was a punishable offense to see the Torah as a collection of songs, as David did.[43] Daniel *deliberately* constructed his narrative against the elementary rules of historiography and rhetoric, introducing an appearance of disorder because he did not wish it said that it was "the work of a poet."[44] He wanted everyone to know that divine inspiration alone had guided him—not a concern for artifice, ornamentation, and trickery, which may make literature good and discourse convincing, but to which the real and simple truth can and must remain alien.[45]

As the rabbis saw it, the Bible was evidently imperfect as history or literature, but that very imperfection attested to its genuine, infinitely superior, perfection. In no way did the Bible belong to the same genre as the works of Homer; it was a unique document of its kind. Only "sacred writings" make your hands dirty[46]—not the works of Homer. This is a radical difference of nature, not of degree, and that is why it has precise implications at the level of ritual. "Sacred writings" are to the books of Homer what the remains of a great priest are to the carcass of a donkey.[47] And if the truthful discourse of Scripture has none of the rhetorical ornaments that make "fine" literature, this should be seen not as the result of something it lacks, but as an indisputable sign of superiority.

In a sense—to put it a little abruptly—the rabbis were not far from thinking of the Bible in more or less the same way that Celsus regarded it. Only they drew opposite conclusions.

The Bible as Non-Literature

For a long time, this rabbinical reticence about any "consecration" of the Bible as a literary work clearly differentiated Jewish attitudes from those prevalent in the Christian world. We read in the *Zohar**: "Woe to those who say that Torah has been given to show us mere stories and profane things!"[48] And although it accepts that the profane books of the Gentiles are much better, from a strictly literary point of view, the *Zohar* further warns: "Shall we then follow them, and make a Torah out of them?"[49]

In the mid-twentieth century, Abraham Heschel echoed this: "Some people hail the Bible as 'literature,' as if such juxtaposition were the highest praise, as if 'literature' were the climax of spiritual reality. What would Moses, what would Isaiah have said to such praise?"[50] Eliezer Schweid, for his part, though agreeing to regard the Bible as literature, does not forget to emphasize that it serves a "metaliterary" purpose.[51]

In this connection, it is not unreasonable to think that the seemingly "disproportionate" interest of Jewish academic scholarship in *literary* study of the Bible, and questions of intertextuality within it, is a way of evading, not only the solvent effects of contemporary biblical criticism, but also the religious ("metaliterary") status of the sacred texts. Although such literary study may appear to be a kind of "neo-midrash*," posing in principle or revealing in practice the ultimate unity of the scriptural text, it still marks a sharp break with the classical posture of rabbinical Judaism. James Kugel is not wrong in pointing out that to read the Bible as literature is to read it as a human book, to establish an analogy between prophet and poet or divine inspiration and inspiration *tout court*, whereas in essence there is nothing strictly "literary" about the Bible; the legal, historical, predicatory, sapiential, and oracular dimensions account for ninety percent of the canon. For Kugel as for the *Zohar*, the author of the biblical text never aims simply to "narrate adventures." And those whose adventures it narrates are never "characters" in the literary sense of the word, but rather "ancestors:" *your* ancestors, *our* ancestors.[52]

Although hellenized Jews and early Christian commentators had no trouble identifying tropes and rhetorical figures in the Bible, Jewish readers in the Pharisaic* and rabbinical tradition always refused to see in it anything "decorative" (that is, strictly "literary"),[53] on the grounds that everything in it, down to the slightest graphic detail, was there to convey a meaning.

God does not do things for the sake of style. His speech escapes all the constraints, and all the easy options, of human speech. He can say two different things at exactly the same time—which no human mouth could ever do. This explains certain discrepancies between the versions of the Decalogue* given in Exodus and Deuteronomy.[54] It was in a single breath, we are told,[55] that God ordered people to "remember"[56] and to "keep"[57] the Sabbath; only the limitations of man's use and understanding of language made it necessary to transcribe the two simultaneously uttered injunctions separately. Conversely, when God seems to say only one thing, He actually broadcasts an almost endless number of messages; it is up to the exegete to bring out this multiplicity of signifieds imprisoned in a single signifier, just as a hammer striking a rock produces multiple sparks.[58] Finally, God never repeats Himself, because He never speaks to say nothing. It is only for the ordinary human reader, keen on ordinary human literature, that Scripture seems full of duplication.

While the ancient rabbis consciously used rhetorical parallels in formulating their prayers and aphorisms, they remained curiously blind to the same device when it appeared in Scripture.[59] Yet from a strictly literary point of view, parallelism—repetition of the same idea in slightly different terms—is characteristic of biblical poetics.

Thus, when Deuteronomy 33.10 evokes the pedagogic role of the Levites by saying that "they teach Your laws[60] to Jacob and Your doctrine[61] to Israel," an exegete cannot see this as repetition, as simple redundancy, as rhetorical insistence on a single signified. If the formulation is twofold, then it is because the signified is twofold. This is precisely what a midrash[62] implies: the first pair of words ("Your laws") refer to the *written* Torah, while the second pair ("Your doctrine") serve to remind us of the existence of a second body of law, the *oral* Torah. In this way, it establishes the transmission of the Oral Law as a Levitic obligation equivalent to the transmission of the Written Law and insists that this Oral Law, like the other, is of Mosaic origin.

This example—just one among countless others—has the dual merit of rescuing the Bible twice from a common-or-garden "literary" reading. On the one hand, it reminds us that the "omnisignificance"[63] of the sacred text defeats any trivially stylistic or aesthetic reading of it; on the other hand, it rules out any explanation of the Bible by itself, since the ultimate meaning of the Book is revealed only through elucidation of its dialectical link to the other, equally inspired, body of the Oral Law.

Of course, in ancient Judaism and to a large extent subsequently, the status of the language in which the Torah was written remains an object of controversy. Is it strictly, inherently divine, to the point where—as Rabbi Akiba believed—each word (even prepositions and other function words), each letter, or each purely graphic detail of the manuscript text conveys a hidden meaning that the commentator has to draw out? Or was Rabbi Ismael right in arguing—against the exaggerations of his colleague—that the Torah expresses itself "as humans express themselves," so that its language needs to be interpreted in accordance with the rules governing ordinary usage?[64]

After all, if we could not approach the Bible also as literature, if we did not have access to the meaning of the Law by the same means that we use for human communication, would we, as human beings, ever be in a position to read and understand it?[65] This being so, even the principle issued by Rabbi Ismael is perhaps only an apparent concession to the exigencies of ordinary rhetoric and hermeneutics; it does not even go so far as to cover parallelism.[66] In the end, it was only the birth of Islam, in the seventh century, that compelled Jewish teachers to rethink—in a clear identity framework—all the questions linked to the literary status of the Bible.

Facing the Koran, Facing the Arabs

After the death of Muhammad in 632, the Muslim empire soon expanded across a vast territory from the Atlantic to the borders of India and China. The numerous Jewish minorities living there gradually dropped their vernacular languages—above all, Aramaic and Greek—in favor of Arabic, thereby entering directly into contact with Arab-Islamic culture. Born in the East, spreading progressively westward, attaining new heights in Spain, that culture enjoyed extraordinary prestige among non-Muslims too (above all, Jews and Christians). It was not simply "religious" but also "secular." It grew richer through contact with the huge philosophical and scientific corpus inherited from ancient Greece, which was translated first into Syriac and soon afterwards into Arabic. The Koran naturally occupied a central position, but one that was not exclusively theological.

Islam and its Book certainly posed more than one challenge to the Jews and their Bible. But the debate between them did not suffer from the dual burden of appropriation and addition, as it did in the case of Judaism and Christianity. The Bible did not enter the canon of the sacred writings of Islam, and the Koran, unlike the New Testament, was not "added on" to any kind of "Old Testament." Muslims revere only the Koran; it does not compete directly with the Scriptures of the two older monotheisms, which have value for it as first, essentially genuine, revelations. To be sure, the Torah is supposed to have been abrogated by the Gospel, then by the Koran. But both the Torah and the Gospels are reputedly derived from the same Tablets as the Koran, and these make Jews and Christians "peoples of the Book," who as such enjoy the status of *dhimmis* (protected ones) in Muslim society.

No doubt the Koran and Muslim theologians reproach their monotheist predecessors with having distorted or "falsified" their own scriptures, by changing either the meaning or form of certain words. The Jews in the dock are Moses, a number of Israelite kings or priests, and Ezra the Scribe; some contemporaries of Muhammad are said to have deliberately concealed biblical material that, for example, prescribed stoning as the punishment for adultery or even foretold the mission of the Prophet. Finally, Muslim critics consider that a number of details—chronological inconsistencies, geographical errors, contradictions, theological incongruities—clearly testify to the unreliable transmission of the biblical corpus.[67]

In a way, however, such challenges to the correctness of the text were much less problematic for Judaism than was Christian acceptance of its integrity and authenticity, since such recognition went together with a general appropriation and reinterpretation of the Bible along Christian lines.[68] The philologist, exegete, translator, halakhist*, and philosopher Saadia Gaon (882–942),[69] for instance, living in a majority Muslim world, saw fit to polemicize against Christianity rather than Islam, no doubt because it represented a greater threat to Judaism.[70]

In fact, the challenge that the Koran and the Arabs posed to the Jews was perhaps much more literary than theological.

This challenge came down to three propositions: (1) the Koran is the best of the writings ever to have come from Heaven; (2) Arabic is the best of the languages in which God spoke to believers; and (3) the best poetry is Arabic poetry, which serves the angels to praise God on High.[71] Here literary excellence is no longer dissociable from theological excellence; in a sense it may be said to precede and ground it. In establishing the language and text of the Koran at the heart of a particularly effective system of self-enhancement, in developing an exemplary science of philology, lexicography, and grammar, and in raising the art of Arabic poetry to hitherto unsuspected heights, medieval Muslim culture exerted an undeniable pull on the Jewish elites.

They responded to this pull by coopting the values of the dominant society, appropriating its aesthetic canons, and imitating its products. But at the same time they actively promoted Jewish cultural referents: the Bible came to play the role of the Koran, while the Hebrew language—vehicle of Revelation, to be sure, but also language of poetic expression—played the role of Arabic.[72]

From this point of view, the Oriental, Sephardi* moment of medieval Jewish culture would seem to have revolutionized the status of the Bible as both linguistic testimony and literary text (hence also revealed text). For the Jewish world then developed a new Hebrew philological science (grammar and lexicography), as well as a Hebrew poetry (secular and religious). Both used Arabic models and precedents, but they also lastingly installed the Bible and its language at their center; philology made them an object of exclusive study, while poetry appropriated them as its near-exclusive linguistic material, as a store of images and formulas, and, more ambiguously, as its source of inspiration and ultimate justification.

This shakeup did not, however, entail an unambiguous revaluation of the Bible as literature. Most of the medieval commentators continued to ignore the aesthetic dimension of the sacred text; only a handful conceded, for example, that certain repetitions or parallelisms might have a strictly stylistic value without necessarily providing new information.[73] Jewish scholars remained torn between asserting the absolute superiority of Scripture over all extant literature and recognizing that biblical verse was well below the demanding standards of the Arabic and Hebrew poetry of their time—unless, of course, they followed the poet, theologian, and physician Judah Halevi (c. 1075–1141) in seeing this formal inferiority as the other side of a higher superiority.[74] After all, the Bible, unlike medieval poets, did not torture the laws of Hebrew syntax and semantics; on the contrary, with the *te'amim*, it allowed for proper recitation, without ever sacrificing sense to meter.[75]

One Spanish Jewish poet, Moses Ibn Ezra (c. 1055–1135), conceded in his poetic art (written in Arabic) that it was impossible to demonstrate that Israel in biblical times—the age of its independence and power—had developed a poetry comparable to that of medieval Jews and Arabs. Moreover, in keeping with the scientific theories of his time, he held that the Arab lands (and not the Holy Land) were climatically the best situated in the inhabited world for the development of fine literature; he even explained in this way the beneficial effects of exile for Jews who had settled in those lands and experienced a remarkable cultural blossoming there. Nor did he fail to mention the principle of the *imitation* of the nations (and of the Arabs, in the case of poetry), which seemed to have presided over the development of Jewish culture in exile. In spite of the new centrality he accorded to the biblical heritage, he argued that there was an unbridgeable *aesthetic* gulf between the Bible and later Jewish literary output.

No doubt that was for the better. For if, as Moses Ibn Ezra put it, "the best thing about a poem is its deceptiveness"—that is, its figurative language—what should one think of biblical poetry? How to approach Song of Songs, for example, which can be included in the scriptural canon only on a purely allegorical interpretation?[76] How to justify the manifestly "deceptive" (poetic) language that the biblical author uses when he pretends—only pretends—to be telling of a thoroughly human amorous idyll? The answer is not in doubt: by reaffirming, in spite of oneself and as a last resort, the fundamental difference between the Bible and literature. Scriptural poetry used a figurative language that, though false in expression, was always true in content. Indeed, that sharply differentiated it from medieval poetry and, more broadly, from all secular verse.[77]

The Bible as Marker of Sephardi Identity

Even when it is uneasy or ambivalent, this primary, in some cases almost exclusive, concern with the Bible as language, literature, model, pillar of Jewish identity, as chief source of a sometimes arrogant self-promotion, was uncontestably new. And more than "typically Jewish," it perhaps appeared in the medieval world as typically Sephardi. A good illustration of this is the bitter complaint in the early fifteenth century of Isaac ben Moses ha-Levi (known as Efodi).[78]

Using a critical-historical approach in his famous treatise on grammar, Efodi told the sad tale of a gradual, centuries-long degradation of Hebrew biblical scholarship (in the philological and linguistic sense) among the Jews—a process due as much to the rigors of exile as to culpable negligence on the part of those involved. He dwelled on the devastating effects of this negligence, also for observance of the commandments of the Torah, a little as if only a good grammarian could be a good Jew. This "sickness,"[79] he wrote, blighted all his contemporaries; even "Israel's sages and great men" thought someone "stupid" if he spent his time studying Scripture, and, since for them it was the Talmud that was essential, they might well be unable to identify the source of a biblical verse. But worst affected were the Jewish scholars of France and *Ashkenaz**, a million miles from the ancient Sephardi tradition of promoting biblical and philological studies, but also from the scriptural and talmudic erudition of one of the principal teachers in their own tradition, Rashi.[80]

Similarly, the blossoming of Sephardi historical literature shortly before and above all after the expulsion of the Jews from Spain in 1492 may be regarded as one of the last and most revealing manifestations of this "biblocentrism." Saturating their writings with scriptural allusions, and giving a "biblical" turn at the level of language and form to their account of the postbiblical history of the Jewish people, all these authors naturally injected a sacred and strongly ahistorical element into their discourse. At the same time, however, they exhibited a partly secular relationship to the Bible, which became for them not only the vehicle of an incomparable divine revelation but a perfectly imitable model of historiographic *literature*.[81]

Thus, having at one point been among the markers of Hellenistic-Jewish "identity"—for Philo or Josephus, for example—the Bible seems to have become much later one of the markers of a certain Sephardi "identity." It might well be thought that it was for this reason—albeit, as we have seen, among others—that the Bible played such a role in the return of some Marranos to Judaism, at a time when the Muslim context of the emergence of a Sephardi identity was no more than a distant memory.[82]

✳

In neither the Hellenistic nor the Arab-Islamic world did the surrounding society appropriate Holy Scripture at the very beginning. Non-Jews, whether pagan or Muslim, recognized it as the special possession of the Jews. It could naturally come in for criticisms—of its literary mediocrity and/or the emptiness or unreliability of its content. But for the Jews it could, even must, serve to underpin their claims to literary and theological greatness; the Bible was respectively the Homer of the Jews or something like their Koran. In both cases, response to attacks was mixed in with a clear form of emulation. The idea was to achieve—or claim to achieve—on their own terrain (Greek and biblical, Hebrew and biblical) something as good as or better than the culture of the Other. "Imitation" of that culture, at least partial identification with it, was a paradoxical but real form of self-affirmation.

In the medieval Christian context, as we shall see, almost the exact opposite was observable. This was a further illustration, different but ultimately convergent, of a constant principle: the Jews' relationship with the Bible—and the function of that relationship, as recognized or rejected in the image they had and sought to reflect of themselves—largely depended on the particular challenges posed by their environment.

Facing the Christians: Their Scriptures and Ours

Throughout its history, Christianity has been tempted to reject the Old Testament out of hand, in favor of the New Testament alone. In the second century, Marcion—who saw the Jewish Bible as a "truthful ac-

count of actual history,"[83] certainly not just a collection of falsehoods—
nevertheless discerned in it "the frightful countenance of the cruel God
of the Jews, the creator of the world,"[84] the enemy of the fundamentally
new Redeemer-God manifest in the person of Christ. In his view, Christianity should purge the Old Testament from Holy Scripture and base
itself purely on the message of the Gospel. This radical position was
vigorously rejected by the early Church, but thirteen centuries later, it
echoed more softly in the Reformation contrast between the Old and
the New Testament (or the "book of law" and the "book of grace").[85]

The Protestant theologian Adolph Harnack (1851–1930), historian of
the Church, and author of the classic work on Marcion, spoke of the
inability of the Reformation to take the decisive leap of removing the
Jewish Bible from the Christian canon as if it were a kind of "fate." Its
preservation "in Protestantism as a canonical document [not merely
a historical testimony] since the nineteenth century" was "the consequence of a religious and ecclesiastical crippling."[86]

For Harnack, then, Christianity and Judaism were mutually exclusive; the Old Testament was specifically Jewish, and for that very reason it should be kept outside the canonical limits of Christianity. Other
great names in modern and contemporary thought took the same or a
similar line. Either they rejected the Old Testament en bloc or, judg-
ing it a heterogeneous collection, promoted a kind of Bible without
the slag of the Law, animated only by the spirit of the early prophets.[87]

Nevertheless, however circuitous or attenuated its forms, and whatever the disguises it sometimes assumed, the Marcionite temptation
never overcame Christianity in general. Had it done so, the relationship of Judaism to Christianity—and by extension to the Bible in
Christian countries—would surely have been profoundly affected.

In the Christian world, the Bible—understood as the indivisible
sum of its two "Testaments"—played and continues to play a crucial
role. It is true that, unlike the Torah in Judaism or the Koran in Islam,
and in spite of the demands periodically raised by various zealot currents, it did not became a fundamental source of law in the Latin West.
Its authority was essentially spiritual; it did not substitute itself for preexisting Roman law, nor did it cancel barbarian legal systems.[88] Yet it
was the "locus of Christian identity"[89] in the Middle Ages, and it has
probably never ceased to be so.

This adoption of the Hebrew Bible (in its authorized Greek or Latin versions) as the centerpiece of the *Christian* scriptures—in short, its Christianization—inevitably confronted the Jews with a problem that neither the pagans nor the Muslims nor the "Marcionites" ever posed. Or, to put it differently, this conflictual proximity and appropriation proved to be much harder to manage than indifference or a real break would have been. If the Bible, even expanded by a New Testament, was the "locus" of Christian identity, how could it still be—for Jews as well as Christians—the "locus" of Jewish identity?

The "Guardians" of Our Books

The textual authenticity of the Old Testament and the reliability of its transmission are not usually questioned by its Christian readers. In the second century, Justin Martyr accused certain Jewish teachers of having suppressed "many Scriptures from the [Greek Septuagint] translations" because they proved that "this very man who was crucified was God and man."[90] Moreover, Christian authors sometimes accepted the Greek text when it conflicted with the Hebrew original. Nevertheless, when the Manicheans in the late fourth century were denying all value to the Scriptures handed down by the Jews, Saint Augustine asserted their exactitude and authority, as well as the perfect harmony of the two Testaments: "All Moses wrote is of Christ."

The Old Testament, Augustine argued, offered indisputable testimony of the truth of Christian history and theology; the New Testament, which revealed its deep meaning, was already hidden within it. Nothing could be removed from the Old Testament; all of it had to be accepted, and the disciples of Jesus continued to observe its precepts, although in a spiritual sense. In the case he made vis-à-vis the Jews, however, Augustine established a hierarchy between the two inseparable parts of the scriptural diptych: the Old Testament, engraved in stone and imposed on man from without, was promise; whereas the New Testament, rooted in everyone's innermost being, inscribed in their heart, was fulfilment.[91]

The position of Augustine, and of those who mostly followed in his wake, was decisive in more ways than one. It recognized the Jews as genuine and absolutely reliable transmitters of books (the Old Testament) that basically testified to the truth of Christian doctrine.

Though precious librarians, "custodians of our books," the Jews did not grasp their deep meaning. "They are like servants who, when their masters go to the audience room, follow behind carrying their files but remain waiting outside."[92] Exhorted not to forget the Law, they thus carry it wherever they are dispersed and wherever the Church is present, both as proof for the Gentiles and as opprobrium for themselves.

This blindness of the Jews, who do not hear what Christians say because they do not understand what they read, is a recurrent theme in medieval Christian polemics against Judaism, where it is presented, paradoxically, as further testimony to the truth that the Jews ignore. By the nature of things, they do not understand the books that foretell that they will not understand them. But this is itself a salutary phenomenon: for, as Rupert of Deutz (c. 1075–1129) points out, would they not have "burned all the Scriptures and put to death all the prophets if the Scriptures had not been closed and sealed for them, and if the prophets had clearly told them everything that would come to pass concerning the Christ?"[93] The Jewish people is here like Uriah,[94] whom David sent to Joab with the letter that would lead to his death: "It carries the Law," said Saint Gregory the Great (c. 540–604; Pope Gregory I), "through whose accusation it will find death."[95]

The Jews are also like Hagar, seated near a fountain she cannot see (Gen. 21.19), like Leah, the wife of Jacob, whose eyes are weary (Gen. 29.17), like Pharaoh himself, whose hardened heart remains closed to the divine message (Exod. 10.1). Their dispersal and humiliation, visible punishments for their wilful blindness and refusal to recognize in Jesus the predicted Messiah and Son of God, are further testimony to the truth of Christianity. They must not die. Slaves of a signifier whose signified they do not know, the Jews have a role to play that no other people can assume in their place: they preserve, or indeed *embody*, the literal sense of the Law. For that reason too, it is necessary that they do not disappear. The "Do not kill them" of Psalms 59.12 applies to them.

Real Judaism and Biblical Judaism

The Augustinian teaching is paradoxical in more ways than one. It fully identifies the Jews with the Old Testament and reduces Judaism to a kind of "biblism"; the Jews are Jews thanks to the book they bear.

However—first paradox—the Jews supposedly do not understand a word of it. And—second paradox—the Christians have appropriated this Book and claim to hold the only keys to it. Jews therefore are recognized as legitimate bearers of what makes them Jews—the Bible—but at the same time they have been dispossessed of it (by Christianity). Thus Justin Martyr speaks to his Jewish interlocutor Trypho of "your Scriptures, or rather not yours, but ours. For we believe them; but you, though you read them, do not catch the spirit that is in them."[96] This custodianship of "our" books is even what justifies and guarantees the survival and protection of the Jews. And yet—third paradox—the books convict them of pernicious errors and pronounce mortal judgment.

It is as guardians of the *letter* of these books, as literal observers of the Law, as scrupulous and blinkered disciples of Moses, that the Jews are permitted and even encouraged to remain what they are until their final conversion. But—the fourth (and by no means the least) paradox—the "biblical" Jews who must not perish do not actually exist. By reducing Judaism to "biblism," Augustine justifies its right to endure—but that Judaism is, of course, a pure fiction.

Thus, the biblocentrism of the traditional Christian perception of Judaism makes the Jews doubly alien while claiming to recognize them. The Bible that supposedly defines them escapes them, and it is a matter of historical fact that that book alone has never defined them.

When the mendicant orders realized in the thirteenth century that that was not the Judaism of the actually existing Jews, they accused them not only of being unable to grasp the spiritual meaning of the Bible but of deviating from its literal meaning; the Talmud and the Oral Law—the heart of actually existing Judaism—seemed to distance the Jews not only from Christianity but also, perhaps above all, from the Mosaic Law recorded in the Bible. And once they no longer played the role of faithful witnesses to the truth of Scripture, they could not claim the protection that Augustine had accorded them by virtue of that status. Condemnations and burning of the Talmud, campaigns of aggressive proselytism, persecution and even physical elimination received a new and terrifying rationale; betrayal of the Book had turned Judaism into common heresy. In attaching sole authority to the Talmud, a human creation, Judaism had placed itself outside the family of religions rooted in divine revelation.[97]

Nicholas of Lyra (c. 1270–1340) remarked that the Jews placed the Bible on the same plane as talmudic literature and treated as authentic the teachings of "the Hebrew commentators on the Old Testament." This dual allegiance, biblical and talmudic, was not without parallels in Christianity, although, as Nicholas noted, the Jews revered the rabbinical texts even more than Catholics the writings of Saint Jerome or Augustine.[98]

In a polemical context, this simple observation became a central item in the charge sheet. When Nicholas Donin (d. 1240), a Jewish convert to Christianity, presented Pope Gregory IX with thirty-five charges against the Talmud, ten specifically concerned the status that Jews attached to the Oral Law. The Jews, he said, claimed that God first communicated the Law (which they called the Talmud) to them by word of mouth; that it was engraved in their minds and only then put in writing by their Sages. This Law, whose written version greatly exceeds the Holy Scriptures in size, teaches among other absurdities the superiority to the prophets of the sages and scribes; it authorizes them to take liberties with the explicit provisions of the Written Law; credence should be given in them, whatever the occasion and whatever they say; and anyone who does not observe their precepts is deserving of death. Worse still, if one may say so, is that the Jews deny their children access to the Bible and consider that anyone who studies rabbinical doctrine in this world will enjoy life in the hereafter.[99]

At issue here are not only "the mass of deceptions and shameful things"[100] that (according to Donin) fill the Talmud, but the special or even exclusive reverence that Jews show for it. In the end, the Catalan Dominican theologian Ramón Martí (d. 1284) delineated three different types of Jews, corresponding to three moments in Jewish history. First, there were the Old Testament Jews, who observed the divine Word in so far as that was possible for humanity before its redemption by Christ. Then there were the Jews of the Talmud, who quite consciously turned away from the religion of the Old Testament, even if it meant distorting the biblical text to erase allusions to Christ and passing from worship of the true God to worship of Satan. And finally there were the "modern" Jews (Martí's own contemporaries), who did no more than follow in the footsteps of the second category.[101] Having broken with the Bible—which could confer on them a degree of legitimacy—and relying solely on the Talmud, the Jews had become creatures partly in league with the Devil. They therefore had no right to the protection accorded by Saint Augustine and should be fought without mercy.

The People of the Oral Law

Judaism reacted in various ways to the challenges that Christianity posed from the beginning—challenges that, though fluctuating in their expression and sharpness over the centuries, touched the very identity of Judaism and the legitimacy of its survival.

Tactical adjustments were sometimes made to counter the adversary in polemical contexts. In his typological and kabbalistic exegesis, the talmudic scholar and poet Moses ben Nahman (1194–1270; Moses Nahmanides) relied unreservedly, for example, on the midrashic* heritage that the Oral Tradition placed at his disposal.[102] On the other hand, at the Disputation of Barcelona in 1263, when he tried to refute claims that certain talmudic* sources clearly attested to the coming of the Messiah, he maintained that the Jews had *three* kinds of book (and not, as one might have expected, only the written and the oral Torah): namely, (1) the Bible, in which they had "total faith"; (2) the "Talmud," an explanation of the 613 commandments, in which they had "confidence"; and (3) the "Midrash" or the Aggadah*, in which they were permitted to believe or not believe (a freedom that made it easier to reject pro-Christian arguments drawn from certain messianic midrashim*).[103]

If we leave aside such contexts, where the terms of the debate were set by the opponent, the Jewish teachers consistently organized their position around three inseparable principles: (1) the Oral Law, a divine revelation entrusted to Israel, grounds the identity of the Jewish people and its claim to speak the truth; (2) the Written Law (the Bible) remains a closed book to those who do not read it in the light of the Oral Law; and (3) the Oral and the Written Law are not *two* laws, but one and the same law, to which Israel holds the keys. The Jews thus took back the Bible of which Christians claimed to dispossess them, but they did so while intransigently reaffirming the supremacy of the Oral Law.

The Oral Tradition is in effect the distinctive possession of Israel; better than the Bible, it *makes* and legitimates Israel. When Moses, having smashed the first "Tablets of Testimony" out of anger at the sight of the Golden Calf, was seized with remorse (as Rabbi Akha taught), God reassured him as follows: "Do not be sad about those first tablets, which contained little more than the ten commandments; on the second tablets, I shall give you *halakhot**, midrash, and *aggadot**."[104] What are these "ten commandments" whose smashing was not supposed to distress Moses so much? A simple fragment of the Written Law. And what are these "*halakhot*, midrash, and *aggadot*," which, when added to them, have the capacity to console the prophet for the initial loss? The Oral Law.

Similarly, if God eventually forbids Moses to put in writing the Oral Law—the Mishnah*—revealed to him on Mount Sinai at the same time as the Written Law,[105] it is because "the Mishnah is a mystery of the Holy One, blessed be He, and because the Holy One, blessed be He, unveils His mysteries only to the just [that is, Israel], as explained:[106] 'The counsel of the Lord is for those who fear Him.'"[107] The Oral Law is the ultimate touchstone; it enables those who possess it to confound the usurpers. It is the wall that stands between Israel and the nations—which is probably why a Gentile who studies it may be punished with death, and why Jews are forbidden to teach it to the Gentiles.[108]

Even if the nations of the world had not appropriated the Scriptures, it would still be the Oral Law—not the Written Law—that differentiated Israel from them. For which nation does not glory in its own books and its own "scrolls"? How is Israel different in this regard from the Gentiles?[109] The Mishnah and the Talmud, which have been handed down to Israel orally, will differentiate it forever from the rest of the nations.[110] The singularity and confidentiality of this transmission guarantee de facto—and in a way independently of its divine origin—the singularity and persistence of Judaism, also and above all in the context of the Jews' subjection to non-Jews.[111] The Covenant was contracted through this "word of mouth," spoken and heard rather than written and read, and it is what makes it possible to say that Israel was "chosen."[112]

As the inalienable possession of Israel, *ungraspable* in every sense of the word, the Oral Law eludes God Himself as well as persecutors who seek to stamp it out.

Persecutors can burn the books in which the Law is recorded, but it does not cease to live in people's hearts and elsewhere. As Rabbi Yechiel of Paris put it in his debate with Nicholas Donin: "And though your wrath should well up against us, are we not dispersed throughout the world, is our Torah not found in Babel, among the Medes, in Greece, and among the seventy nations? . . . Here our bodies are in your hands, but not our souls, and you will never be able to eradicate the Torah but in your kingdom."[113]

But the Torah also eludes God Himself; the Torah, since the moment of its revelation, has no longer been in Heaven but on earth.[114] And God Himself is bound by the unshakable authority of the commentaries and rulings of the rabbis. The time of prophecy is long over: no one can rely on a special revelation to impose his point of view; no miracle, not even a "divine voice," can authenticate the slightest teaching; any issues are now settled by a majority.[115] God, rejoicing at his defeat, says to Himself with a smile: "My children have vanquished me, my children have vanquished me."[116] No doubt it is this ancient victory that still today continues to animate the radical talmudocentrism of the most Orthodox fringes of Judaism. The Bible may be granted primacy in terms of *holiness*, but the Oral Law still has absolute primacy in terms of *authority*.[117]

This ultimate authority of the Oral Law and the ultimate decision-making power of the sages of each generation are closely bound up with each other. The two have equal necessity, as Leon of Modena forcibly argued in the seventeenth century. The existence of an Oral Law—which guarantees correct reading of the Written Law and precise observance of the divine commandments, which it sets out only elliptically (not explicitly)—is alone capable of guaranteeing the unity of practices among the people to which the two Laws were given, and therefore the unity of that people per se. Similarly, the patent inadequacy of the Written Law as a guide to action—an inadequacy willed by God Himself—means that each generation must have providential recourse to the opinions and wisdom of the sages of the day; they are the undisputed masters of the Oral Law, and it is necessary to comply with their rulings.[118] The Oral Law thus appears to play all the roles: it is the Jews' distinctive possession and as such defines their very being;

it guarantees and justifies their perennial existence; it ensures their religious unity and a kind of political cohesion that counters the corrosive effects of dispersion. The Oral Law. Not the Bible.

＊

In a way—and beyond any directly polemical intent—the Christian (especially Catholic) world eventually acknowledged this nonbiblical, or metabiblical, definition that Judaism gives of itself. But it did so at the price of three new paradoxes.

First paradox: it underlined the proximity of form (not content) that this definition finally established between Judaism and Catholicism. Thus, long after Nicholas of Lyra, the Oratorian Richard Simon (1638–1712), a contemporary of Leon of Modena and French translator of his work, could write: "The Jews concur with most Christians that their religion is based upon tradition as well as the word of God."[119] And he immediately added: "As Tertullian once said that only the Church truly possessed Holy Scripture [*Scriptura Sacra Ecclesiae Catholicae possessio est propria*], the Jews say that only the Synagogue possesses it, and that the other nations have only its letters, not its spirit."[120] In the end, even the commentaries produced by the Jews about the "letter" of the Scriptures are "quite few in number, since, especially in ancient times, they mostly preferred to stick to the allegorical meaning rather than explain the text."[121] The recognition of the otherness of Judaism is in keeping with its image of itself, but this is immediately coupled with the affirmation of a structural homology between Judaism and Catholicism.

Second paradox: this recognition of Judaism as a nonbiblical or metabiblical religion by no means prevents Richard Simon from arguing that the Jews' essential, and no doubt only real, contribution to civilization (by which is meant Christian civilization) is . . . the Bible. Apart from what may be usefully gleaned from them for a literal interpretation of the Old Testament, "or to explain certain passages in the New Testament,"[122] the other books of the Jews essentially serve no one other than themselves or those who wish to know their religion, or else provide access to certain lost works of the Arabs.

Third and last paradox: for Richard Simon, as well as for some of his Christian contemporaries or successors, there is nevertheless a type of Jew incomparably more respectable than the great majority who venerate the Oral Tradition as the essence of Judaism. This type is the Karaite. Through their attachment to Scripture (*Mikra* in Hebrew) and their rejection of the rabbinical legacy, the Karaites (*kara'im*) sometimes remind Richard Simon of those self-styled "evangelical" Protestants who "nowadays" claim "that we should base ourselves only on the Gospel and reject traditions."[123]

As Simon concedes, however, the Karaites do not disqualify all traditions, "only false and absurd ones"; they keep those that are "reasonable and well founded."[124] Placing "no faith in the kabbalists' explanations or in baseless allegories," their theology is "purer and farther removed from superstition."[125] The chief merit of the Karaites is this: "They do not consult the text of the Bible in the same way as the rabbis, who at the slightest opportunity delight in inventing new rulings"; rather, "they explain Scripture by itself," discarding "everything that Scripture, reason, and constant tradition do not teach them."[126]

A century later, Abbé Grégoire is more straightforward. Rejecting the absurdities of the Talmud and regarding the "Pharisees" as "bridled asses," he presents the Karaites as "the most honest of the Jews,"[127] a genuine countermodel to the Rabbanites, whom it is clearly "more difficult to enlighten."[128] So, despite everything, there are something like ideal Jews (for Christians), whose merit is to differ from all others in finally placing the Bible, and the Bible alone, at the center.

The Karaite Temptation: Scripture Alone?

I shall not trace in detail the history of the Karaites—a minority current within Judaism, to be sure, but (at least in its early period) a strong and active one that upholders of rabbinical norms saw as a major threat and combated accordingly.[129] Challenging the authority of the Oral Law, either en bloc or selectively according to the context, Karaism placed extreme, though not exclusive, value on the letter of the sacred texts. It was born in eighth-century Babylonia out of the gradual crystallization of several Jewish currents, at a time when the religious, political, and economic effervescence of the Muslim Orient was coupled with socioeconomic tensions and power struggles at the very heart of Persian-Babylonian Judaism. The richness and diversity, even the internal contradictions, of its centuries-long existence in various regions (the Muslim Orient, North Africa, medieval Spain, Byzantium and the Ottoman Empire, eastern Europe) naturally mean that it cannot be presented with the simplistic aspect that both adversaries and adulators like to give it.

Its basic position was actually less radical than one would gather from an often quoted recommendation attributed to its putative eighth-century father, Anan ben David: "Study Scripture closely and do not support yourself on my opinion." As we have seen, even Richard Simon accepts that the Karaites were never content with an exclusive, personalized, unmediated reading of the sacred text. Over time, their legal theory came to be based on four elements: the biblical text, of course, but also new laws derived by analogy from scriptural prescriptions, agreement within the community, and Karaite tradition itself (the "burden of inheritance"). A Byzantine Karaite like Aaron ben Joseph the Physician (c. 1250–1320), writing a commentary on the Pentateuch, even permitted himself to quote directly from nothing less than the Mishnah: "For most of these sentences," he said, "were spoken by *our* Fathers. And we have not departed from all [of their teachings], but only from what Scripture does not support, what is disputed, and what conflicts with Scripture."[130]

This being so, the interesting aspect here is not so much the historical complexity of the Karaite case as the polemical or apologetic use that could be made of it. The arguments in support of Karaism put forward by non-Jews—mostly Protestants (and we can see why), but also Catholics such as Richard Simon—were often no more than direct or veiled attacks on majority rabbinical Judaism, which no doubt disturbed them more than Karaism appealed to them. Such apologies helped to forge an idealized image of Karaism, one built on actual knowledge of its historical doctrines, texts, and communities, as we can tell from the erudite interest shown in them by Europe's Christian Hebraists from the mid-seventeenth century on. But this image could also serve as justification for a particular Jewish "deviant" in his struggle with rabbinical Orthodoxy, even if he had no direct access to Karaite literature or real contact with the Karaites of his day.

It was thus possible to declare oneself a "Karaite" without being one, or to be accused of "Karaism" without belonging to an actual Karaite community. This appears to have been the case, for example, with three "Karaites" excommunicated in 1712 by the Sephardi community of Amsterdam. What was the charge against them? That they "entirely den[ied] the Oral Law, which is the foundation and underpinning of our Holy Law."[131] This was obviously not enough to make genuine Karaites of them; apart from anything else, it was an attitude shared by other conversos or descendants of conversos,[132] whose return to Judaism via the Bible, in Amsterdam, the "Jerusalem of the North," could not involve unreserved adherence to rabbinical norms and sometimes resulted in a radical challenge to them.

What was the essence of this (ideal or real) "Karaism" that caused such fear in Judaism and was so much to the liking of Christianity? First, it represented what Judaism *might have been*, what it was perhaps still tempted to become, and what it stubbornly refused to be. Seen in this light—as a temptation never wholly overcome or a potentiality within Judaism that could always become actual—Karaism has something essential to tell us about normative Judaism and its fundamentally ambiguous relationship with the Bible (stubborn claim to the scriptural heritage together with an equally stubborn refusal to be reduced to it). Nor are we talking here only of the Bible.

When Natronai, the head of the academy at Sura, in Babylonia, went onto the attack against the Karaites around 860 CE, did he accuse them of placing the Bible at the center of Judaism and wishing to see nothing else besides it? Not at all—or anyway not only. He also reproached them with "deriding and scorning the words of the Doctors," "turning their back on the words of the Mishnah and Talmud," and fabricating their "own Talmud," an "evil and depraved" Talmud.[133] Four centuries later, when Yechiel of Paris laid into Nicholas Donin, a Jewish convert to Christianity who was attacking the Talmud, he charged that "for fifteen years," before his apostasy, he had been "a rebel against the words of the wise men and believed only what was written in the Torah of Moses, without interpretation [*pitaron*]," whereas everyone knew that "everything must have an interpretation [*pesher*]."[134] It was somewhat as if Donin had been a "Karaite" before becoming a Christian—as if denial of the authority of the Oral Law and an exclusive attachment to the letter of the Bible had inescapably led him to embrace the alien new Law of the Christians and their New Testament.[135]

Functioning as an archetypal "heresy" in the eyes of rabbinical Judaism, Karaism was not strictly speaking a biblicism; it did not simply reduce to Scripture the corpus of inspired or authoritative writing. It also, perhaps mainly, involved denial, rejection, or disqualification of the nonbiblical authoritative corpus (the Oral Law), substituting for it a *different* corpus of the same nature (the other "Talmud," according to Natronai, but also the Christians' evangelical tradition). In this optic, the "Karaism" that frightened Judaism was far from contenting itself with "Scripture alone." It removed something (a true tradition) and added something else (a false tradition).

"You shall not add anything to what I command you or take anything away from it," God says in Deuteronomy 4.2. Subtraction and addition always go hand in hand. That was certainly the reproach that the Karaites directed against their Orthodox adversaries, the Rabbanites: "When they add and when they subtract, the upholders of the [Oral] Tradition contravene what the Torah prescribes, and thus add one sin to another."[136] It was also, of course, a charge leveled by the Jews against the Christians: that they took away the Law and added the Gospel. But, as we have seen, it was no less what Rabbanites such as Natronai could and did accuse the Karaites of doing.

Emmanuel Lévinas once said that "the Jew is he who has no direct relationship with the Bible."[137] Perhaps it would be more accurate to say that the Jew is he who does not believe there could ever be a direct and exclusive relationship to the Bible; he who thinks that to believe in the possibility of such a relationship cannot but lead to heresy, which involves submission to a *different* mediation, acceptance of a relationship inescapably mediated by a *different*, unauthorized tradition.

It seems to me, however, that we need to go even farther. The "authorized" tradition in question here is perhaps something other, or anyway much more, than a simple, at least partly petrified, corpus (Mishnah, Talmud, large midrashic collections duly edited, copied, and printed). It is the *living tradition* that lives in "souls" and, unlike bodies and books, as R. Yechiel tells us, will always escape the fury of persecutors and the flames of the pyre[138]—the living tradition within which the Bible and that corpus are reread and tirelessly subjected to reinterpretation that is never complete.

On another occasion, Lévinas compared the Bible read by Jews to "a text stretched over a tradition like the strings on the wood of a violin."[139] This image conceals real complexity beneath its appearance of simplicity. Sound (meaning) gives itself up to be heard (understood) only through the dynamic union of the strings (the Bible) and the wood (tradition). The strings without the wood are nothing. The wood without the strings is nothing either. But the strings and the wood together are still nothing. For the sound to resonate and meaning to appear, the musician must still tune and play his instrument; the correctness of the sound and the harmony of meanings depend on the tuning of strings on wood and the skill of the musician's performance. This tuning and the art of playing have not been learned from the strings (mere reading of the Bible) or the wood of the violin (mere reading of vestiges of the Oral Tradition finally put in writing), but rather from a teacher. That teacher in turn learned them from his own teacher, and so on *ad indefinitum*, in the unbroken line of a living, inspired, authorized tradition that overhangs and justifies everything: the strings and wood, the musician, the teacher, and the teacher's teacher.

This living tradition, resonating with all the harmonies of reading and interpretation, is the only genuine (though ever shifting) "locus" of a living Jewish identity that is paradoxically never identical with itself. The fixed score can guide the musician, but each musician reinvents the music each time he plays.

In this "site," there is certainly no playing that does not risk a wrong note, nor any reading that does not risk a wrong meaning. But it is solitude—the state of being "offsite"—that engenders true dissonance, real heresy properly so called: solitude of the text that the reader abstracts and isolates from the tradition bearing it, and/or solitude of the reader who abstracts and isolates himself from the chain of readers who precede and surround him and show him the way.

Four   Reading the Bible at the Risk of Heresy

Read the Bible? Give it to others to read? Yes, the tradition seems to answer, and two or three times rather than once. The believer is expected to read the weekly pericope, twice in its original Hebrew version and once in the Aramaic paraphrase attributed to Onkelos. It is an ancient exhortation: read "the Bible twice, the targum* once [*Shnayim mikra, ehad targum*]."[1] In his halakhic* code, Moses Maimonides clearly distinguishes this duty from simple attendance at the public reading of the Torah* during the Saturday morning service at the synagogue. It is a duty requiring personal, private reading, *le-atsmo* ("to oneself"), he specifies.[2] The Shulhan Arukh (literally "Set Table"), the halakhic compilation of the Sephardi* Joseph Karo (1488–1575),[3] for its part, widens this obligation to include a reading of the commentary by the exegete par excellence, Rashi, saying: "If [the believer] has studied the pericope in Rashi's commentary, it counts as if [he has read] the targum; he who fears Heaven will read the targum as well as Rashi's commentary."[4]

So, read the Bible and give it to others to read? In fact, the codified practice to which I have just referred raises more problems than it solves. We can certainly see it as an expansion in concentric circles of the field of prescribed study—from text to translation, and from translation to commentary. But this expansion remains limited. However private and personal the obligation described, the rhythm of its fulfilment is directly dependent on the liturgical calendar and accords an exclusive privilege to the Five Books of Moses. Nor is anyone under any illusion: access to this minimal study is not open to all and sundry. There are not usually many believers capable of reading and understanding by themselves, even at a basic level, the biblical text in its original language, its Aramaic paraphrase, and Rashi's commentary. The question I am posing is therefore more fundamental, more strategic, than it appears to be at first. It concerns the actual access that each individual has to the letter and the meaning, to the reading and the interpretation.

What is the place for the Bible in the ordinary education of men and women, adults and children? What is its place in the curriculum of those who devote all or part of their time to study? What is the place for biblical exegesis in the creative activity of knowledge-producing scholars? Why should Scripture be interpreted: for what purpose(s) and by virtue of which inherent or incidental necessities? How should it be interpreted: by which methods, and in accordance with which format(s) of literary exposition? For whom should it be interpreted, what is its target audience? Evidently my initial question breaks up into a multiplicity of others. That is hardly surprising.

Everything in the preceding three chapters shows that the Bible is an important issue in Judaism. On the one hand, it is never thought about or experienced alone, but always in connection with something else (Revelation, tradition) that both includes and surpasses it; on the other hand, it willy-nilly sets up a tension in the relationship to self and in the relationship to the Other, whether the Jewish Other, the non-Jewish Other, or God Himself. The multiplicity of questions is therefore inevitably echoed in a multiplicity of ambiguous, sometimes contradictory, answers, since these are inevitably split between the reserve inspired by the Bible and the devotion it imposes.

Children, Women, the People

It is said that, when Rabbi Eliezer ben Hyrkanos (a Jewish sage of the late first and early second centuries) fell ill, his disciples came visiting and asked him to teach them the "paths of life." In particular, what should they do to have some chance of entering the afterlife? Rabbi Eliezer answered with four pieces of advice. The first three are straightforward enough: be solicitous for the honor of your peers; ensure that your children spend their time with wise people; and when you pray be aware of whom you are standing before. Collegiality principle, primacy of education, awareness of the greatness of Him to whom our prayers are addressed: these are clear and coherent rules of life. A fourth, however, is expressed in a negative manner, signaling a danger and urging abstention: "Keep your children away from *higgayon*."[5]

"*Keep your children away from* higgayon"

The word *higgayon*—which I have deliberately not translated—poses a problem here. It appears four times in the biblical corpus, where it evokes thought or meditation, but also whispering or speech, or even music and song.[6] What can it mean here, in the mouth of Rabbi Eliezer shortly before he departs this world? Medieval Jewish exegetes gave two different answers.[7] For some, *higgayon* here refers to the secular sciences, from whose pernicious influence Rabbi Eliezer wishes to keep young people. For others, it is from Scripture itself that he seeks to protect them. Far from being banally recommended as a pious activity, the reading of the Bible therefore holds such dangers that children should not be exposed to it without due consideration.

For Tsemah ben Paltoi, the ninth-century head of the Babylonian talmudic academy in the city of Pumbedita (near present-day Fallujah in Iraq), the point was that the very young should avoid studying too closely passages from Scripture that might astonish them, since this could lead them to question basic religious truths and to lapse into heresy. For the eminent French Jewish biblical and talmudic commentator Rashi (1040–1105), Rabbi Eliezer had been suggesting that young people should not get "too used" to reading the Bible (*Mikra*), since its very "seductiveness" could become an obstacle to profound study.[8] For still others, the main intention of the dying master had been to warn against any literal interpretation of the Bible, that is, one unduly disconnected from the equally authoritative teachings of the Oral Tradition and the Talmud*.[9]

Far from being contradictory, these three interpretations of Rabbi Eliezer's supposed reservations about Scripture teaching to children are perfectly consistent with one another. Any "naïve" reading of the Bible is dangerous, and children are inclined as if by nature to that kind of naïveté. As regards the substance of the matter, the Bible's relationship to the truth is complex: what it seems to say is not what it really says, and to stick with what it seems to say—as children may be tempted to do—is inevitably to mistake the Truth and to risk sliding into heresy. As regards form, since the Bible first presents itself as a sequence of fine narratives, it misleads readers about its true nature and purpose, which are to speak the Truth and the Law, not to charm minds fond of grand adventures. And as regards status, although the Bible is the main vehicle of divine Revelation, its text is far from constituting the whole of Revelation, and to isolate it from the teachings of the Oral Law is to miss its meaning entirely. From one or more of these points of view, Christians and Karaites may be thought of as "grown children," who in their different ways have extensively updated the dangers of any reading of the Bible not controlled by tradition.

"Five [is the age to study] the Bible"

These are the dangers from which children have to be protected. It is a question not so much of forbidding them to read the Bible as of closely structuring how they learn to read it. In fact, a new paradox arises here: the Bible reaches children first of all, and that is even what their education should begin with.

"Five," says an ancient mishnic* tradition, is the right age "to study the Bible."[10] But even earlier, as soon as he begins to speak, a child should be taught a *biblical* verse: "Moses charged us with a Law, as the heritage of the community of Jacob [*Torah tzivvah lanu Mosheh, morashah kehilat Yaakov*]" (Deut. 33.4).

In this case, it is not unimportant that the first Hebrew word a child should utter is none other than *Torah*, which evidently includes both the Written and the Oral Tradition; that the second is *tzivvah* ("charged" or "ordered"), which underlines the legal dimension of Revelation as a body of commandments (*mitzvot*) revealed by God to his people; and that the third is *lanu* ("to us"), which recalls the function of communal bonding or identity referent that this Revealed Law has for "the community of Jacob."

Thus, although the first teaching received by the child is a verse from the Bible, its message already seems metabiblical. The focus is not the Bible but the Torah; not a founding narrative but a Law; not a divine message to humanity in general and each of its members individually, but rather to a selected community—the "community of Jacob"—that is defined by its reception, interpretation, and implementation of that message.

According to another ancient tradition,[11] the first book of the Pentateuch studied by children should be Leviticus: partly because it collects the laws regarding ritual purity, and children are pure beings; and partly because it contains nearly half of the 613 commandments of the Law, and nearly a half of the debates recorded in the Talmud base themselves on this book. A further reason, however, is that Leviticus is incontestably the most arid, austere, and legalistic, as well as the least narrative, of the Five Books of Moses, and hence the least likely to favor a kind of aesthetic emotion or literary identification that might push the essence—the Law—into the background.[12]

Filled with "gory instructions," descriptions "fit to turn the appetite," and "sins lusty and punishments violent," in the words of the anthropologist Mary Douglas, Leviticus—which opens with an exposition of the laws governing sacrificial worship—is not "a book for the squeamish." What is there in it, Douglas asks, "to attract the young mind?"[13] No doubt nothing—or almost. Yet perhaps this is precisely what justifies its place right at the beginning of children's schooling.

"A virtue that isn't really one"

Everything about this prioritization of Scripture reveals an ambivalence that, especially in the Ashkenazi* world, is subsequently confirmed by the ordinary curriculum. The Bible is indeed the earliest moment in any self-respecting Jewish education. But it is and must be only that. Although some teachings advise Jews to divide their years into three—"a third for Scripture, a third for the Mishnah*, a third for the Talmud"[14]—while others, without disqualifying the Bible, establish a hierarchy with the Talmud at the top,[15] the fact remains that, between the eleventh and thirteenth centuries, the Talmud established itself as the unchallenged core of the curriculum, the text requiring to be tackled at all costs.

Since, in a sense, the Talmud "includes" the Bible (quoting it in abundance) and the Mishnah (commenting on it at length), these no longer really have to be the objects of special study after a certain age.[16]

Scripture is essentially the resource for the ignorant.[17] And for ordinary Jewish students, the study of it goes no farther than Rashi's commentary, which, as we have seen, may even replace the targum for those studying the weekly pericope.[18] Thirteenth-century Christian polemicists were therefore on the right track when they accused Jews of deliberately keeping their children from study of the Bible.[19]

This marginalization of Scripture in study and scholarship was largely characteristic of the Ashkenazi cultural universe. To be sure, it did not take hold there unanimously or all at once; the emblematic case of Rashi himself, who devoted himself no less to explanation of the Bible than to that of the Talmud, as well as the work of many of his disciples and successors, certainly encourages one to avoid any sweeping judgment in this regard. Later, too, there would always be Ashkenazi masters who insisted on the need for profound knowledge of Scripture (if only to assist a correct understanding of the Talmud). Nevertheless, the Ashkenazi tendency to talmudocentrism—which the Tosafists[20] clearly reinforced from the very beginning—became more and more apparent over the centuries. The *Sefer Hasidim* (twelfth–thirteenth centuries)[21] summarizes the mainstream doctrine quite well when it states that he who busies himself with Scripture acquires a virtue that is not really one,[22] because he will spend all his life dealing only with *pshat** (the obvious sense, the letter of the law).[23]

The Sephardi world, despite its dominant biblocentrism, does not present just an inverted image of the Ashkenazi. It certainly tended to see the Talmud more as a juridical source than as one essential to the development of Jewish intellect and subjectivity, and it hesitated to make it the object of study as if this were a religious end in itself.

Thus, in his *Guide of the Perplexed*, Maimonides did not place at the top of his hierarchy of scholarship those whom he called "jurists": that is, talmudists who "believe true opinions on the basis of traditional authority and study the law concerning the practices of divine service, but do not engage in speculation concerning the fundamental principle of religion and make no inquiry whatever regarding the rectification of belief."[24] In the Mishneh Torah, his halakhic code, moreover, he devised a plan to make it unnecessary for practitioners of the Law to consult the Talmud and the other sources of rabbinical law. Maimonides—whose *Guide* opens with clearly hermeneutic reflections on expressions in the

Bible that cannot be understood in a literal sense—thus makes scriptural exegesis the locus par excellence of a crucial comparison between the truths of Reason (philosophy and science) and the truths of Revelation.

Here, we may note in passing, the two competing interpretations— the biblical and the secular-scientific—of the term *higgayon* as it appears in the teaching of Rabbi Eliezer come together; a philosophical (allegorical) exegesis of Scripture is presented as the best way of saving the Jewish faith philosophically and of according to philosophy its full *droit de cité* within Judaism. In this light, it is hardly surprising that those who sought to relegate the Bible to the margins of Jewish wisdom were also very often adversaries of philosophy.

Nevertheless, unlike many of his disciples and successors, Maimonides never wrote a sustained commentary on Scripture. And not everyone in the Sephardi world unreservedly shared the master's opinions or endorsed the barbs that the philosopher, biblical commentator, and philologist Joseph ben Abba Mari Ibn Kaspi (1279–1340?) directed against legal idlers who wasted their days in debate on obsolete (no longer applicable) rules.[25] In fact, in the Sephardi world too, the high value accorded to biblical studies—whether of philosophical or philological inspiration—suffered certain exceptions, and they tended to decline if only because the enlargement and greater diversification of the curriculum required sacrifices to be made somewhere.[26] And in the end there is a very "Ashkenazi" ring to the warnings of Sephardis like the Lisbon-born Joseph ben Abraham Hayyun (d. 1497 in Constantinople), for whom study of the Bible should occupy children only from their fifth to tenth years, or his contemporary Joseph Garçon, for whom those familiar only with Scripture are not worthy of great reward.[27]

The Women's Bible

The temptation was thus constant in Judaism to leave Scripture to boys (for as short a time as possible), to popular strata, and of course to women. There was no need for any of these to have access to higher levels of knowledge, but study of the Bible, suitably framed and adapted, might edify them. The case of women, even more than boys or "the people," illustrates particularly well the demotion of a certain kind of biblical science.

For the *Sefer Hasidim*, the talmudic judgment that "teaching one's daughter the Torah comes down to teaching her licentious practices"[28] concerns only "deep study of the Talmud, the reasons for its precepts, and its mystical teachings." Women "are not required to enter into the detail of the discussions." The aim—and obligation—is to teach them the precepts that concern them directly and that they must apply, and to do so "in a language they know," not in Hebrew (the language reserved for men).[29]

For Maimonides, women are no more liable than slaves or young children to the legal obligation of studying the Law. It would even be inadvisable to teach it to them, "since most women do not have minds suitable for study, and in keeping with the poverty of their understanding they transform the words of the Law into idle chatter." But Maimonides does make one exception: if the teaching of any part of the Law is not absolutely forbidden to his daughter, it is the *Torah she-bi-khtav*, the Written Law:[30] in other words, the Bible, or at least the Five Books of Moses.

In the late Middle Ages and early modern period, the main literary works of religious inspiration in the vernacular, intended for the people in general and sometimes for women in particular, belonged to the biblical register. For traditionally in the Jewish world scholarly and "popular"[31] literature never differed from each other only in the language they used (Hebrew rather than Yiddish or Judeo-Spanish, for example) or in their target audience; they also involved the creation of different "repertoires." And the popular repertoires always gave a central, though not exclusive, place to the Bible.

Thus, the first book printed in Yiddish—in Krakow in 1534—was none other than a scriptural glossary and concordance;[32] literal translations of the Bible into Yiddish, known as *Taytch-Humesh*, followed soon afterwards. But right up until World War II, the best-known Yiddish work, the most widely distributed and read in the Ashkenazi world, was undoubtedly the commentary on the Pentateuch by Jacob ben Isaac Ashkenazi of Janow (1550–1626), whose first publication seems to date from the 1590s. This collection of tales, midrashic* interpretations, and medieval exegeses, organized around a Yiddish paraphrase of the biblical text, was aimed at a popular, female readership, as we can tell from its title: *Tseenah u-reenah* ("Go forth and gaze"), borrowed from Song of Songs 3.11, which uses the feminine plural form of the imperative.[33]

Nearly a century and a half later, in 1730, the first volume of a somewhat similar compendium appeared in Judeo-Spanish in Istanbul: a commentary on Genesis by Rabbi Yaakov Kuli (c. 1689–1732) entitled *Me'am Lo'ez*.[34] Kuli's untimely death prevented him from continuing with his monumental project, but others took up the commentary on other books of the canon, and the collective enterprise reached completion only in 1899 with the publication of Hayyim Yitzhak Shaki's volume on Song of Songs.

The *Me'am Lo'ez* is a huge compilation that draws on both ancient and recent rabbinical sources, offering the Judeo-Spanish reader an abundance of material for the exegesis of biblical verses.[35] This time, the target audience was not specifically female. Making a form of biblical knowledge available to popular strata that spoke and could read Ladino, the *Me'am Lo'ez*—the most widely read text in all the Oriental Sephardi communities—also enabled illiterate women to gain partial access to it by listening to someone else read it.

Thus, although the Bible permitted a limited and controlled sharing of knowledge, it also unquestionably drew a frontier between children and adults, people and elite, men and women. It was a porous frontier, to be sure, but it still operated as a kind of filter. Transfers of knowledge flowed in only one direction: from adults to minors, from the learned elite to the people, from men to women. And it was always the former who acted as the conveyers and censors, determining the nature and scale of the authorized transfer. On one side of the frontier were the Bible, one form or another of popularized rabbinical culture, and the vernacular language. On the other side were the rabbinical literature itself, the Talmud, philosophy, Kabbalah*—all usually read in the languages closed to the masses, Hebrew and Aramaic.

The Bible therefore delimits a symbolic space, home, or matrix that certain groups cannot (and, in the case of women, must not) leave. It is important, the *Me'am Lo'ez* emphasizes, that women know "they are obliged to be shut up in their houses and not to show themselves at the window to passers-by."[36] The *Tseenah u-reenah*, for its part, insists that "women must remain at home and bear children who will go forth into the world and study the Torah."[37] Only sons will be authorized and exhorted to "go forth": boys will grow up and become adult men, with access to a world where study of the Torah will be of quite a different form and scale.

The Scholars' Bible

However, in that world beyond the frontier, the Bible is always still there. It is present through the innumerable quotations from it in postbiblical Jewish literature. It is there as a springboard, a support, a justification for developments (in law, philosophy, or mysticism) that go beyond it yet cannot but include it. As a red thread running through diverse, contradictory, and therefore fragile (almost brittle) cultural production, it gives it the appearance—and no doubt more than the appearance—of a consistency, solidity, and continuity essential to the survival of Judaism as such. This is the scholars' Bible, tirelessly interpreted and reinterpreted. Here the frontiers it serves to delimit are different: between what is and is not Judaism, between Orthodoxy and heresy, between loyalty and betrayal. It is the locus, but also the main issue and weapon, of a never-ending struggle for existence as well as truth. In this sense, the Bible has played a role in Judaism that no other text has ever seemed likely to occupy.

It is true that the Talmud has functioned as much as, or even more than, the Bible as a normative canon defining standards of conduct, and as a "formative" canon providing the foundation for the cur-riculum of studies.[38] Yet, unlike the Bible and especially the Penta-teuch—whose intent is clearly prescriptive, even if the prescription may sometimes appear ambiguous, obscure, or even contradictory—the Talmud and the Mishnah before it do not settle matters defini-tively; each in its way is a kind of canonization of controversy itself.[39] Besides, unlike the Bible, the Talmud did not obtain recognition from the Jewish world as a whole; Karaism[40] posed a radical challenge to its authority. And finally, again unlike the Bible—even though some medieval Christian polemicists, with tactical ends in view, searched for and claimed to find support for the Church's teachings in the Tal-mud itself and more generally in classical rabbinical literature—the Talmud remained the exclusive property of rabbinical Judaism. This made it a favorite target of attack for Christians, a victim of ecclesiastical censure and many an auto-da-fé.

The *Zohar**, the third literary pillar of Judaism—which is often presented as enjoying comparable authority—generally occupied a place close to that of the Talmud and the Bible. Like the Talmud, it assumed the prior existence of the biblical referent. Like the Talmud, it never obtained the recognition of the whole Jewish world, and as early as the fifteenth century, it even came under strong suspicions that it was not genuine. Like the Talmud but not the Bible—and despite the emergence of a Christian Kabbalah—the *Zohar* became neither the focal issue nor the locus of an absolutely vital debate between Christianity and Judaism.

Since the Bible, and only the Bible, was always common property—shared by Orthodox and heretics, Jews and Christians—it occupied a unique strategic position within Judaism itself, imposing an exceptional duty on scholars to engage with it. For while the Talmud, or even the *Zohar*, could provide the basis for an internal specificity and legitimacy well-nigh unassailable from outside, the Bible could not just be handed over to the Other. Scripture appeared as a kind of front line, where it was impossible, without incurring major risks, to allow the slightest breach in the defenses. And if rabbinical Judaism never ceased to affirm and demonstrate—by means of ever new interpretations—that Scripture was indeed *its* Scripture, the reason was simply that its own credibility and integrity were on the line in biblical exegesis.[41]

On Interpretation

As sign and condition of continuity, not only of Judaism but more generally of Jewish culture as such, biblical exegesis is in a paradoxical sense *prior* to the Bible itself. It precedes the Bible and dominates and invents it. Was it not to some extent the condition for the definitive crystallization of the text and the closure of the canon? If Esther or Song of Songs had not been subjected to a particular type of interpretation and justification,[42] would they ever have made their way into the canon?

Interpretation of the Bible actually developed *in parallel* to the process of its composition, as the work of James Kugel has illustrated.

Before Scripture had taken its final form, its narratives, songs, and prophecies had already begun to be interpreted. This tradition would never be dissociated from the Bible itself, and it is that "already interpreted" Bible that found itself at the heart of rabbinical Judaism and nascent Christianity.[43] Whatever the ambition of fundamentalist currents, ancient or modern, to "return" to Scripture and a supposedly primal text, there is not and never has been a "naked" Bible.

Lastly, the Bible *interprets itself.* What are the Chronicles if not (at least in part) a rewriting—that is, reinterpretation—of the books of Samuel and Kings?

In this way, the Bible already asserts itself as the point of origin and crystallization of a form of creativity perceived as "typically Jewish." Indeed, starting from the Bible and the earliest rewritings and "narrative expansions,"[44] so richly illustrated by ancient exegesis and the rabbinical midrash*, some authors have felt able—exaggerating a little, but not without some truth—to present the whole of postbiblical Jewish literature as an unflagging effort to "reimagine" the Bible.[45]

According to the same authors,[46] this reimagining continued deep into the twentieth century, as well illustrated by the monumental publication of *The Legends of the Jews* by Louis Ginzberg (1873–1953), an eminent Talmudist and leader of the North American conservative current, which collected and wove into a continuous narrative a vast store of data from the available midrashic literature, thereby representing a tendency at work in Judaism since its origins to keep reconstituting a kind of "Book of the Book."[47] Even the contemporary Jewish novel is sometimes cited as a new form of exegesis that has survived secularization and the dissolution of the Jewish faith.[48]

Besides, the Bible *demands* to be interpreted—and it does so explicitly. This is what God urges on Joshua after the death of Moses: "Let not this Book of the Torah cease from your lips, but recite [*ve-hagita*] it day and night, so that you may observe faithfully all that is written in it" (Josh. 1.8).

The Hebrew *ve-hagita*, which the 2004 *Jewish Study Bible* translates as "recite," but which may also be rendered as "meditate upon," is a verb with the same root (*hgh*) as the famous *higgayon* that we came across above.[49] This is precisely because the "meditation" in question (*higgayon* in the biblical sense) is, not just a preoccupation with the text (*higgayon* in Rabbi Eliezer's sense), but an effort at appropriation, internalization,[50] or—in other words—*interpretation*, this being essential to promulgate the Law and to guide action.

The perfect biblical example of this interpretive posture is the following: "Ezra had dedicated himself to scrutinize [*lidrosh*] the teaching of the Lord so as to observe it, and to teach laws and rules to Israel" (Ezra 7.10). This verse and the one from Joshua clearly echo each other. But here the verb is different: *lidrosh*, whose root (*drsh*) is the same at that of another word that, though present only twice in the whole of Scripture,[51] has had a remarkable career in postbiblical language: midrash. The expression *beit midrash*, "house of study," appears for the first time in Sirach [= Ecclesiasticus] 51.23. At Qumran, *drsh* was used in the sense of "to interpret." And in its current acceptation, the term *midrash* came to denote classical rabbinical exegesis of Scripture as it developed mainly in the Holy Land.

Imperceptibly, then, we slide from "book" to "meditation" thereon, from "meditation" to "scrutiny," from "scrutiny" to "interpretation." The book itself urges, encourages, explicitly enjoins such interpretation. But it also enjoins it, in a less direct, though no less decisive, manner.

Faced with a difficult passage from Scripture, or one whose strategic importance impels him to go beyond the obvious meaning, the reader feels an implicit call to redouble his effort to understand it: *darsheni*, "interpret me," the passage seems to call out.[52] From this point of view, the position of the Christian reader is no different, although he may express it in other imagery. When God seems to deliver an obscure or even shocking message, Saint Augustine tells us, He "blinks."[53]

In fact, given that the definitive sanctification of the scriptural text prohibits any updating in the form of additions, corrections, or rewriting, it inevitably becomes—or threatens to become—ever more alien to its readers as language and culture evolve over time and the community bearing it undergoes social transformation. The context in which the book is read is no longer the one in which it was produced; and either the Hebrew of its authors is no longer the same as that employed by its readers or Hebrew has altogether ceased to be the vernacular language of the community. Suddenly, the meaning of a word loses its transparency; certain unspoken assumptions are no longer self-evident. Suddenly, the obvious meaning of certain passages becomes unacceptable to the customs and morals of new times.[54] Interpretation then becomes essential.

Of course, beyond these more or less objective exigencies born of historical transformation or changed ways of thinking, more patently ideological constraints carried great weight. It was also, no doubt mainly, because of the status that rabbinical Judaism conferred on the Bible—a divinely inspired and authorized document supersaturated with meaning—that its interpretation became a major imperative.

Only the work of exegetes made it possible to bridge the inevitable gap between the biblical text and its readers. It alone enabled the text to escape the contingencies of time and chronology; for there is "no before and no after" in the Torah,[55] all parts of Scripture are contemporaneous in the eyes of the Absolute, regardless of the circumstances of their production or the supposed identity of their "authors," and the whole is already given in each minutest part. The work of exegetes is supposedly capable of resolving the contradictions of a thoroughly consistent totality, each part of which can and should explain each of the others.[56] In short, their work ensures the permanence of the sacred character of Scripture, while at the same time making it manifest.

Their work preserves the status of Scripture as the word of a living God, as the still living word of that God, or even as the manifestation of God's own essence and inner life.[57] In its interpretation, and only in its interpretation, can a virtually dead text like the Bible (dead because frozen and untouchable) manifest the power of life within it. It is through interpretation that a text from the past, a "dated" text like the Bible— "a corpus of sacred texts, whose words [constitute] a body of divine instruction given to each generation"[58]—reveals its unalterable actuality, its unchanging capacity to speak to men in the present. It is through interpretation that a text reputedly born out of dialogue between God and His people, and transmitted via His prophet, can remain—despite the apparent suspension of dialogue and the end of prophecy—the primary vehicle of a still active Revelation.

The text is potentially imperfect because it is materially finished and "perpetually incomplete."[59] But through interpretation it reveals its true perfection and its infinitude that supposedly differentiates it from any secular, merely human text. Since the canon is closed, "everything must be found in it."[60] And conversely, if—God forbid!—the least word of the biblical text should appear "empty of meaning," the emptiness could only be the sign of inadequacy on the part of its interpreter.[61]

On the Community of Interpreters

The exceptional status of Holy Writ is thus both ensured and expressed by the reading made of it—and so too is the exceptional status of the community that claims it for itself. Or, in other words, this text "exists, in the final analysis, thanks to the community, for the use of the community, with a view to giving shape to the community." And it is by interpreting it that "the community in question interprets itself."[62]

In fact, what is this "community" in question? The community of the Jews, to be sure. But, to be even more precise, it is the community of Jewish *scholars*: Pharisees*, then legitimate heirs of the Pharisaic* tradition, the only authorized decoders of a text permanently seen as encoded.

But where does the authority of the exegete come from? What does it draw upon? How can it somehow outdo the authority of the prophet himself, on the grounds that he does not know the exact meaning of his own prophecy?[63]

It is not certain that the "faith" of the exegete—or, to put it in more Christian terms, the "welcome" he gives to "the Spirit"[64]—is the decisive factor in the eyes of Judaism; nor that it is the safest guarantee of the correctness of the exegesis. To believe is certainly not sufficient to understand, even if belief is no doubt necessary to understanding.

It is his expertise, his scholarship, that authenticates the legitimate exegete—if that expertise and scholarship have been acquired in the straight line of an authentic tradition, and they are deployed within, and in interaction with, a community of legitimate experts and scholars.

That community is established right at the beginning of the first chapter of the Avot tractate of the Mishnah: "Moses received the Torah from Sinai and passed it on to Joshua; then Joshua to the ancients; then the ancients to the prophets; and the prophets passed it on to the men of the Great Assembly." The scholar is the sole inheritor of Moses, at the end of the chain stretching through Joshua, the ancients, and the prophets; therefore no one—not even a "prophet" or some visionary claiming to be one—can ever contest his legitimacy.

The scholar appears as nothing more or less than a new Moses, as we can see from a fine passage in version B of the Avot of Rabbi Nathan: "Rabbi Eliezer was seated there, expounding [*doresh*] more things than were said to Moses on Sinai, and his face shone like the light from the sun, its rays issuing like the rays [from the face] of Moses, and no one knew whether it was night or day."[65]

But, as the Mishnah Avot stresses, the community of scholars, masters, and disciples stretching across the generations from Moses without a break crystallized around the Torah, not the Bible. And the Torah, we must remember, is not only Scripture but above all the Oral Tradition rooted in Sinai. Thus, when the exegete interprets the Bible, he appears as the final relay and player in a continuous Revelation. If, in exegesis, there must be a "Spirit" animating the "Flesh" that is the "letter" of Scripture, then it should be sought in the Oral Tradition.

Exegetic Challenges (1): Pshat *and the Law*

One of the main challenges for medieval rabbinical exegesis was simultaneously to maintain and reveal the unbreakable links between the Written and the Oral Torah—a challenge it had to take up both against the Karaites (who denied the existence of such links) and against the Christians (who in a way substituted Jesus and the teachings of the Church for the Oral Torah). In the final analysis, it was consonance with tradition that validated a scriptural exegesis, which was further legitimated by the polyvalence or polysemy of the text.[66] At the same time, the exegesis had a mission in principle to demonstrate tirelessly the consonance of text and tradition.

This was precisely the aim of what Geza Vermes calls the "applied" exegesis that appeared at the beginning of the Christian era.[67] It no longer started from the text itself, but rather from the practices and beliefs of the day, the role of the exegete being to link them to the text and in so doing to justify them. The Pharisees, being laymen unable to claim any hereditary status (unlike the priests or Levites), undertook to defend their doctrine by grounding it on Scripture whenever it departed from the common norm. Such was the function of the halakhic midrashim* (*midreshei halakhah*) of tannaitic[68] origin, which bore on the legislative sections of the Pentateuch. Unlike the Mishnah—

which usually refrained from adducing biblical evidence in support of a law[69]—these midrashim forged a formal link between the Written and the Oral Torah. Such was one of the purposes of the *middot*, hermeneutic "measures" or "rules" that underwent several attempts at formalization in antiquity.[70]

It is remarkable that the same kind of concerns, though arising from the different historical and ideological context of the Karaite challenge, impelled much of medieval biblical exegesis.

"Literalist" commentators of the Middle Ages often invoked for polemical purposes a principle that appears only infrequently in the talmudic corpus:[71] namely, "a scriptural text does not go outside its simple meaning." However, this "simple" meaning (*pshut** or *pshat*) is not what we would today call the "literal" or "obvious" meaning. The *pshat* of rabbinical literature is the interpretation that everyone accepts as authoritative, the traditional meaning usually given to the text, which may be quite remote from the "literal" or "obvious" meaning.

The *pshat* to which Rashi himself, the undisputed master of medieval exegesis, devoted his energies is also not the narrowly literal meaning. Drawing selectively on the resources in talmudic and midrashic literature, he aimed first of all to restore the coherence of the narratives he analyzed, and it often happened that he would consider a midrash as the actual *pshat* of the text on which he was commenting.[72]

Things became distinctly more complicated, however, when exegetes themselves, as in the Spanish school exemplified by the polymath Abraham Ibn Ezra (1089–1164),[73] identified *pshat* more and more clearly with philological and grammatical meaning, and when, in one legislative passage from Scripture, this philological and grammatical meaning came into blatant conflict with the explicit provisions that rabbinical law (Halakhah*) claimed or appeared to derive from that passage.

Such a contradiction was—if I may put it like that—manna from heaven for the Karaites. They could argue that it showed the human rather than divine origin of the Oral Tradition, and that it was the best proof of its being incompatible with, and its doing scandalous violence to, the letter of Scripture.

Faced with such a challenge, medieval scholars had only two real options: sometimes, in a hazardous philological exercise, they tried to show that the philological meaning of a passage was perfectly consistent with the rabbinical Halakhah, which then appeared as the correct interpreta-tion of the text; sometimes, in a kind of tactical retreat, they pointed out that the ancient rabbis established only a formal link[74] between a legal provision of the Oral Tradition and a particular verse of the Written Torah, that the legal provision was not and never had been strictly con-sidered as an interpretation of the verse, and that in the end it did not really "need" the verse in order to be authoritative, since the authority of the Oral Tradition, having been given by God to Moses on Sinai, and therefore enjoying a fully autonomous legitimacy, did not fundamen-tally depend in any way on conformity to the Written Tradition.[75]

This problematic character of the links between the Oral and the Writ-ten Law haunts the entire medieval (and, when Orthodox, also modern) history of the rabbinical exegesis of Scripture. It is clear, for example, that the scholars' enumeration, categorization, and localization (within the scriptural corpus) of the 613 commandments that God, according to a talmudic tradition, revealed to Moses on Sinai was the result of a new reading of the Bible; and that the authors of these "books of com-mandments" were seeking to proclaim the unity and integrity of the Halakhah, while at the same time underlining correspondences between the Written Law of the Pentateuch and the Oral Law of tradition.[76]

The same concern was unquestionably shared by Abraham Ibn Ezra, for whom the Oral Law was no less revealed than the Written Law, and any questioning of the reliability of the preservation or transmission of the biblical text was a questioning of the authority of the traditional canon, the masoretes, and at the same time of the rabbinical tradition itself.[77] Ibn Ezra's resolve in his exegesis to go down the path of *pshat* was closely associated with his unshakable confidence in the masters of the Oral Law concerning "laws, statutes, and rules": "Heaven for-bid that we should get mixed up with these Sadducees* [by which is meant 'these Karaites'], who say that the tradition [that of our Mas-ters] contradicts the written biblical text and grammatical [rules]!"[78]

Exegetic Challenges (2): Pshat *and Allegory*

In the history of ancient and medieval exegesis,[79] *pshat*—whose explicit or implicit definition can vary considerably from one source or author to another—is always strategic.

Sometimes it proves to have been opening a space of encounter with the Other, or even a space of possible conciliation. For, at least in an ideal world, whatever the tradition to which they lay claim, all exegetes "of good faith" are in theory likely to come together around it, provided they agree to bracket it temporarily, tackle the same text in the same language, and submit to the same rules of hermeneutic rigor.

In the real world, however, that is far from how things always present themselves, and *pshat* most often proves to be fertile ground for conflicts over the fundamental legitimacy of each of the rival camps. It then becomes a weapon to be used *against* the exegesis of others, who can always be accused of betraying the *pshat* in question.

We have seen this in the case of the Karaites, who tried to discredit the Rabbanites' Oral Law by showing that it clashed head-on with the obvious sense of Scripture, but the upholders of "Orthodoxy" never failed to wield the same weapon against those who contradicted them within or outside Judaism. Although all exegetes, Jewish or non-Jewish, "Orthodox" or "heretical," agreed that Scripture contains a plurality of meanings, and that a well-conducted exegesis should bring out multiple levels of meaning, none ever hesitated—at least tactically—to counterpose the *pshat*, the obvious meaning, the letter, to nonliteral interpretations that their opponents sought to promote.

From antiquity on, the distinction between the obvious and the deeper meaning was a hermeneutic principle common to the pagan, Jewish, and Christian traditions.[80] Greek-speaking Jewish writers such as Philo naturally adopted the Greeks' allegorical method of interpretation,[81] though with the (essential) difference that for Philo, it did not cancel the legitimacy or fundamental importance of the obvious meaning[82]—on the contrary, it was a precise extension of that meaning and had the effect of strengthening it.

The ancient rabbis, who distinguished between *pshat* and *drash* (allegory and homiletic development), were similarly reluctant to downplay *pshat*. That is also the purport of the previously mentioned teaching that "a scriptural text does not go outside its simple meaning";[83] the second meaning adds to the first without making it disappear.

Christian exegesis adopted a similar position, distinguishing between the obvious (historical or literal) sense of Scripture and its deeper, "spiritual" sense, where the second is opposed to the first as spirit to flesh, light to shadow, or sap to the bark or fruit. Medieval Christian commentators saw in the very existence of spiritual meaning the essential uniqueness, in contrast to secular culture, of the Bible and the Christian faith; in any case, that meaning relied on the literal sense and did not exclude it.[84] "The spiritual sense must be established on the solid foundations of the letter; it is from them that the 'mystical meanings' can be derived with some effort."[85]

Medieval Christians and Jews did not rest content with a simply duality of meaning; the profundity of the divine message contained in the limited human words of the Bible led the commentator to etch several exegetic layers in succession. No doubt it was under the (unrecognized) influence of the four meanings of Christian hermeneutics that a comparable doctrine eventually commanded acceptance in the Jewish world too, even if the categories of the two systems did not overlap exactly.[86]

Apart from the literal sense, Christian exegesis identified three others with a spiritual character: the tropological sense that contributed to the moral and spiritual training of the soul; the typological sense that mostly interpreted Old Testament realities as "types" prefiguring the realities of the New Testament; and the analogic sense that concerned the celestial world and the "Last Things."[87]

On the Jewish side, to take but one example, the highly popular commentary of Bahya ben Asher (c. 1260–1340) on the Pentateuch follows a fourfold approach: the path of *pshat*, the path of midrash (homiletic meaning), the path of "intellect"[88] (that is, reason or philosophy), and the path of "secrecy"[89] (or Kabbalah). Before him, however, Moses Nahmanides (1194–1270) had developed a four-level hermeneutic inspired consciously or unconsciously by Christian exegesis; he went farther still, making typological exegesis a methodological shift away from the linguistic-textual resonances typical of classical midrashim to the structural correspondences among events, people, and things, with the past heralding or even predetermining the future.[90]

Allegorical, symbolic, or "spiritual" exegesis is therefore not alien to the Jewish tradition. It won recognition among both philosophers and kabbalists.[91]

For the philosophers, the biblical text was stratified by dint of the equivocal nature of all language, but also because the text addressed—

and in fact adapted to—a distinctly heterogeneous community of readers. In this framework, the philosophers had intensive though limited recourse to allegorical readings; Maimonides, for instance—who used the image of the "golden apple overlaid with a network of silver"[92]—thought that a second level of interpretation should be postulated only if the literal meaning of the text was contrary to reason, as in the exemplary case of the anthropomorphisms used by the Bible to speak of God.

For the kabbalists, the biblical text was stratified for almost the opposite reasons: its essentially divine language, ontologically distinct from all conventional human languages, is the one in which the world was created and the very essence of God is expressed. They also considered that the *whole* of the Torah, not just certain passages, should be read in this way, since each word in it has both a literal meaning and one or more symbolic meanings.

In fact, the kabbalists distinguished several (classically four) thresholds for the disclosure of meaning. They evoked this hierarchy by means of various images, including the walnut encased in its shell, the tree with its roots and branches, or the garment, body, soul, and soul of souls;[93] mystical (zoharic*) exegesis of the Bible permits the exegete who assimilates the properties of what he studies to ascend "exegetically," by stages, toward God.[94]

The scriptural controversy between Christianity and Judaism cannot therefore be reduced to a conflict between two mutually exclusive methods of exegesis: allegorical (for Christians) and literal (for Jews). The rabbis did set some inviolable limits to the allegorization of Scripture: it cannot cancel the letter of the text or encroach upon halakhic exegesis of the Pentateuch, without running into danger in the minefield laid by Christianity, for which not all provisions of the Law have equal validity, and for which some ceremonial requirements are of only limited duration and require to be interpreted in such a way as to bring out their prefigurative value or their purely spiritual significance.

On the Christian side, Bartholomew of Exeter (twelfth century) reproached the Jews with never accepting allegory except as a last resort, and with sticking to the letter of Scripture except when it could provide "testimony clearly in favour of Christ."[95] In reality, for Jews too, the Torah had countless faces (seventy, to be precise).[96] And what they rejected was not allegory as such but the arbitrary use they thought Christians made of it.

Conversely, when Christians finally realized the nature and importance of the Oral Tradition for Jews—a tradition from which allegory is far from absent—they accused them this time of "fabrication."[97] The allegory of others is always their folly . . .

In Judaism, far from clearing a path to consensus, the return to *pshat* and the reaffirmation of its supremacy were thus often a defensive reaction, a posture of rejection. *Pshat* was never an absolute value or an untouchable principle, especially as it necessarily suffered exceptions.[98] If *pshat* won acceptance in the Latin West in the eleventh century, it was in an anti-Christian polemical context. Jewish assertion of the preeminence of the literal meaning was still very closely bound up with refutation of Christian spiritual interpretation.[99] Abraham Ibn Ezra, for example, had no words harsh enough to stigmatize Christian allegorists;[100] they wander on "a path of darkness and obscurity," imagining "mysteries" everywhere or "enigmas" behind every law or statute, whereas everything should be weighed in the balance of the "intellect," that God-given faculty of judgment that replaces the literal with the figurative only when the former clearly contradicts the evidence of the senses or the exigencies of reason.[101]

At the same time, similar tracts could be directed by Jews against *fellow Jews*, "enemies within," with kabbalists, but also philosophers, as natural targets. Thus, when the Hebrew translation of Maimonides's *Guide of the Perplexed* sparked major controversies, first in 1230, then again around 1303, because of its wide circulation and the extreme value that certain milieux (especially in Languedoc and Provence) attached to scientific and philosophical culture, traditionalists used the excesses of philosophical allegorization as a pretext to disqualify their opponents. What should we make of Jacob ben Abba Mari Anatoli (c. 1194–1256), for example, who interpreted Abraham and Sarah as allegories of form and matter rather than actual historical characters, or the seven branches of the candelabra in the mobile desert temple as evocations of the seven planets?

Was this not leading irresistibly to allegorization of the commandments of the Torah themselves, to dissolution of their objective content and binding nature through a symbolization likely to ruin the practice of Judaism? Does the fact that prophetic language uses images—like dreams—allow all prophecy to be regarded only as images? The danger is not hard to see. And we can understand why Nissim of Marseilles (fourteenth century)—who suggested that correct exegesis of the prophetic word means above all filtering out everything drawn from the prophet's all-too-human imagination—also protected the Books of Moses from deviant interpretation by distinguishing them as sharply as possible from all other revealed texts, on the grounds that they did not show the slightest element of imagination (or dream).[102]

Biblical Exegesis as a Combat Sport

"Potentially infinite" though the exegetical process may be, "precise rules formulated over time" in both Christianity and Judaism have periodically sought to banish "arbitrariness, randomness, or what today we call overinterpretation."[103] Such rules, however, do not only positively define an exegetical program; they have also—perhaps mainly—been an instrument in the hands of commentators to delegitimize the Other's interpretation. For in the end all biblical exegesis involves combat.

Placed at the interface between inside and outside, the Jewish Bible functions as a kind of filtering airlock. What exegete would not be tempted to insert into it every truth acquired or demonstrated outside (talmudic truth, kabbalistic truth, philosophical truth), in the belief—or make-belief—that he actually found it inside the Bible? After all, the Truth is one, the God who speaks in the Bible is precisely the God of Truth, and He is reputed to have spoken the whole Truth there. Here the airlock is open, sometimes gaping wide.

Another exegete, no less an exegete than the one preceding him, was therefore always found to make the airlock as tight as possible and to expel from it anything that, in his view, had nothing to do with the Truth. He could always argue that others, acting in a dubious cause and concerned only to "torture Scripture," had inserted into it the Rabbanites' Oral Tradition, or the "Aristotelian quibbles" of philosophers, or the "childish lucubrations" of mystics, the spiritual interpretations of Christians, and so on.[104]

At the interface between inside and outside, the Bible is also at the intersection of the particular and the universal. For a Jew, therefore, to comment on the Bible is first and foremost to affirm (against any external claim or attempt at expropriation) the sole, exclusive, essential legitimacy of the rights he has over it—in short, to reaffirm its definitive Jewishness.

A particularly eloquent case in point are the exegetical efforts in the Talmud to exclude Gentiles from the obligation to "increase and multiply" (Gen. 1.28), as a result of which a divine benediction addressed to the first human couple—and therefore in principle to the whole of humanity—is transformed into a Mosaic commandment, a legal obligation of the Torah; it applies only to Jews,[105] in the framework of the Covenant and within a messianic perspective, procreation being a sine qua non of the coming of the Son of David.[106]

In the same way, when Christians argued that God meant to dispense Gentiles from the ritual provisions of the Law, Jews were not so far from thinking the same. But whereas the former saw this as a token of the futility, or at least obsoleteness, of those provisions (which retained no more than symbolic significance), the latter proudly claimed them for themselves alone as clearly defined obligations, interpreting them as "the sign of divine favor."[107]

But although the particularity and permanent election of the Jews were affirmed in biblical exegesis, that was not all it involved. Just as essential was its affirmation of the universality of Judaism. The discovery of *all* truth in the Bible along with Jewish truths—or at least, should one not wish to go that far, the demonstration that, if only because it is situated at another level and aims at something different,[108] the Bible as the Jews understand it does not conflict in any way with the great scientific and philosophical truths accepted by human reason—was thus a means, for Jews themselves at least, of opening up Judaism and refusing the slightest support for its relegation to the sidelines of universality where its adversaries thought it belonged.

This being so, the self-affirmation project that seems to drive all Jewish exegesis of the Bible remains stamped with the seal of irreducible ambiguity. For the Other is always present, and adversaries never stop partly dictating the agenda of those who respond to or preempt their objections.

In the long history of Jewish-Christian polemics, it is unquestionably Christianity that imposed its themes and even the tone of its responses on Judaism, often compelling Jewish masters to void or neutralize the messianic dimension of so many biblical promises.[109] Unquestionably too, it was the Karaite challenge that forced so many Rabbanite exegetes to operate on the (not necessarily favorable) ground of *pshat*, philology, and grammar, and at the same time to appeal to the undisputed authority of tradition, to prove both that rigorous philology guards against doctrinal error and that pure belief offers protection against philological error.[110]

More generally, a biblical commentator was never alone before his text. The shades of his predecessors, the expectations and prejudices of his audience, the objections of his opponents inevitably haunted the terrain. God Himself was doubtless watching sardonically from on high, regarding his commentary as no more than another modest and ephemeral wave on the surface of an ocean.

The "Immense Ocean" of Commentaries

A fifteenth-century Byzantine-Jewish commentator once remarked that "it would be good if the content of all books were intelligible without a commentary," and that that would "fully achieve the author's intention."[111] One would think that, as an exegete, he would have considered it fortunate that the ideal never essentially corresponded to reality. Indeed, medieval—and more generally premodern—Jewish culture was fundamentally a culture of commentary.[112] Everything in it was material for exegesis; all its output was structured as commentary, or at least presupposed a whole labor and experience of exegesis. From this point of view, the Bible was no exception to the rule—although the rule did not apply to it in exactly the same way as to purely human productions.

The latter require commentary for various reasons that have to do either with their relative imperfection—excessive brevity, elliptical quality, ambiguity, errors in need of clarification or correction—or with unjust handling on the part of previous commentators (necessitating rehabilitation work), or with the real or alleged imperfection of their usual readership (necessitating pedagogic work). In placing himself at the service of the preexisting text, the exegete therefore naturally wavers

between two tasks: a search for the *meaning* or truth of the *text* (trying
to understand, and help others to understand, what the author really
meant, whether it was true or false), and a search for the actual *truth* of
things (whatever the text may say about them).[113]

Until Spinoza, the truth of the biblical text was identified precisely
with the truth of things:[114] to disclose the meaning of the text was to
gain access to the truth of Being itself. (This distinguished the Bible
from secular works, and commentary on it from exegesis of the latter.)
Moreover, as we have seen, biblical commentary is not just an intellectual exercise: it is also a religious duty and, so to speak, the social duty
of every member of the caste of scholars.

This is where the difference ends, however. For biblical commentary
is *also* an intellectual exercise. And like all secular commentary, it is
an opportunity for the commentator, not only to show his reverence
for the text (and for the chain of commentators in which he is the
latest link), but also to display a certain autonomy or inventiveness,
sometimes audacity, which is no less real for being usually hidden behind a veil of conspicuous modesty. God is his one and final judge, his
one and final guide. The truth that the exegete aims to bring to light
makes no distinctions between individuals; it grants him a right to take
stock and imposes on him a duty of criticism.[115]

In these circumstances, it is not surprising that a biblical commentary—especially one on the Pentateuch—should classically crown an
author's oeuvre and often, if not always, form its cornerstone or one
of its centerpieces. The exegete may bring all his skills to bear on it,
whether religious or secular, rabbinical or scientific. He enters into
dialogue with his sources, quotes his predecessors, sometimes copies
them without saying so, completes, corrects, and discusses them, criti-
cizes them indirectly and refutes them openly. It is out of this endless
face-off between loyalty and treachery, reproduction and emancipation, that *his* commentary emerges. It sorts, selects, rewrites, contrasts,
or combines material, underlining conflicts of interpretation or, on the
contrary, seeking to reconcile the irreconcilable. Even the most sober
commentaries, the ones most attached to *pshat* of the biblical text, the
ones least dependent on rabbinical, philosophical, or kabbalist tradition, resonate with a thousand presences hidden in their very silences,
in the very things they forget or leave unspoken.

The reader has a responsibility to be attentive to them. The commentary is *always* a "supercommentary," a commentary on a commentary. More than two hundred supercommentaries have been written on Rashi's commentary on the Pentateuch—and he was far from alone in enjoying such popularity. As early as 1170, just six years after the death of Abraham Ibn Ezra in England, a Bulgarian Jew by the name of Avishai of Zagora signed a supercommentary on Ibn Ezra's commentary on the Pentateuch—a text mentioned in the fourteenth century by Yehuda Leon Moskoni (born at Ohrid, in today's Macedonia, in 1328), himself a great lover of and (super)commentator on Ibn Ezra's texts, who reported having seen with his own eyes some thirty different supercommentaries on the master.[116] Five and a half centuries on, the Ibn Ezra fever had still not subsided, and in 1722, forty-five years after the death of Spinoza (himself an attentive and rather indulgent reader of Ibn Ezra),[117] Yekutiel Lazi ben Nahum Ashkenazi published in Amsterdam his *Sefer Margali(o)t Tova*, an anthology of supercommentaries on Abraham Ibn Ezra's commentary on the Pentateuch . . .

Here a new paradox inevitably arises. When its primary function is precisely to foreground the Bible, biblical commentary cannot but eat into all the space on its own behalf. Perhaps nothing better illustrates this phenomenon than the way in which the scriptural text, its Aramaic paraphrases, and some of its medieval commentaries and supercommentaries were organized in relation to one another, in what is commonly known as the rabbinical Bible (in Hebrew, the *Mikra'ot Gedolot*, literally, the "Great Readings"), first printed in the early sixteenth century.[118] This was in fact a continuation of an old medieval tradition, observable also in Christendom.

What is usually to be seen in the *Mikra'ot Gedolot*? Most often, only a few biblical verses could find room there, in large vocalized square characters above and on the right side of the right page. The size (big or small) and nature (square script or "Rashi" script)[119] of the characters chosen for each of the texts on the two pages that present themselves for reading once the book is open are the reflection of a certain hierarchy, and it is clear that the scriptural text—however short the fragment reproduced—occupies the summit. These typographical choices and the actual arrangement of the texts in relation to one another (e.g., how far they are from the biblical text to which they refer) also suggest a quite precisely drawn reading itinerary, the first stages of which are the masoretic text, its targum, and Rashi's commentary, in that order—all the rest coming only afterwards.

We should not be misled, however, by these seemingly indisputable signs of the preeminence of the biblical text. For there is another way of viewing the balance among the texts laid out together; we may also think that, in a particular page-setting or "staging," the biblical text is literally squashed by the huge mass of commentaries around it. The size of the disproportion, which can vary from case to case, is instructive in itself; even the least informed observer can at a glance make an initial estimate of the relative importance or difficulty of the scriptural passage in question, as well as of the scale of the debates that it may have provoked among various exegetes. But the main effect of the layout actually adopted is to distract the reader from a close reading of the biblical text, and to involve him in a complex to-ing and fro-ing both between text and commentaries and—a process virtually independent of the biblical text—between the commentaries themselves.

The reader is thus invited to hear the echoes of a "dialogue" that the typography establishes in advance between texts sometimes very different in status and nature. Of course, this "dialogue" is not totally imaginary, and the whispering of the intermingled voices is sometimes highly audible. All the commentators have read the same scriptural text; they have often fueled their reflections from the same external sources; and, having in many cases read one another, they sometimes quote and refute one another too. The fact remains that the spatial arrangement of the text unquestionably threatens (perhaps even seeks) to maintain more illusions than one in the mind of the reader.

The first, and the easiest to eliminate, is the illusion of exhaustiveness. The commentaries may seem to occupy four-fifths of the two facing pages, but they represent a choice whose criteria of selection and exclusion deserve to be spelled out, since it tends to confer near-canonical status on the chosen commentaries.[120]

Another perverse effect—or, if one prefers, a second illusion—compounds this impoverishing focus on a small number of endlessly reproduced texts. It is one that the traditional reader (by which I mean the reader trained in a traditional approach to texts) will doubtless be the least capable of dispelling. I shall call it the illusion of contemporaneousness—as if spatial crowding corresponded to temporal crowding, as if the different authors were really there in one another's company, freely conversing on the same biblical text.

Various other elements contribute to this flattening of historical perspective, but it will be sufficient if I mention just one. Many commentators who appear in the *Mikra'ot Gedolot* are commonly designated by acronyms rather than their full names, and this does not fail to confer on them a curious (but false) family resemblance. Do not Rashi, Rashbam,[121] Ra'aba,[122] Radak,[123] Ramban,[124] and so on—at least when they are named in that way—have the strange appearance of being cousins? At first sight, anyway, nothing clearly indicates that they lived in periods and cultural zones sometimes quite distant from one another. This may well be an item that should be added to the file on the complex relationship of rabbinical Judaism to historicity, so brilliantly explored by Yosef Hayim Yerushalmi.[125]

What does all this show? A single, exemplary exaltation of the Bible, by a mass of commentators from different times and places squeezing into the service of a never-complete elucidation of its meaning? Or a Bible covered, almost hidden, by a swell of commentaries that often seem to be an end in themselves?

The continuous scriptural commentary, completely organized around the Bible, taking the Bible as its point of departure and constantly returning to it, was a medieval invention.[126] Those who invented this type of commentary clearly promoted the Bible, emancipated it, freed it from a stifling rabbinical tradition, and saved it from seemingly inevitable drowning in what it has become customary to call "the sea of the Talmud" (*yam ha-Talmud*). Yet the same medieval scholars threatened another kind of drowning: in the "immense ocean" of their own commentaries,[127] fueled by a thousand other things than the Bible itself, including the Talmud.[128]

All things considered, it is only with the moderns (neo-Karaites of a kind) that the "vessel of Scripture"[129] finally reached port. No doubt the price was the almost complete evaporation of what for centuries had been the flesh and the spirit of rabbinical Judaism. The ship's holds were empty, as it were.

Five   The Bible of the Moderns

The modern age of the Bible is in a sense the age of its triumph. Perhaps at no other point in the history of the West or of Judaism has the Bible enjoyed a symbolic, cultural, and political position as central as it has during the past four centuries. In the Christian world, the tendency first crystallized with the birth of Protestantism and its orientation to "Scripture alone." Then it developed and reached fulfilment in a new "Promised Land," with the emergence of a power that may be described in more ways than one as both "biblical" and "messianic": the United States of America. In the Jewish world, the process was in many respects comparable, though spread over a longer time period. Rooted in the Haskalah*, the Jewish Enlightenment movement that appeared in eighteenth-century Berlin and gradually moved into eastern Europe, it developed in the late nineteenth century into a new "Palestinophilia," as in the case of the Lovers of Zion.[1] And it finally led to Zionism and the creation in 1948, on the ancient land of Canaan, of a state no less "biblical" and no less "messianic" than its predecessor: Israel.

This modern triumph of the Bible, however, has been more complex than it may seem. It did not conflict at all with the advance of a certain secularization, especially as it unfolded at the expense of the centralized churches and traditional clergies. Moreover, the two trajectories mentioned in the last paragraph did not run strictly in parallel. Nor did they develop inevitably, in a straight line from one point to another, in accordance with some mechanical historical determinism. A critical observer must, of course, resist any temptation to engage in teleological reconstruction, bearing in mind the ambiguities and contradictions, the splits and internal conflicts, and the side tracks that were never lacking in either case.

The novelty of the phenomenon is certainly relative for Judaism, and it requires at least to be precisely identified. Before the modern age, the Bible had more than once played the role of springboard for reform and renewal. Scripturalism had permitted Karaism to shake off its rabbinical straitjacket and to propose another way of being Jewish. It was through a return to the Bible, its language, and the model it suggested that the Oriental and Sephardi* moment in the history of medieval Judaism had been able to come forward as one of the most creative. These past triumphs of Scripture had gone together with—and supported themselves upon—a profound renewal of (often critical) biblical scholarship among grammarians, philologists, and lexicographers initially trained in the Arab-Muslim school. With the Karaites, the Bible had taken over the whole space and stripped the Oral Tradition of its authority. But against all odds, amid tensions and in sometimes complex forms, the Bible had maintained a solid (but renewed) link with that tradition in the Oriental and Sephardi cultural area.

Although some of its features were not unfamiliar, the movement that first got under way in the sixteenth century was new from at least three points of view. First, with the exception of Spinoza (a noteworthy exception, to be sure, but was he still within Judaism?), the renewal of biblical scholarship characteristic of this third modern trend was almost exclusively Christian, and mainly Protestant, in origin. It also undermined the position of the Old Testament to an unprecedented extent, casting into doubt almost everything hitherto believed about it. Second, this new modernity of the Bible worked itself out in politics; and among the Jews, at least in the case of Zionism, it came to serve a political project that was at first distinctly *secular*. Finally—and this too was unprecedented—the relationship of Jews to the Bible tended to become aestheticized. Scripture was for the first time perceived as literature, to be protected from critical attack and treasured as a legacy providing the foundation for a renewed Jewish identity and an epic novel of the Jewish nation.

In the end, these three dominant tendencies were fairly congruent with one another. All tended to "trivialize" the Bible. All threatened to cut it off from its celestial roots, by historicizing, politicizing, and aestheticizing it. And all, in their different ways, exposed Judaism as such to a major danger.

The Critical Age, or the Bible Humiliated

There was no "absolute birth" of biblical criticism. On the Christian side, no one can maintain that it was an invention of nineteenth-century philologists or even sixteenth-century humanists.[2] A critical sensibility and critical works were observable as early as the first centuries after Christ, when scholars sought to improve the available version of Scripture by methods that may be described as scientific (comparison of texts with one another, and of translations with their originals). This approach picked up again in the Middle Ages, especially the twelfth and thirteenth centuries, finding expression in recourse to the Hebrew original; this first meant consultation of Jewish men of letters, but then it came to involve participation in the researches of Jewish converts to Christianity, and finally mastery (at least passive) of Hebrew by Christian scholars themselves.[3]

Comparable in nature, on the Jewish side, was the work of the masoretes.[4] Later, again in the Middle Ages, Jewish commentators on Scripture sometimes displayed a critical awareness that went well beyond a mere concern for textual correctness. The new value placed on *pshat*[5] opened the way for some more fundamental questioning. Rashi and Rashbam accepted that the obvious sense of a verse could not overlap exactly with its halakhic* sense. And Abraham Ibn Ezra implied that certain passages in the Pentateuch might have been written after the death of Moses[6]—one of his bolder suggestions, which did not stand in the way of his becoming (and remaining) one of the major references of traditional exegesis, and which may therefore not have been quite as radical as Spinoza liked to imagine.[7] Indeed, it could be argued that, despite certain flattering appearances (flattering in the eyes of the moderns), Ibn Ezra never deviated from an intransigent conservatism on such matters as the integrity of the masoretic text, and that this enabled him to adopt less conformist positions on other issues.[8] Joseph ben Eliezer Bonfils (second half of fourteenth century), a successor of Ibn Ezra and commentator on his work, implicitly defined the limit that critical Jews in the Middle Ages did not intend to cross: "What should I care whether it was Moses or another prophet who wrote it [the Pentateuch], since the words of all of them are true and inspired?"[9]

It was precisely that limit that modern criticism would cheerfully cross. Even the paternity of texts—basically a secondary issue for medieval thinkers—acquired a new centrality. In the eyes of the moderns, to identify the author was a sine qua non for any correct and responsible interpretation of the text.

A New Biblical Scholarship

What characterizes the modern age of biblical criticism, at least with regard to the Old Testament, is its historicism. To be modern, it is necessary to be not only (outrageously) historicist[10] but also (preferably) Christian and Protestant.[11]

The new biblical scholarship was certainly furthered by the interest of Christian Hebraists in the whole of rabbinical culture, including Kabbalah*. Paradoxically, however, this interest grew in a West that, following the wave of expulsions that closed the medieval period, was almost entirely devoid of legitimate representatives of that culture. For a time, rabbinical culture could be seen as part of the continuity of biblical civilization, and therefore as a reliable and useful source for the solving of interpretation difficulties that the Bible presented for Christian readers. But it soon suffered a battering from Protestantism and its attachment to direct confrontation with Scripture. If the words of the Bible alone were seen as authoritative, and if the new biblical scholarship claimed to demonstrate the falsehood of old "papist" interpretations, bypassing all intermediaries in the shape of saints or ecclesiastical hierarchies, it is not easy to see how the old Jewish interpretations could have had greater legitimacy to interpose themselves between Scripture and its readers.

Drawing on established methods in the study of Greco-Roman literature, the new biblical scholarship aimed to discover things *about* the Bible, not from it. Scripture thus became a particular document from the history of the ancient East.[12] This distancing permitted, indeed called for, every possible doubt, as the researcher approached the text from a position of a priori distrust.[13] Everything could and should be challenged. Virtually no question was viewed as illegitimate or scandalous.

Can the Text really be attributed to those whose paternity has been recognized by tradition for centuries? Can its unity be considered

certain? Do not its manifest duplications, contradictions, and inconsistencies reflect a multiplicity of original sources, produced at various
times in the history of ancient Israel by authors belonging to different
social milieux? Is not the very historicity of the narratives open to doubt?
What should we make of the institutions of ancient Israelite society, such
as we can imagine them from the Bible? What relations did the Hebrews of antiquity really have with their neighbors? What debts did their
civilization contract toward them? Was the "monotheism" of the ancient
Jews really more than just "monolatry,"[14] or indeed more than just henotheism?[15] Was Jewish monotheism primal, in the sense of originary, or
did it prevail among the Judeans only at the end of a long process?

Of course, all these questions were not posed immediately or all
at once. But nothing could stop the process begun in the sixteenth
century. From a Jewish traditionalist point of view, the consequences
of this were nothing short of disastrous. First consequence: at the very
moment when printing was finally establishing a single authoritative
text in the Jewish world,[16] the Christian world was questioning its
unity, authenticity, and reliable transmission, cutting it up into multiple sources, and revealing its composite nature. Second consequence:
this text could no longer be assumed to speak the Truth, and the
transparent meaning of history that it presented—above all, its narrative history of the people of Israel—could no longer be taken at
face value. Third consequence: it was no longer God alone, through
the mouths of the prophets, who expressed a divine truth; rather, the
prophets were historically and culturally determinate human beings,
their message was a datable document susceptible to normal literary
and historical analysis, and the worst sin an exegete could commit was
anachronism. Fourth consequence: faced with the traditional Protestant insistence that only the originating moment of a text benefited
from divine inspiration,[17] or with the critical idea (only seemingly a
secularized version of the same) that a biblical text "has one meaning,
the meaning it had to the mind of the Prophet . . . who first uttered
or wrote, to the hearers or readers who first received it,"[18] what legitimacy could the reworkings of the text itself still have: the midrashic*
and talmudic* tradition, the centuries of exegesis, the whole tradition
that basically made Judaism what it was and grounded its relationship
to the Bible as an essentially polysemic text?

Although the critical approach to the Old Testament evidently clashed head-on with certain commonplaces of the Christian tradition, and although it could eventually gnaw away at the Christian faith from within, it still corresponded to the needs of the (Christian) community in which it was born. It made it possible—or gave the illusion of making it possible—for the reader to come to grips directly with the original text, rid of the slag that had weighed it down for centuries. Above all, it made it possible to inscribe the Old Testament within an oriented history that led by stages to the New Testament.[19] Beyond that, the critical approach might in some respects and in certain cases resonate with the old Christian contempt for Judaism, lending it every semblance of scientific rigor. The challenge to the biblical account of the ancient history of Israel certainly got off to a "slow and sporadic start," but it "sometimes took on virulent forms."[20]

Thus, one of the first great masters of the historico-critical method, Julius Wellhausen (1844–1918), who identified three successive layers in the Pentateuch, quite naturally developed a new evolutionary conception of the history of Israel that broke it down into three major periods: the monarchy, the reforms of Josiah (622 BCE),[21] and the post-Exile reconstruction. This history was one of decline, concluding, not in apotheosis, but in sclerosis. The prevalence of Law, far from being the *fons et origo* of ancient Israel, was only the late sign of a decay that broke with the spirituality of the early period; rabbinical Judaism, a pure product of post-Exile legalism, appears as the final manifestation of this decay.[22]

Spinoza

This reduction of Judaism to an arid legalism was a leitmotif of Christian anti-Judaism, and the new version of it proposed by Wellhausen and his followers was certainly not likely to win the allegiance of any Jewish readers they might have. Nevertheless, the historico-critical approach does not have only Christian, Protestant, or Germanic roots; it can also claim a prestigious Jewish precursor, in principle less suspect of anti-Semitism: Spinoza.

After Thomas Hobbes, in his *Leviathan* (1651), presented the Pentateuch as a fundamentally post-Mosaic book, but before Richard Simon, in his *Histoire critique du Vieux Testament* (1678), claimed that Moses cannot be the author of all the books attributed to him, and certainly long before all the Wellhausens of the nineteenth century set to work, it was Spinoza, a "heretical" Jew of Marrano* origin living in Amsterdam, who, in his *Theologico-Political Treatise* (1670), railed against the teachings so "obstinately defended" by the Pharisees* and declared in no uncertain terms that "it was not Moses who wrote the Pentateuch, but someone who lived long after him."[23] And a little farther on he noted: "If anyone pays attention to the way in which all the histories and precepts in these five books are set down promiscuously and without order, with no regard for dates; and further, how the same story is often repeated, sometimes in a different version, he will easily, I say, discern that all the materials were promiscuously collected and heaped together, in order that they might at some subsequent time be more readily examined and reduced to order."[24] It is Ezra whom Spinoza "suspects" of being the final editor of the Pentateuch, and of not having finished the job properly.[25]

Spinoza's offensive has a degree of radicalism that few later devotees of the historico-critical method would attain. The fact that he saw, or pretended to see, Abraham Ibn Ezra as a kind of precursor should not give us the wrong impression. Similarly, try as one might to "explain" his approach as a typically Sephardi biblocentrism taken to its limits, or as the result of his "Marranism*," neither of these reduces the sharpness of the break. It does not concern only Scripture, nor, of course, only Judaism, but rather the place that the Bible and theology occupied in seventeenth-century European politics. Spinoza saw the source of all the ills of Europe in the belief of every sect that it could read its own opinions in the Bible without bothering about textual rigor.[26] In establishing that the biblical text was uncertain, contradictory, and imprecise, Richard Simon aimed to show—against the Protestants—that its authority could only come from outside, and that it was therefore not possible to dispense with the authority of the Church.[27] Naturally that was not Spinoza's intention; nor was he susceptible to the fascination that the text held for Protestants (a fascination that, as we have seen, eventually led them into a paradoxical labor of deconstruction).

Spinoza's radicalism expressed itself at several levels. He separated the truth of the text once and for all from the Truth of things, and it was the truth of the text—what it meant in its historical context, the "signification of the words"[28]—that he sought to track down. To do this, one had to be imbued with a simple principle: "The method of interpreting Scripture does not widely differ from the method of interpreting nature—in fact, it is almost the same."[29] Everything that can be known about Scripture should be drawn from Scripture alone, just as all knowledge of nature should be drawn from nature itself.

It is sheer folly, "harmful, useless, and absurd,"[30] to expect to find the conceptions of a particular philosophical system in the Bible—unless one supposes, like Maimonides, that the meaning of Scripture cannot be established on the basis of Scripture itself. Theologians indulge in a comparable folly when they seek to derive "their inventions and sayings" from the sacred text, in order to "fortify them with divine authority."[31] And then there are the rabbis who "let their fancy run wild,"[32] who pride themselves—like Roman Catholics—on a certain "tradition,"[33] think they can find strange mysteries behind the form of every letter, strive by all means to reconcile irreconcilable texts, and claim to explain an obscure passage from one prophet by a clearer passage from another, as if all these texts had not been written by different authors, in different historical contexts, and for different audiences.

That is already a lot, but it pales beside Spinoza's attempt to devalue, depreciate, and marginalize the biblical text itself. The points he makes may be summarized in five propositions:

1. The Bible is not and cannot be the source of exact knowledge of God and things; it speaks of them "inaccurately," because "its object is not to convince the reason, but to attract and lay hold of the imagination."[34]

2. The Bible is only Law, and if Moses taught the Hebrews "a rule of right living," he certainly did not do so as a philosopher, "as the result of freedom, but like a lawgiver compelling them to be moral by legal authority."[35]

3. The laws revealed in the Bible to Jews were "ordained to the Jews only"; furthermore, it is only in respect of their "society and government" that they may be considered "God's chosen people."[36]

4. The Bible testifies to a childhood of humanity, since if "religion was imparted to the early Hebrews as a law written down," this was "because they were at that time in the condition of children."[37]

5. Reading the Bible is not indispensable for "a man . . . [who] has right opinions and a true plan of life," since "he is absolutely blessed and truly possesses in himself the spirit of Christ."[38]

In short, the Bible of which Jews are so proud is not a book of philosophy or science but only a Law, revealed to them alone and valid for them alone, at a time when they were but children who had to be constrained and whose imaginations had to be captured. For an enlightened citizen, its utility was in the end very relative.

*

The challenge that the critical age posed for Judaism did not therefore come only from the "historico-critical approach," the premises of which can be found both in Spinoza and in non-Jewish (especially Protestant) precursors from the school that would eventually triumph in Wellhausen and his successors. This challenge had two dimensions, and what I have called the "critical age" had two faces: one Protestant and "scientific," the other Spinozist and secular.

On the one hand, Protestant science consecrated a militant Christian reappropriation of the Old Testament, making it a central object of study. It took it out of the hands of the "traditions"—Catholic, to be sure, but also Jewish—that claimed to hold the keys to it. It invented itself with the text, even as its criticism dismembered and dissolved it, in a supposedly "authentic" face-to-face encounter that could alone reveal the "original" meaning of the text—a meaning that eluded Judaism, which from that point on ceased to be even the source religion.

On the other hand, the Spinozist and secular tradition ended up destroying the very status of the Bible, effectively denying it any status or legitimacy. It was seen as nothing but testimony to a primitive age, ancient and Oriental; read as the expression of a Hebrew-Jewish particularism, or even chauvinism, little in keeping with the universalist aims of the new times; blamed for having been the pretext or underpinning for a theologization of politics, whose noxious character had been sufficiently illustrated by history.

These two tendencies of the modern "critical age" were not convergent. But they were both perceived, in the Jewish world, as fraught with dangers. They prompted in it a whole range of (often contradictory) responses, in line with the hopes and expectations of a Judaism now split into different currents and confronted with sociopolitical contexts that varied widely according to time and place.

Toward a Postcritical Age, or the Bible Redeemed

The Rejection Option

In the face of danger, it is always possible to turn a blind eye. That was certainly the attitude taken by Orthodox, especially ultra-Orthodox, Judaism. In eastern Europe, the Talmud* served more than ever as the exclusive reference for the identity and culture of the Jewish elites. And in the nineteenth century, there was an organized struggle against all currents within Judaism tempted to come to terms with the corrosive spirit of the new times.

Rabbi Meir Loeb ben Yehiel Mikhael (1809–79), known as Malbim,[39] forcefully reaffirmed both the divine origin and the absolute unity of the Written and Oral Law in biblical commentaries that won him huge popularity. Similarly inspired, Rabbi Naftali Tsvi Yehuda Berlin (1817–93),[40] the head of the Volozhyn yeshivah* for forty years, attempted to show that the talmudic interpretations of the Pentateuch were perfectly consistent with the plain, obvious sense of Scripture and the rules of the Hebrew language. Although he preached dual allegiance to the strict principles of the Torah* and the values of Western secular civilization, the father of Jewish neo-Orthodoxy himself, Rabbi Samson Raphael Hirsch (1808–88), expected people to get to know Judaism by themselves, urged them to ignore the scholarly work of non-Jews, Reform Jews, or Jews outside Judaism, and held that only the Bible and the Talmud counted in learning, teaching, and practicing the Law.[41]

Things were naturally less simple for all the others: that is, for all those who, from the second half of the eighteenth century and over the next two hundred years, did not reject the progress of science and reason en bloc or in principle, even in cases when this seemed to be undermining the very foundations of Judaism. They might be inheritors of the Jewish Enlightenment, the Haskalah, which crystallized in Prussia in the 1760s,[42] or practitioners of *Die Wissenschaft des Judentums* (the new "Science of Judaism" that in the early nineteenth century embraced the rigor of modern scholarship),[43] or promoters of reform who sought to adapt the thought and practice of Judaism to the expectations of the new times. They might also be Orthodox Jews who had combined an education at the rabbinical seminary and at university. They might be believers or nonbelievers, supportive of Zionism or distant from it, resident in the Diaspora or (before long) in Palestine. Yet they all inscribed their action or scholarship within a kind of loyalty. Faced with the challenges of the historico-critical approach to the Bible, they soon began a long period of wavering between two positions: either to ignore the adversary in one way or another, or to refute his method point by point.

The Refutation Option

The refutation option was not necessarily more difficult, but the question arose as to whether it was already playing the enemy's game. Was it enough for a refutation to maintain that the disputed approach was based upon three false postulates: that the moderns knew scriptural Hebrew better than the masters of the Pharisaic* and rabbinical tradition; that they had the means to rediscover the original intention of the "authors" of Scripture; and that the Bible, or at least the "documents" comprising it, had only one meaning?[44] In a way, supporters of the historico-critical approach may be said to have considerably helped their own critics. For the conflicts, doctrinal reversals, and extreme caricatures that permeated the long history of this approach are so much grist to the mill of its opponents. And there is certainly a history of Jewish refutations of the method.

Take the Italian Samuel David Luzzato (1800–65), for example, who, though rather traditional in his approach to the Bible, cultivated the idea of a radical antagonism between the spirit of Judaism and what he called "Atticism" (Hellenism). Seeing himself as a follower of Rashi and Rashbam—whom he considered genuine seekers after truth—but hostile to Abraham Ibn Ezra and Maimonides, he was one of the first to engage in debate with modern biblical criticism in his commentaries on the Pentateuch and the Book of Isaiah. This countercritical vein continued with the first great modern Jewish historian, Heinrich Graetz (1817–91),[45] David Tzvi Hoffmann (1843–1921),[46] Benno Jacob (1862–1945),[47] and Umberto Cassuto (1883–1951),[48] among others.

Practitioners of countercriticism did not necessarily reject the "documentary" theory out of hand. Indeed, some accepted that the text we read today contains traces of documents, strata, and fragments woven together by a later editor-compiler. What they contested, first of all, was the reading strategy induced by that statement—a purely diachronic reading that abstracted from the synchronic perception that the natural community of readers had of the text historically. What they contested next was the conclusions drawn from that observation. Yehezkel Kaufmann (1889–1963),[49] for example, thus tried to show that Jewish monotheism was not the result of a long slow evolution culminating in the Judaism of the prophets.[50]

The Denial Option

Intellectuals and scholars have often been discouraged from addressing the subject head-on, not only because of the "unsettling effect" that "critical exegesis has had upon religious minds," to quote Emmanuel Lévinas,[51] but in view of the "higher anti-Semitism" that Solomon Schechter detected and denounced behind the biblical "higher criticism" of Wellhausen and his associates.[52] Silence, withdrawal, and the surrender of academic biblical studies to their "natural" masters have often constituted a response of a kind.

Biblical studies were not especially popular among representatives of the *Wissenschaft des Judentums*. Concerned to promote the eventual legal emancipation of central European Jews, the new-style Jewish scholars of that era undertook to present scientifically (that is, in accordance with the demands of contemporary science), both inside and outside their community, those aspects of the culture and history of Judaism that they considered the richest and the most capable of assisting recognition of its values—or, to be more precise, of its *value*. From this point of view, to submit rabbinical literature or medieval Jewish philosophy and poetry to the philological and historico-critical scrutiny that the great texts of antiquity had hitherto enjoyed would "lead to a revalorization of the subject and enable Judaism to be compared and related to other cultures."[53] Such revaluation *in* and *through* comparison involved an assertion of equality and made it possible to face up to the traditional hostility of Christian scholarship, as well as the open contempt and poorly disguised ignorance shown by the Orientalists of the day. However, scientific treatment of the Bible as the epitome of historical Israel living on its land threatened to underline Jewish "separatism."[54] And the champions of the *Wissenschaft des Judentums* were generally more eager to highlight the diversity of ways in which the Bible was received and interpreted within Judaism than to elucidate the original meaning of its text.[55]

This form of Jewish scientific modesty regarding the Bible as such would survive the disappearance of the sociopolitical context that had favored the birth of the *Wissenschaft des Judentums*. The development of "higher criticism," the Protestant grip on the field, and the fact that many of the categories in biblical studies were perceived as deriving from patently Christian doctrines,[56] were unlikely to contribute to rapid or significant change. The defiance would prove to be tenacious. Everything seemed as if made to sustain it: the lack of interest shown by biblical studies in post-Exile strata; the marked predilection for prophet, word, and spirit to the detriment of priest, sacrament, and institutions (especially those supposedly expressing a "degradation" of early Israelite religion within "halakhic" Judaism); the voluntary limitation of the field and period, which suggested that there was not a continuum between biblical Judaism and rabbinical Judaism, and so on.[57]

In fact, certain things had to happen for Jewish biblical scholarship—scholarship that incorporated the critical dimension, without losing itself in it—to find the occasion and the means to assert itself and to gain acceptance of its legitimacy. In particular, the method itself had to suffer some setbacks; a degree of skepticism had gradually to affect its champions; a return to models of synchronic analysis had to begin to take shape; and—on the Jewish side itself—Zionism and the creation of the State of Israel had to help put the Bible back at the center of things.[58] When it began to be accepted that "modern critical approaches are no more or less than our own midrash*," the Bible naturally ceased to be perceived on either side "as a sphere apart from later Jewish tradition."[59]

The Literature Option

Although it is sometimes difficult to pin down what is specifically "Jewish" about Jewish academic biblical studies over the past half-century, one characteristic feature does seem to have been a "disproportionate" interest in *literary* study of the Bible and aspects of intrabiblical textuality.[60]

We should hardly find this surprising. To approach the Bible as a literary work allows us to take it as it is given to us to read, independently of the history of its creation—hence as a single whole. Traditional Judaism always viewed this as a misunderstanding of what the Bible really was, or even a negation of its authentic, deeper nature that posed a major danger to its status as a sacred text: in short, a desecration. But in the secularized context that is ours today, literary analysis of the Bible appears the best way of gaining recognition at least of its unity, its resistance to atomization and endless dissection, as well as its irreducible polysemy. Paradoxically, it enables one to maintain a kind of Jewish loyalty or exegetic continuity within the academic world, without departing from the critical exigencies of the latter.[61]

Literary analysis of the Bible helped to lay the foundations, if not exactly of a "postcritical age" (criticism is not dead), then at least of a possible postcritical (or paracritical) stance.[62] It did not do this only by reestablishing the material unity of the Bible or by sewing together the broken threads of an exegetic tradition at the price of its secularization. Paradoxically yet crucially, literary analysis restores in a novel form the relationship of the Bible to Truth. And it thereby indirectly rehabilitates its religious value.

It will be recalled how the ancient sages of Judaism liked to contrast Homer to the Bible, seeing the first as mere literature, the second as part of an absolutely different, absolutely *non*-literary register.[63] In his book *Mimesis* (first published in 1946), the famous Jewish critic and academic Erich Auerbach (1892–1957),[64] who was originally from Berlin, took up this old debate in his way, sometimes in terms that seemed directly reminiscent of it; both Homer and the Bible were literature, and both were susceptible to a literary approach, but they still belonged to two different orders of literature.

Despite a composition "incomparably less unified than the Homeric poems," the type of "connection" that holds together the biblical narratives and groups of narratives is of a very different kind. This connection, Auerbach writes, is "vertical," whereas in the *Iliad* or *Odyssey* it is only "horizontal." This vertical connection—"entirely lacking in Homer"—unites the biblical stories under "one concept."[65] Furthermore, the Bible has a unique relationship with the Truth: it asserts a "tyrannical" claim to it. Its "religious intent involves an absolute claim to historical truth."[66] Unlike in Homer, the stories in Holy Scripture "do not flatter us that they may please us and enchant us"; their aim is "to subject us, and if we refuse to be subjected we are rebels."[67] The very content of the biblical text calls for interpretation, and without believing in the objective truth of the sacrifice of Isaac (Gen. 22) "it is impossible to put the narrative of it to the use for which it was written."[68] No doubt this is why "Abraham, Jacob, or even Moses produces a more concrete, direct, and historical impression than the figures of the Homeric world."[69]

Auerbach, who lived in exile in Istanbul from 1936, began work on *Mimesis* in 1942. In 1944, Elias Canetti, another German-speaking Jewish writer, this time of Sephardi origin and born in Bulgaria, who from 1938 on divided his time between London and Zurich, described his own relationship to the Old Testament as that of a Jew and a poet. He eloquently illustrated Auerbach's "literary" analysis:

> The greatest intellectual temptation in my life, the only one I have to fight very hard against, is to be a total Jew. The Old Testament, wherever I open to, overwhelms me. I found something suitable to me at almost every point. I would like to be named Noah or Abraham, but my own name also fills me with pride. I try to tell myself, when I am about to sink into the story of Joseph and David, that they enchant me as a writer, and what writer have they not enchanted! But that's not true, there's more to it.[70]

Here the Jew and the writer are one. The Bible speaks to and "subjugates" both; it threatens to "subject" them, as Auerbach would have put it. It puts both in danger, more than any other text could do. To be a writer, the Jew must resist the "intellectual" temptation of being "a total Jew." *As literature*, however, the Bible awakens and stimulates this temptation, by placing itself on the ground of the writer while taking him further and deeper, and threatening to "swallow him up."[71] In the face of open secularization that dissolves the traditional references of Judaism, and in the face of humiliations inflicted on it by the historico-critical approach, *the Bible as literature* becomes the pillar of a modern Jewish identity wholly imbued with a new kind of religious sensitivity.

A detail (a lapsus?) may not have struck the reader here; Canetti could have seen himself bearing two *biblical* forenames. One of these, Abraham, is hardly surprising: it is the name of the founder of a line, the ancestor of the people, the very first believer. The other, Noah, is more unexpected. It is the name of the ancestor of all human beings, and therefore especially of the Gentiles. Even when redeemed—that is, re-habilitated, reunified, rejudaized—and even when playing to perfection the role of rejudaization that so many nineteenth-century Jews wanted it to play, the Bible never ceases to be the Book of the nations too.

As such, over the past two centuries, in an age of modernization and secularization, it has been revealing itself to Jews and non-Jews as a frontier book, whose patent ambiguity, the fruit of a long ancient and medieval history, remains insurmountable.

The Political Age, or the Bible Manifesto

Translating and Sharing

The modern age of the Bible is also the age of its great Jewish translations. This massive phenomenon, political as well as literary in scope, remains problematic and often contradictory in its implications. To be sure, there is a wish not to hand over this field of work to non-Jewish translators alone, to assert and display one's rights to a heritage. But what, in fact, are the ends of translation? For whom is it done, and in which language?

When Moses Mendelssohn (1729–86),[72] the father of the Jewish Enlightenment, worked on a German version of the Psalms for no less than thirteen years and finally published his translation in Gothic script in 1783, he had a mainly Christian readership in mind, with two apologetic and polemical purposes. He wanted to remind them of the aesthetic and poetic heights that ancient Jewish literature had been capable of achieving, and to show that Psalms definitely contained no allusion to Jesus as the Messiah.[73]

His intention was evidently different, however, when he launched the great collective work with which his name would remain associated for posterity: a German translation of the Bible printed in Hebrew characters, accompanied with the original text and a Hebrew commentary, the *Be'ur* (a kind of condensation of the medieval exegetic tradition of *pshat**).[74] The target readership was Jewish and cultured. His aim was to spare it the need to use existing Christian translations, as well as Yiddish ones that in his view did insufficient justice to the beauty of the original.

However real this new departure was, it was not as absolute as one might think. Since the seventeenth century, the style of scriptural translations into Yiddish had itself evolved, as we can see from two Bibles published in Amsterdam in 1676 and 1679.[75] These combined two influences—from earlier Protestant translations in the Netherlands, but also from the great Sephardi Bibles published in Italy.[76] The authors of these works in Yiddish broke with the old model of the carbon-copy translation and sought to respect the spirit of the destination language. But they also aimed to restore the obvious sense—the *pshat*—of the scriptural text, without burdening it, as was the custom, with an abundance of midrashic* and exegetic material.[77] Their success was certainly qualified. But a movement got under way, marked on the one hand by a determination to return to the Bible as the founding text of Judaism, and on the other hand by a literary, stylistic, and aesthetic concern that was in itself a sign of relative secularization.

It was in this slipstream, a little more than a century later, that Mendelssohn set out to place the study of Scripture back at the center of Jewish education (wrongly focused, in his view, on legalist learning of the Talmud) and to combat the lack of interest among his contemporaries in deeper mastery of the Hebrew language. For all these reasons, Mendelsohn's Orthodox opponents vigorously denounced his venture. They also saw a danger that his translation of the Bible into German would educate young Jews—who mostly spoke traditional Jewish German—in a language that gave them access to German literature, the sciences, and the ideas of the age, leading them insidiously toward assimilation.

To be sure, assimilation was not part of Mendelssohn's agenda. Nor would it be correct to see his translation as a "manual of the German language"; he himself continued to show his practical attachment to Jewish German "internally."[78] All the same, his project remained ambiguous.

In a letter of 1779 to his (non-Jewish) friend August von Hennings,[79] Mendelssohn explained that he had originally conceived his project as a "service to [his] children and perhaps a sizable part of [his] nation, making available to them a translation and explanation of the holy books better than those they had had until then." But he immediately added: "*This is the first step toward culture*, from which my nation has unfortunately kept itself so apart that one might almost despair of the possibility of improvement."[80] Mendelssohn thus explicitly presented his translation as the first stage of a regeneration, the "first step" toward a culture that was evidently not synonymous with traditional Jewish knowledge, but also included the culture of the Other.

Mendelssohn was a trailblazer. There was no lack of successors, and Jewish translations of the Bible succeeded one another throughout the nineteenth century, on the initiative of various public figures or groups, and aimed at either a specifically Jewish or a mixed audience. These works depended to a greater or lesser extent on the work of Christian scholars and translators, whether or not the debt was openly recognized—up to the time when Franz Rosenzweig (1886–1929) and Martin Buber (1878–1965) embarked on their monumental achievement.[81] But Mendelssohn had emulators outside the German-speaking world—in France, for instance, where legal emancipation (in 1790–91) had preceded effective integration, and the condition of Jews was not comparable to that of their fellows in central or above all eastern Europe. As early as 1791, in fact, Berr Isaac Berr (1744–1828), syndic of Alsatian Jews and spokesman of the delegation of Jews from eastern France to the Constituent Assembly in 1789,[82] expressed the wish that the "Holy Bible" might be taught to Jewish children "in a French translation . . . as faithful as that of the immortal Mendelssohn."[83]

Samuel Cahen (1796–1862), the first to execute this project, brought out the eighteen volumes of his "new translation" between 1831 and 1851.[84] To his mind, "the reading of the sacred text should make it possible to refute the accusations of archaism and legalism still directed against Judaism."[85] Less conservative than Moses Mendelssohn, he benefited from scholarly notes provided by a circle of eminent colleagues, so that he was able to base himself both on the Jewish rationalist tradition of exegesis (extracts from which he published) and on the critical scholarship of his day. With regard to the Pentateuch, one already finds in his writing the documentary hypothesis borrowed from the German Protestant theologian Wilhelm de Wette (1780–1849). The fact remains, however, that Cahen's monumental Bible was aimed at cultured readers,[86] and a "universally accessible, affordable, and popular" Jewish Bible continued to be lacking in French.[87]

For a short time, in 1867, there was a plan to produce an ecumenical translation involving Catholics, Protestants, and Jews, Hellenists and Hebraists, but it fell through after the Catholics withdrew their support. It was necessary to wait until 1899 and 1906, more than a century after the appeal issued by Berr Isaac Berr, for a complete Jewish translation of the Bible to appear in French in two batches, carried out by members of the French rabbinate under the direction of the Grand Rabbi of France, Zadoc Kahn (1839–1905).[88] His introduction presented it as a "pious undertaking." It certainly filled a gap that had not affected members of other faiths or Jews living in other countries. It was "truly a people's French Bible, in a convenient format, modestly priced, agreeable to read, and devoid of any scholarly apparatus"; in other words, not a "work of science or criticism," but "a modest work of translation, meant to satisfy readers who ask for religious and moral inspiration from the Bible."[89] The rabbinate Bible was clearly a Bible for Jews; it aimed to reach people who did not know Hebrew, and to "inspire" them at a moral and religious level, sparing them the weight of excessive scholarship and assuming the traditional functions that Judaism had attributed for centuries to a certain form of biblical culture.[90] But it was a Bible in French: or rather, Zadoc Kahn said, a "French Bible" that made "agreeable" reading. The aesthetic dimension was thus underlined,[91] and so too, indirectly, was the dimension of sharing.

For a modern Jew, to read the Bible in translation was not simply a *retour à soi*. And to translate it was not simply to claim something valuable of one's own, in the face of others and against attempts at dispossession. The Jewish Bible in a "non-Jewish" language also served to ratify a break with oneself—a traditional self already largely dissolved—and constituted the springboard for a culture shared with others.

Samuel Cahen himself was aware of this. As the translator of the Bible into French, he required rabbis to express themselves and to teach others in that language; yet he was still eager to maintain and develop the practice of Hebrew, not only, of course, as the language of the Old Testament, but as a mark of Jewish identity and guarantee of the continued existence of the Jewish people.[92] Whether it was a question of giving German or French a Hebrew inflection, or Hebrew a German or French inflection, whether the aim was to catch hold of believers tempted by assimilation or simply of people ignorant of the sources of Jewish culture, or to ensure that a particular modern version of Judaism prevailed through the interpretation presupposed in any translation, such initiatives—German no less than French—placed the Bible at the center, underlined its status as literature, and established it as both a medium of self-affirmation and a space of dialogue. And however religious the explicit motives of the translators may sometimes have been, their enterprise undeniably bears the mark of secularization.[93]

In nineteenth-century Europe, the Bible was both a special object that Jews claimed as their own and one that they shared, and intended to share, with non-Jews. In a way it allowed them to remain themselves while universalizing their condition.[94] Unlike the Talmud, whose exclusive study marked life in the ghetto, the Bible identifies Jews without particularizing them. It is a universally appreciated masterpiece, which shows to the world the ancient literary creativity of the Jews and awakens among them a precious aesthetic sensitivity that sadly lay dormant in the confined atmosphere of the yeshivot*. Hence the new importance that all reformers and modernizers of Jewish education in Europe sought to give it in their teaching programs. But the Bible is much more than that: for the *maskilim** of central Europe, contemporaries or successors of Moses Mendelssohn, the Bible offered a complete model of political and economic life, including agriculture, war, and government; it was an "optimal bridge to the life of citizenship."[95]

It was this also for the contemporaries and successors of Samuel Cahen and Zadoc Kahn in France. In 1822, the French scholar Joseph Salvador (1796–1873) described "biblical Judaism as the ideal political system."[96] And in the view of the Orientalist James Darmesteter, who published his book *Les Prophètes d'Israël* seventy years later, in 1892, Israel was only "the first convert of the Bible," and "the god of the

Prophets was only human reason projected heavenward."[97] This could equally well read: Israel was only the first convert of human reason, and the saga of the prophets only the start of the march of human reason toward universal triumph . . .

Israel's mission and "the achievement of human rights" became perfectly identifiable with each other.[98] In the end, it was the French Revolution and the ensuing Republic that achieved here and now the aspirations held by Israel since time immemorial and first expressed in the Bible (especially the prophets). This privileged role of prophetism—extended in Jesus and fulfilled above all in the eternal principles of 1789—was characteristic of the special "Franco-Judaic" synthesis of Judaism and republic produced by nineteenth-century "Israelitism." It also enshrined the downgrading of a traditional, primordial Jewish concern for the Law and observance of the commandments.

Judaism (rid of its pharisaical ballast) and Christianity (rescued from its medieval darkness) could then rejoin and together inspire the grand history of human civilization. The Bible and the Prophets justified the republican faith of the Jews emancipated by the Republic. The Republic itself justified an authentic, but purified, Jewish faith, which in essence could be shared by all sincere republicans. The Republic was the long-awaited Messiah; Paris, the New Jerusalem. And Darmesteter's *Les Prophètes d'Israël*, more than the Bible itself, was the "Bible of Franco-Judaism." It was the first present that the poet Edmond Fleg (1874–1963) gave to the young fiancée he would marry in 1907.[99]

Redemption: Book, Land, and People

On the rugged byways of Palestine, far from Paris, Edmond Fleg, and his young bride, what people offered as a gift in those early years of the twentieth century was certainly not Darmesteter's beautiful work but the Bible itself. For a good century, nurtured by Romantic Orientalist dreams as well as a whole new scientific and popular literature consisting of studies, dictionaries, atlases, and so on, Western Christian travelers and pilgrims had been scouring a Holy Land once again within reach, half as tourists, half in a spiritual quest, with Scripture as their guidebook.[100] Some Jewish pioneers of nascent Zionism were beginning to do the same.

Sometimes it was at their peril, as in the case of some students from the Bezalel Academy of Arts and Design,[101] founded in Jerusalem in 1906, who explored the area in search of biblical experiences. For them the biblical figure par excellence was the Palestinian Arab, and as they approached a village, they saw a group of women drawing water from a well. A biblical scene if ever there was one! One of the art students, a tall Russian Jew, rushed up to one of the women to help her place her jug on her head (closely reproducing Jacob's gesture to Rachel in Gen. 29.9–11). But she shouted out in surprise and covered her face. Men then came from the village, piled into the intruders, and robbed them even of their shoes and pants.[102] All they gave back to them in the end was the Russian Bible that had brought them to the scene of their rout.

Strange though it may seem at first sight, the Bezalel art students, as much as Fleg or Darmesteter, were inheritors of the biblocentric tradition initiated by Mendelssohn and his disciples and successors. Basing itself at times on the medieval Sephardi precedent, idealizing its harmonious combination of a creative Jewish culture with an openness to universal culture,[103] the Haskalah was not only the opening act in an evolution that, passing through the *Wissenschaft des Judentums*, reform movements in Judaism, legal emancipation, and the promotion of modern Jewish education, led so many European Jews toward acculturation or assimilation. As the Haskalah spread to eastern Europe, the Habsburg Empire, and Russia, where the prospect of citizenship could not but seem remote, it also inaugurated a renewal of Jewish culture itself, centered both on the Bible and on its language: Hebrew.

Yiddish, the "jargon" held in contempt by so many *maskilim*, was not abandoned, especially since Hebrew remained the language of a small intellectual elite, and Jews did not usually master the language of the local non-Jewish majority. Moreover, important Yiddish works disseminating the ideas of the Haskalah developed in parallel with the new Hebrew literature. Nevertheless, the Bible appeared in this context as a specifically Jewish literary monument, conjuring up a glorious national past in contrast to the current predicament of the Diaspora in eastern Europe. Rich in pastoral and agrarian imagery, it was the testimony—and became the model—of a Jewish contact with nature from which ghetto life had been severed. It was also a combat weapon against the "retrograde" Talmud-centered forces in traditional Jewish society, which for their part did not fail to see this as so much apostasy and license, even accusing the *maskilim* of being accomplices of the hated ruling powers.[104]

Ahavat Zion (Love of Zion) by Abraham Mapu (1808–67), the first modern novel in Hebrew, was published in Vilna in 1853. Mapu had worked on it for more than twenty years and was then living in Kovno (today's Kaunas in Lithuania). It is a biblical novel, both in its language and in the time and place of the action: the Judea of the prophet Isaiah. And one of the countless readers to be deeply impressed by it was Boris Schatz (1866–1932), the founder of the Bezalel Academy in Jerusalem, where the bold excursionists of the "biblical" misadventure mentioned above were studying.[105]

Mapu was also well regarded by certain Parisian Hebraists. *Les Archives israélites*, the periodical founded by Samuel Cahen, was quite favorable to his second novel, *Ayit Tzavua* (Hypocrite Eagle). According to the reviewer, Cahen himself, Mapu wrote "in the pure biblical Hebrew," demonstrating that, whereas in Paris "even several of our chief rabbis seem to make more of so-called translations than of faithful translations," at least in eastern Europe "the intelligence of the Hebrew language, the art of expressing with clarity and elegance," had not been lost; there, "the sacred language ha[d] remained a living language." But, Cahen wondered: "Do you think people will start speaking Hebrew again?"[106] In his view, the answer was: obviously not.

He was wrong, of course, since the eastern European Haskalah would open onto new forms of Jewish cultural and political expression, brilliantly illustrated by Mapu and his successors in the field of literature, in which the return to the Bible and to Hebrew as the national spoken language would play a central role, inseparable from a return to the Land.

To be sure, the triumph of Hebrew did not happen overnight. For the language to become capable of evoking all the worldly realities and competing with Yiddish literature, it was first necessary to break with the (biblical!) purism and classicism of an earlier period and to build on all historical strata, including Aramaic ones. Also required were all the stubbornness and inventiveness of Eliezer Ben Yehuda (1858–1922)[107] and a few other writers in imposing what for Orthodox Jews as well as champions of Yiddish was nothing short of a "sacrilege." Hebrew, they showed, was capable of saying everything and, suitably enriched and transformed, could once again become a language of education as well as daily use, in the end winning the allegiance of the Jewish street in Palestine.

In a sense, perhaps Samuel Cahen was not altogether wrong: no one did ever really begin to speak biblical Hebrew again. And the Hebrew spoken by Israelis today is not as biblical as one might think. The Bible is indeed the heart and foundation of their culture, but to Israelis the language of their culture seems "biblical," and the Bible itself seems "familiar" only through a kind of illusion.[108] It is this illusion that Zionism set out to create and foster. It made of the (secularized) Bible a national manifesto, the breviary of a return to body, strength, and nature—and to the Land.

The Bible and the Land existed to transform the Jew into a new Hebrew. They reembodied those who until then had been phantoms, only shadows of themselves, saving them from the alienation of two thousand years of exile and Diaspora culture. The Bible was no longer the narrative of God's history; it was the narrative of the history of the Jewish people. Most of its books expressed the struggle that the Jewish people waged on its Land, for its Land, and for its existence as a people. The Bible was par excellence the product of an original Jewish genius, whose luster had paled in exile, but that shone again on its Land. For a Jew, to know the Bible was nothing other than to know himself at last. And only those who read it in the Land of its birth could really know it, finally stripped of the deceptive veils of traditional rabbinical hermeneutics.

David Ben-Gurion (1886–1973), the man who in 1948 would proclaim the independence of the State of Israel, undoubtedly went farther than others in this extreme Zionist revaluation-appropriation of the Bible. But he was not the only one. The Bible was the "identity card" of the new Hebrew.[109] It was also a title deed: which is how the Zionist banners called it in 1939, at the demonstrations against the British White Paper imposing new restrictions on Jewish land purchase in Palestine: "Not the British Mandate but the Bible is our claim to this Land."[110] The Bible even became a cadastral guide, to be consulted for the frontiers (sadly fluctuating from one book to another)[111] of the ideal Land of Israel. Lastly, sometimes at the price of interpretive somersaults, it became a presocialist manifesto, making it "kosher*" even in the eyes of Jewish socialist "heretics."[112] In short, it became "the holy book of secular Zionism."[113]

The Bible was the core of the new Jewish education. On the eve of World War II, in the secular schools of the *yishuv** in Palestine, it became a national literature sensitizing children to the unique "perfume" of the Land of Israel, an introduction to Oriental lifestyles,[114] a first testimony to sovereign national existence, a means of initiation to the general categories of the historical approach, and also, of course, a path giving access to world literature.[115] The Bible—which taught, as much as the nation's past, its future destiny and the ingathering of exiles—was also capable of serving the unity of the Jewish people after their return. For Ben-Gurion, it constituted the ideal common heritage for young Israelis of Ashkenazi* origin cut off from eastern European Jewish culture, and for young immigrants from Islamic countries, for whom Zionist ideology was largely alien.

In offering active and positive heroes, the Bible provided Hebrew writers with the narrative of a mythical past—a golden age saturated with models of glory and power that could be contrasted to the negative image of the Diaspora Jew as passive victim. Even art—or at least the art that originated and developed at Bezalel—was mobilized to serve the national-biblical interests of Zionism. The Zionist leader Nahum Sokolow (1859–1936) was convinced that only the Jewish artists of the future would be capable of giving a full plastic dimension to the heroic age of the kings and prophets, which had hitherto been neglected by Christian artists. And Boris Schatz, the founder of Bezalel, was convinced that the Bible, like the Land, awaited redemption, to which the new Jewish art should contribute.[116]

These new readers of the Bible, Zionist pioneers and militants, undoubtedly thought they were returning to its original, primal, foundational meaning. They lived in the Bible, and the Bible lived again in them. It authenticated and legitimized their aspirations, while they in turn gave it additional authority by making it a reality. Uriel Simon hit the mark, however, when he showed that what appeared to be a kind of national *pshat* was in fact a national "neo-midrash*."[117] The Bible could play the role allocated to it only at the price of an *interpretation* no less violent than any it had known in two millennia of exile. God was to be more or less emptied from it, the religious and legal dimension more or less ignored or relegated. Reading became eminently selective. And it was no accident that the biblical circle that met at Ben-Gurion's twice a month from December 1958, and whose members were obliged to disseminate their biblical science four times a year in the country, began by studying the Book of Joshua; for, in Ben-Gurion's view, Joshua, much more than Moses, was the real founder of the Jewish people.[118]

This exclusive, truly revolutionary revaluation of the Bible shattered the cultural equilibrium that had prevailed for centuries in the Jewish world. In 1912, the Zionist writer Asher Zvi Ginsberg (1856–1926), whose pen name was Ahad Ha-Am ("one of the people"), feared—although he nonetheless envisaged a key educational role for the Bible—that Zionist biblocentrism would cut off the young "Hebrews" of the yishuv from the rest of the Jewish people, still imbued with the spirit of Exile.[119] Fifty years later, in 1962, the writer Hayyim Hazaz (1897–1973) maintained against Ben-Gurion that the Bible "would do us no good" and refused to live through it alone. He pointed out that it was not the whole of Judaism, arguing that the Oral Law, rather than the Bible, had enabled the Jews to remain a people despite the experience of exile and dispersion. He also demanded that Israeli schools should teach Jewish culture in its entirety, not just a truncated version of it.[120]

By contrast, for other players in the national renaissance, the Bible remained suspect because it was too closely linked to a Jewish past that had to be overcome. For the man who coined the word "Zionism," Nathan Birnbaum (1865–1937), the Judaism of the Bible was well and truly dead; it would not experience a rebirth. As for Max Nordau (1849–1923), Theodor Herzl's right-hand man, he considered Scripture to be historically unreliable and thought it the bearer of a childish worldview and negative moral values. In 1911, the writer Joseph Hayyim Brenner (1881–1921) caused a real uproar in the Hebrew press of Palestine when he called on Jews to shake off "the hypnosis of the twenty-four books of the Bible."[121]

Of course, one might try to free the Bible from its straitjacket of moralism and prophetism by rehabilitating "negative" heroes such as the accursed king and valiant warrior Saul, who courageously faced his predicted defeat: "Though his countenance was pale, yet betrayed he no fear. / And in the gleam of his eyes lurked a dreadful despair."[122] But was this sufficient? By any standards, was not the Bible decidedly "too Jewish"—as it was for the so-called Canaanites[123] and their leading thinker, the poet Yonatan Ratosh (1909–81)?[124]

And in the end, was the Land of Israel really so biblical? Did Israel's state symbols and national calendar really owe everything, or even their most essential elements, to the Bible? To be sure, abundant use was made of history and archaeology—to confirm, where possible, the historicity of the scriptural text, to demonstrate the continuity of Jewish settlement in the country, and to prove the Jewish character of areas that a partition might leave to the Arabs. But which was the place that held such fascination in the years between 1882 and 1931? It was El Medieh, identified with the Modin of ancient Palestine, where the signal was launched in 167 BCE for the great Jewish revolt against the Hellenistic occupier.[125] Yet the event was clearly *postbiblical*. It is traditionally commemorated at Hanukkah*, which has become a largely secular Israeli national festival. And Hanukkah, for obvious reasons, receives no mention in the Bible.

Another typically Israeli site of commemoration and pilgrimage that has been fervently explored by archeologists is the ancient fortress of Massada, where a particularly dramatic episode in the great Jewish revolt against Rome began in 70 CE.[126] It too is clearly a *postbiblical* site. And until recently Israeli archeological research mostly concentrated on periods for which the Jewish presence can be easily demonstrated—the Second Temple period, or even later. Significantly, the first Jewish excavation took place at Tiberias, in Galilee, the heart of Jewish Palestine after the Bar Kokhba revolt of 132–35.[127]

Much was done, of course, to hebraize or biblicize place-names in parts of Palestine that came under Israeli sovereignty. The same happened to the surnames and given names of individuals, establishing a biblical onomastics often thoroughly alien to the Diaspora tradition. In 1963, the first international biblical competition for young Jews opened with great pomp on the anniversary of Independence. And in 1965, the "Sanctuary of the Book" (*Heikhal ha-Sefer*) was opened in Jerusalem as a separate wing of the Israel Museum, to hold and display some of the scrolls and fragments—including a near-intact copy of the Book of Isaiah—that had been discovered in Dead Sea caves between 1947 and

1956 and found to derive from an Essene* community in Qumran of the late Second Temple period. The same "Sanctuary" also houses the famous Codex of Aleppo, which "returned" to Jerusalem in 1958.[128]

As a matter of historical fact, however, it was mainly in *nonbiblical* regions, along the coasts and in the valleys of Mandatory Palestine, that the Zionist pioneers sank roots and developed. With the exception of Jerusalem, the mountainous areas—and therefore the presumed sites of the biblical kingdoms of Judah and Israel—remained untouched, as the Jews had been unable to purchase land or to establish settlements there before the war of 1947–48. Even during that first conflict, the Zionist forces did not move into the heart of the "historical" Land of Israel. Only in 1967, with the Six Days War and the conquest of "Judea-Samaria" did the State of Israel absorb the biblical territories properly so called—although paradoxically this would initiate the waning of the Bible as the pillar of Israeli identity.

At first the conquered lands seemed very foreign: a different people inhabited them in large numbers. Then a radical religious neo-Zionism—epitomized by the Gush Emunim ("Faith Bloc"), founded in 1974—took over the old Zionist ethos and launched a project of settlement, occupation, and annexation of these new lands, basing itself on a one-sided ultranationalist reading of the Bible that was supposedly its authentic *pshat*.[129] From a locus of consensus, the Bible became one of discord. From the sacred reference of secular Zionists, it became the "holy book" of ultrareligious, ultranationalist neo-Zionists, committing God once again to the struggle for Redemption.

What the average Israeli saw ultimately as an innocent text, which he had got to know at school as the founding document of the people and a component of his identity,[130] suddenly morphed into highly explosive material in the hands of sorcerer's apprentices all the more alarming for their extreme religiosity. "The Bible ceased to be a common heritage, and from a book that in large measure united people it became one that separated them."[131] Now serving as justification for an unjustifiable occupation, it also ceased to be what the Declaration of Independence of 1948 had proclaimed it to be: a gift from the Jewish people "to the whole world," affirming "cultural values of national *and universal* significance," the repository of *"freedom, justice, and peace* as envisaged by the prophets of Israel."[132]

Since its origins, Zionism had wavered between aspirations to become normal and exemplary. The Jewish people of Palestine had indeed wanted to become an ordinary nation, "like all other nations" (Ezek. 25.8), gathered in a definite territory and disposing of a state of their own. But it had also claimed to be a "light" (Isa. 42.6) for the whole of humanity. The divide of 1967 and the interminable aftermath of occupation destroyed the foundations of this fine paradox.

Judea-Samaria witnessed the rise of an extreme particularism, a conception of the chosen people that left no place for the rights of others, and whose exemplary value (moral, political, even religious) was to say the least questionable. "In the rear," if that is the right term for it, the landscape developed in the opposite direction: erosion of Zionist ideology among large sections of the population (despite all the public discourse and official rhetoric); growing awareness of the wrong done to the Palestinians; deconstruction and rewriting (since the late 1980s) of the "national epic" by a new generation of "post-Zionist" historians and sociologists;[133] hopes of an agreement and normalization aroused by the Oslo process.

On the West Bank, the Bible—or the offensive and violent reading made of it—held undivided sway. Elsewhere, its power to crystallize the collective identity could only decline. In the end, remembrance of the genocide—the "galutic myth par excellence,"[134] sustaining a victim-centered imagination—replaced it to such an extent that young Israelis were more tempted to make a trip to Poland than to archeological sites at home.[135] The task thus became less to (re)constitute the country of the Bible than to spare its inhabitants a new Holocaust. This latest obsession,[136] encouraged by the failure of the Oslo process, could naturally serve politicians to inspire and justify the most radical and brutal of Jewish nationalisms.

✳

This is what archaeologists have learned from their excavations in the Land of Israel: the Israelites were never in Egypt, did not wander in the desert, did not conquer the land in a military campaign, and did not pass it on to the twelve tribes of Israel. Perhaps even harder to swallow is the fact that the united monarchy of David and Solomon, which is described by the Bible as a regional power, was at most a small tribal kingdom. And it will come as an unpleasant shock to many that the God of Israel, Jehovah, had a female consort and that the early Israelite religion adopted monotheism only in the waning period of the monarchy and not at Mount Sinai.

On October 29, 1999, the Israeli archaeologist Zeev Herzog, a professor at the University of Tel Aviv, was sharp and to the point. The few sentences quoted above are from a lead story in the Saturday supplement of *Haaretz* entitled "The Bible: No Facts on the Ground."[137]

Some have seen this as an expression of "archeological post-Zionism." But Herzog's article does not claim to be innovative; it simply notes discoveries and conclusions on which there has been a consensus, often for a long time, among researchers. The raison d'être of academic archaeology is no longer to confirm the biblical narrative by digging material facts out of the ground. Indeed, by invalidating that narrative, it shakes one of the foundations of secular Israeli identity: that of the Bible as national manifesto establishing the reality of a people's ancient link with its Land and justifying its return to that Land. All of a sudden, if I may dare put it like that, the "Book of the Site"[138] seems to have become the "Book of a Non-Site."

Still, Zeev Herzog is scarcely under any illusion. Although many Israelis are now willing to recognize the injustice suffered by Palestinians, and although they are prepared to go down the road of equality between men and women, they do not yet seem "solid" enough to accept archeological facts that "blow apart the biblical myth." Yet Herzog offers a kind of "consolation" to those who might need it: it is possible to demonstrate the historical existence of the kingdoms of Judah and Israel from the ninth century BCE on.

For my part, I do not think that consolations are useful or even necessary in this domain, nor that the relationship of science to myth is simply that of truth to error.[139] Science can deconstruct myth as much as it likes; that is what it is for. Perhaps it can also help us to qualify the political lessons we draw from myth: in short, help us to negotiate. But I am not sure that science can ever do away with myth or totally obliterate its effects on the imagination. Similarly, "evidence" that "the Jewish people"—another "myth"—was "invented" will never suffice to entail that the Jewish people has never existed, does not exist, and will not continue to exist.[140] And just as the historico-critical approach born two centuries ago could not erase the literary and more-than-literary fascination that the stories and characters of the Bible have had on modern Jewish readers (Elias Canetti being one good example),[141] archaeology will never prevent Israelis from feeling tied to the Land where they live—through the Bible and a thousand other threads—even if they are fully aware that the Bible does not speak the Truth and was not written for that.

There is something that fascinates us in Herzog's article, though: its deliberate brutality (dare I say violence), a determination to shock, and a kind of pleasure in doing so. Here I cannot resist a comparison. Let us switch from science to literature, from a real to a fictional character, from Ashkenazi man imbued with academic culture to Oriental woman devoid of all science.

It is 2002, three years after Zeev Herzog's article appeared in the columns of *Haaretz*. The Israeli female novelist Orly Castel-Bloom has just published her *Halakhim enoshiim* (Human Parts). Nothing is going well in the life of its main character, Kati Beit-Halahmi. She is a cleaning woman. Originally from Kurdistan, she lived in transit camps and got no further than primary school in Israel. Her husband was badly injured in a road accident and is now unemployed. They have four children and are virtually penniless, in a country exposed to daily terrorist attacks—and, what is more, to an exceptionally harsh winter. Kati cannot take any more. Kati dreams. She wants to get away.

> She went to the cupboard and took out the Yellow Pages. Kati was looking for a way out. Perhaps she would have been wiser to open the Bible at those melancholy moments, when she felt that her life was a lie, and to read a verse or two of Psalms. But she found the Bible too complicated to read, and she didn't feel the need for anything holy. She needed immediate, practical and efficient first aid.[142]

What is the connection, we may ask, between the Bible and Yellow Pages? Both are certainly large books with no mention of an author's name. And although the Bible is more varied in content, it also contains long and pretty boring lists of names, less useful, it would seem, than those in a telephone directory. To speak of the two in the same breath appears unusual and vaguely sacrilegious. Kati will find in the Yellow Pages the way out she is looking for,[143] but that is not what matters to us here. Rather, it is precisely that vague sense of sacrilege. After all, to waver between reading Psalms and consulting the Yellow Pages: the irony is latent, the desecration gentle enough. Once again, the modern age of the Bible appears for what it is—the age not only of its triumph but also of its dissolution. But here the dissolution takes place without violence, as if it is not actually thought about. We are a long way from the "virile" outburst of a Zeev Herzog.

It is not at all that modern Jewish *women* do not have a problem with the Bible. They do have one, that's for sure, and not all men do: Scripture is an androcentric, misogynist book. For that very reason, feminists today will hesitate between simply writing off the Bible as the historical foundation of their faith and embracing a neo-midrashic hermeneutic capable of transforming it into a book with which, and through which, a woman can live.[144] Some may even find in it "countertraditions" to subvert or correct the patriarchal bias of the text.[145]

It has been said that Jewish texts—and the biblical text is evidently one of that number—function for their readers (women as well as men?) as "surrogate parents."[146] Uriel Simon once even wrote that "the status of the Bible as the founding book of the people of Israel is similar to the status of parents." You can rebel against it, but you can never "consider the Book of Books as just one book among others."[147]

Indeed. Throughout history, however, until the present day, Jewish women have never had the same relationship as Jewish men to the Bible, or more generally to Jewish books;[148] and some women like Kati Beit-Halahmi, even ones at a far higher social and cultural level, can always shrink from facing the problematic book in the cupboard and get by with a vague, though still radical, sacrilege.

Nevertheless, perhaps the Bible is much less a "parent" than "Father's Book," the Word of the Heavenly Father, the History of the Nation's Fathers, the Law given by the Father to his Firstborn. "Thus says the Lord: Israel is My firstborn son" (Exod. 4.22). The fear, reverential or not, as well as the devastating rebellions that the Bible has prompted in men from Baruch Spinoza to Zeev Herzog, should undoubtedly be measured by this yardstick. Everyone has known—ever since the Bible, precisely—that there is hardly a more gratifying, but also more exposed and fearsome, status than that of a son and a firstborn.[149]

Epilogue

In 1891, Jakob Freud presented his son Sigmund with an "unusual gift" for his thirty-fifth birthday:[1] the family copy of the Philippsohn[2] Bible he had studied as a child, in which the father had recorded in Hebrew and German the event of his son's circumcision. For the occasion, Jakob had had the Bible decked out in a new leather binding and added an inscription in Hebrew that itself resonates with many a biblical harmony.[3] All the love of a father is expressed in this gift and inscription. But the reminder of paternal love is also remonstration, contained anger, exhortation to turn back. Sigmund has forgotten the Book; his father is giving it to him again. Sigmund will thus have received the Book twice from his father—just as Israel received twice the Tablets of the Testimony,[4] from Moses the father-figure, and beyond Moses, from God Himself, the Absolute Father.

But whereas, for the father, the giving of the Book as a gift has only two moments, its receiving, for the son, has four moments—four possible ways of relating to the Book he is given. He can receive it without asking any questions: accept the Book at face value as the genuine record of his father's infallible will. He can smash the Tablets himself and claim to have nothing in common with the Book, destroying, rejecting, or simply ignoring it. He can return to the Book with a new, almost naïve, eye, freed from the chains of obedience as much as the fires of revolt, and actually read it, perhaps for the first time. Or he can dare to comment on it, aiming to become a father in his turn and to pass on the Book he has received, enriching it with a reading of his own that has itself been fed by all that have gone before.

In the present work, the reader will have found many historical illustrations of these four possible ways of relating to the Bible. He or she may even, in some cases, have found them combined with or succeeding one another in accordance with a different logic. I shall not go over these again. Rather, I shall return to Freud himself, since it is with him that I started this epilogue. What did he make of his "Second Tablets" and his "fourth moment?" I shall answer this question neither from Freud's point of view nor, of course, from that of psychoanalysis or its history, but rather from the point of view of this book.

In 1914, Freud published an essay titled "The Moses of Michelangelo" anonymously: not yet a biblical commentary but at most a supercommentary. Freud set out in it what he saw as Michelangelo's almost sacrilegious reading, in which Moses does *not* smash the Tablets, contains his anger, and forgoes satisfying his impulse in the name of his mission. Only in 1934, twenty years later and almost forty years after the death of Jakob Freud (1896), does he really seem to have returned to the theme. The subject of *Der Mann Moses und die monotheistische Religion* (1939; translated as *Moses and Monotheism*) would then occupy Freud right up to his death. Was he finally doing "Jewish work"? Can his *Moses* be read as a new and ultimate "Jewish" commentary on the Bible?

Freud did, of course, make Moses an Egyptian and Israel the murderer of its prophet. And that certainly has a sacrilegious resonance in the ears of many Jews, echoing the sound of the smashing of the Tablets. Freud also imbues his reading of the Bible with the insights, methods, and lines of questioning from two new sciences: the historico-critical approach to Scripture, and psychoanalysis. This may come as a shock to the more Orthodox. But is it really so shocking when we think that so many before him instilled Aristotle and his ephemeral truths into their Bible? In the end, Freud explicitly feared being "classed with the scholastics and Talmudists who are satisfied to exercise their ingenuity, unconcerned how far their conclusions may be from the truth."[5] Yet he too may be said to have "talmudized" in his way.

Freud's aim was to elucidate the distinctive "character" of the Jewish people, its "destinies," the mystery of its resilience and survival.[6] He does this without God, and in a sense even without Moses—at least the Moses of Orthodoxy. But behind his exploration of this "character" and these "destinies" lies something like the secular recognition of a mission. And he, like so many others, looks for a hidden meaning behind the obvious meaning of the text, since the text is the bearer of a *truth*, a "historical truth" if not a "material truth,"[7] and one that reveals itself only to those who know how to seek it out correctly. Sometimes, again like many others before him, Freud will track down this truth *elsewhere* than in the text: in the "rich extra-biblical literature" of the Jews, in the Oral Tradition in fact.[8]

As a Jewish, albeit sacrilegious, reading of Scripture, Freud's *Moses* is perhaps only the farthest (paradoxical) point of a Jewish exegetical tradition that was born with the Bible itself and has never ceased to envelop it, revealing and at the same time hiding it. Freud's *Moses* may be read as a modern midrash*. Treason and revolt still coexist in it with a certain kind of loyalty and even reverence. The Father is not quite dead; his word can still be heard, examined, and interpreted. No more than Spinoza before him does Freud deliver a fatal blow that ends a history going back thousands of years—an ambiguous history of the companionship between Jews and the Bible. Nor is he himself entirely outside that history.

*

Freud's experience therefore always resonates in a way with that of previous generations of Jews, which, as Martin Buber pointed out in 1926, were never able to escape altogether this encounter with the Book. Those successive generations might not have been willing to heed what it had to tell them, still less to obey it. It might have aroused anger or revolt in them. Yet the worry it made them feel was still part and parcel of their lives; their act of denial itself testified to the rights that the Book could claim over them.[9]

After the Nazi genocide, even that no longer seems possible, and it may be that Freud's book belongs inextricably to a bygone age. This time, the hiatus is no longer the (relative) effect of a new reading; it is the result of the massacre. In 1951, Buber asked himself how the verse with which Psalm 118 (in praise of the Redeemer-God) opens and closes, "Praise the Lord, for He is good / His steadfast love is eternal," could still be recommended to those who had survived Auschwitz— the "Job of the gas chambers." Emil Fackenheim notes that Buber gave no answer to his question, and that it retains its full force *today*, after the survivors have died out. It is a question that can never die, and it will forever haunt the *descendants* of the "Job of the gas chambers."[10]

What holds for a partly secularized Judaism may hold less for observant Judaism, and in fact there were Jewish theological responses to the horror of the genocide. From the point of view of the believer, the problem raised by the death of a single innocent is qualitatively the same as that posed by the massacre of six million. And it is always possible to give some account of the genocide, to see it as a punishment or the result of God's deliberately turning away his Face, so that man remained totally free in his actions, and therefore free to commit absolute evil. In short, it is always possible to include the genocide in the "traditional genealogy" of Jewish adversity.[11] Besides, despite the irreducible singularity of the event, contemporary questioning in relation to it is not altogether without precedent. One need only recall the complaints following another historical trauma, the expulsion of the Jews from Spain in 1492: "The Eternal One left his residence to sow havoc and amass booty, and to annihilate . . . our flesh, our children, even our nurslings, leaving us nothing behind. He wanted to exterminate us."[12] Or again: "Which father raised his children to hand them over to public condemnation? To heap on them high wrath and boiling fury? . . . And even if we have sinned, what has become of the just? And if it is out of anger that you drove us away, tell us: what did our children do?"[13]

The fact remains that, for our generations of lesser faith, the God of the Bible, the almighty Heavenly Father present in history, the God of promises, justice, and mercy is well and truly dead. The filial bond that joined us to Him seems irreparably broken. No emissary from the Lord came to stay the butcher's hand; the immolation went ahead without reprieve. Not even the Book of Esther, perhaps the one most in tune with our sensibility (though also one whose entry into the canon met with resistance),[14] can be saved from the rout. It is true that there is no sign of a paternal presence in it: God the Father is absent, nowhere named. It is an orphan woman, Esther, who saves her people. And Mordecai himself, a substitute father-figure, is only her cousin and tutor. Still, the story told in the Book of Esther is one of *rescue*. And there was no rescue in our generation: the Father's absence and silence authorized the massacre. If the Bible really is the Father's Book we say it is, and if that Father is dead, what or whom is the Bible now the Book of? Who speaks to us through it, and why should we still read it? Should we keep from it only the curses of Deuteronomy,[15] the image of the God who "delights" in "causing us to perish" and in "wiping us out,"[16] or chapters 19 and 21 of Jeremiah, of which George Steiner writes: "Auschwitz and Rwanda are there"?[17] What would be the point?

The effacement or debilitation of the Father is not, however, the only threat weighing on the Jewish future of the Bible. Another is his return *in force*, the return in force of the Father consecrated by Zionism. Many secular Jews, but also many religious Jews, have seen (and wanted to see) the State of Israel as reparation rather than restoration: its creation did not bring the dead back to life, but at least it brought back hope; Job did not recover his dead children, but others were born to him instead. Israel was the Redemption, or at least something like its first budding. The whole Zionist venture went from being a simple national adventure to the accomplishment of the biblical prophecies: the ingathering of exiles, the return to the Holy Land, the rebuilding of Jewish power. The Bible, the Book of the founding fathers of the State, became once more the Book of the Father. But now it was that in a new sense: book of the industrious farmer, the conqueror, the warrior; book of the body regained, of strength and combat; book of virility glorified and violence reassumed. The Bible thus became, more than the Book of the Father (the Heavenly Father was pure fiction for all the secular Zionists), the Father-Book. Nothing towered above it any longer, and nothing below could or should subvert it.[18]

We know the radical excesses to which this virile biblicism led after the war of 1967 and the conquest of the West Bank. It made the book itself politically suspect, alienating it from the hearts of so many Israelis and Diaspora Jews. How can one accept without a shudder that the tales of conquest and slaughter in the Book of Joshua should in any way whatsoever serve as a road map for today's Jewish warmongers? Here things are clear: the Letter—the Letter of the Father—kills.

❉

My son, heed the discipline of your father,
And do not forsake the instruction of your mother.

Proverbs 1.8

Many of those presently seeking to return to Judaism are at least dimly aware that the Bible may not be the best or most direct path to their goal. Often, they will prefer to take the edge off their first steps in the practice of Judaism, to curl up in the warmth of a study group, to listen to the real-life voice of a teacher. Not following the codified stages of a traditional apprenticeship, they will perhaps be more seduced from the beginning by some mysterious midrash, some arduous kabbalist meditation, than by the harshness of raw verses. Without knowing anything yet, they already know the main thing: the Bible is not all there is, the Bible is not everything, the Bible alone is nothing.

Dare I say fortunately! For this relative weakness of its status in Judaism paradoxically ensures the possibility of the Bible's redemption; it is the only means of saving it here and now, of wresting it from an isolation against which—as this book has amply shown—almost the whole of Jewish tradition can only protest. Similarly, faced with the Father who speaks to us in the Bible, faced with the all-too-absent Father of the exile and destruction, and the all-too-present Father of the return and conquest, there is perhaps only one way forward: to rehabilitate a femininity that makes it possible both to fill the absence and to hollow out the presence.

Let us therefore end this book as it began: with a free commentary.

The verse from Proverbs extracted above—"My son, heed the discipline of your father, / And do not forsake the instruction of your mother"—seems to say the same thing twice, but we know that such repetition can only be apparent.[19] An ancient midrash gives us the key:[20] the "discipline of the father" is the Written Torah*, while the "instruction of the mother" is the Oral Torah. The Bible is indeed there on the side of the Father, of the masculine and virile—which should not surprise us. Tradition, however, is on the side of the Mother and the feminine. The one cannot be conceived without the other. Heeding the discipline of the Father will depend proportionally on not forsaking the instruction of the Mother.

Better, no doubt, than the Bible alone could ever do, the Oral Tradition enables us to think through the weakness and distress of the Father by making room for the pain of the Mother, by enabling her cry to ring out. The Mother makes it possible for the Father's passion to be converted into genuine compassion. Tradition tells us that the destruction of the Jerusalem Sanctuary in 70 CE, repeating the ruin of the Temple of Solomon six and a half centuries earlier and setting a model for all the catastrophes to come (including those of our own time), was an act of destruction for God himself, within God himself. It sealed the split in him between the male and the female principles, and the beginning of a divine exile parallel to the exile of Israel. "In all their troubles," we are told in Isaiah 63.9, "He was troubled." But the Tradition goes much farther: it echoes in no uncertain terms the heartrending lamentation of the divine "presence," the *Shekhinah*[21] or God's immanence in this world, the Mother who, loving Israel, covers the walls and columns of the Sanctuary with kisses and embraces, and abandons it with regret.[22]

But the Oral Tradition also makes it possible to contain the Father's excesses, the temptations to violence, the seductiveness of force; it forbids us, for example, to stick to the letter alone of the narrative in the Book of Joshua. The Judaism of the Second Temple period no longer believed that conquest alone could ground the legitimacy of a possession. And against the immediate evidence of the texts, against the explicit provisions of the Law requiring extermination of the first occupants of the Land and proscribing any alliance with them, that Judaism tended to rewrite the history of the conquest of Canaan under Joshua in such a way as to make it a legal, negotiated, or even peaceful process.[23] Later, certain medieval authors—good allegorists that they were—were able to find something other than an appeal for further bloodshed behind the rivers of blood scattered through the Bible.[24] Rashi, and others too,[25] could see perfectly that in Psalms 45.4 the "two-edged sword" that makes the "splendor and glory" of the "hero" who wears it is perhaps first of all the sword of the Torah. [26] And the same Rashi, commenting on Proverbs 18.22, "He who finds a wife has found happiness," identifies "wife" precisely with the Torah.[27]

In Song of Songs, according to the Oral Tradition, the female beloved is Israel and the male beloved is God. Within the walls of the synagogue, the lover is Israel and his beloved fiancée, the king's daughter, is the Torah. This gender reversibility permits no end of daring touches. Perhaps it imposes them. The Bible was the Father's share, the (male) gift of the Father to Israel. The tradition, though also supposed to come from Sinai, is the (female) share of Israel. But Moses was outdone long ago by Rabbi Akiba: when God gave his prophet the possibility to cross time and attend one of the Master's classes, Moses, the great Moses, did not understand a single word.[28] God Himself confessed long ago to being outdone by his own children, since no miracle, no divine voice had the power any more to force their decisions.[29] Today, Moses is not only outdone, he may be dead. God—the failed God of the genocide and the abusive God of the reconquests—is not only outdone but may be dead. And whereas, in some kabbalist imagery,[30] it is the Written Torah, the male principle, that irrigates the Oral Torah, the female principle, it could be that the opposite is possible, or even that from now on the opposite alone is possible. It is in the power of sons, and now also of daughters, to bring the Father back to life—or not. And in our world today, beyond all the self-proclaimed orthodoxies, it is in the power only of the living tradition, the post-genocide and post-Zionist tradition, to save the Bible—or not.

Reference Matter

Notes

Prologue

1. See Genesis Rabba 1.10.

2. For words followed by an asterisk, see the Glossary at the end of this book.

3. In the biblical text, it is "Wisdom" (*hokhmah*) or "Reason" (*tevunah*) that speaks (see Prov. 8.1). The identification of the Torah with Wisdom goes back a very long way in Judaism, to the second century BCE (as in Sirach).

4. Genesis Rabba 1.1. Like an artisan consulting his plans to build a palace, God consulted the Torah to create the world.

5. In Hebrew, "head," *rosh*, a word with the same root as *reshit*.

6. Preparation of Israel for the tenth plague destined to strike Egypt. At the time when Egypt's firstborn were exterminated, the Angel of Death spared the Hebrew firstborn by "striding over" their houses, marked with the blood of the lamb sacrificed the day before. The sacrifice of the paschal lamb was repeated every year at the Jerusalem Temple.

7. This passage is freely inspired by Rashi's commentary on Gen. 1.1. On this medieval exegete, see 172, n. 59, below.

8. Babylonian Talmud, Shabbat 88a.

Chapter One: An Elusive Book?

1. Hayyim Rabin, "Bible Study and Hebrew Language Research" [in Hebrew], *Ha-Universita* 14, 1 (May 1968): 15.

2. See, e.g., Sylvain Gouguenheim, *Aristote au mont Saint-Michel. Les racines grecques de l'Europe chrétienne* (Paris: Seuil, 2008), and one of the critical responses to which it gave rise, Philippe Büttgen et al., eds., *Les Grecs, les Arabes et nous. Enquête sur l'islamophobie savante* (Paris: Fayard, 2009). See also Jean-Christophe Attias, "Les racines sépharades de l'Europe chrétienne? Philosophie, théologie et exégèse," in Attias, ed., *Les Sépharades et l'Europe. De Maïmonide à Spinoza* (Paris: Presses de l'université Paris-Sorbonne, 2012), 17–35.

3. Gilbert Dahan, *L'exégèse chrétienne de la Bible en Occident médiéval, XIIe–XIVe siècle* (Paris: Cerf, 1999), 8.

4. See Leo Strauss, "Jerusalem and Athens: Some Introductory Reflections," in id., *Studies in Platonic Political Philosophy*, ed. Thomas L. Pangle (Chicago: University of Chicago Press, 1983), 147–73, esp. 163.

5. On this ritual reading of the Bible, see 45–47 above.

6. On the Sefer Torah, see 36–39 and 41–44 above.

7. Jacob Neusner, *Formative Judaism: Religious, Historical, and Literary Studies*, 6th ser. (Atlanta: Scholars Press, 1989), 29, writes: "If we ask what all Judaisms identify in common, it is the Pentateuch, or the Five Books of Moses." It was the only holy book for the Samaritans, and the Sadducees, too, based themselves on it alone.

8. André Paul, "Les 'Écritures' dans la société juive au temps de Jésus," *Recherches de sciences religieuses* 89, 1 (January–March 2001): 27.

9. Philo sought to harmonize the teachings of Judaism with the principles of Greek (especially Platonic and Stoic) thought. His writings, in Greek, are an essential source on the Jewish reality of his time, comprising historical, apologetic, and philosophical texts, as well as extensive biblical commentaries. They exerted considerable influence on the early Church Fathers, but were ignored by the classical rabbinical tradition.

10. Paul, "'Écritures' dans la société juive," 20.

11. Colette Sirat, *Hebrew Manuscripts of the Middle Ages* (Cambridge: Cambridge University Press, 2002), 27.

12. Babylonian Talmud, Bava Batra, 13b.

13. This took place for Jews around the eighth century CE (Sirat, *Hebrew Manuscripts*, 35).

14. Born in Spain and active in Egypt, Maimonides left a sizeable, wide-ranging body of work, which profoundly marked the whole future of rabbinical Judaism. The author of a number of medical treatises, he first made his name as a halakhist*. Apart from a commentary in Arabic on the Mishnah and a *Book of Commandments*, he produced a monumental codification of Jewish law in Hebrew, the Mishneh Torah, "the double of the Torah*" (Deut. 17.18), also known under the title *Yad ha-Hazakah* (The Strong Hand). Maimonides is also the most distinguished representative of medieval Jewish Aristotelianism. His *Guide of the Perplexed* was written in Arabic but soon translated into Hebrew.

15. Carsten L. Wilke, "Les degrés de la sainteté des livres," in Colette Sirat et al., *La conception du livre chez les piétistes ashkénazes au Moyen Âge* (Geneva: Droz, 1996), 22.

16. In 586 BCE, Nebuchadnezzar wiped the kingdom of Judah from the map and destroyed the Temple of Jerusalem. The Judean aristocracy were deported to Babylon, while the peasantry remained where it was. Jewish settlements took shape among pagan populations in the lands of exile, retaining a strong cultural and national identity, belief in one God, and hopes that their kingdom would be restored.

17. Conventionally, the so-called Hellenistic period covers the three centuries from the death of Alexander the Great (323 BCE) to the death of Cleopatra (30 BCE).

18. Cyrus II of Persia conquered Babylon in 539 BCE and allowed the return of the exiles to an autonomous (but not independent) Judea, as well as the rebuilding of the Sanctuary in Jerusalem. Thousands of exiles flowed back to Palestine in several waves. Far from being egalitarian, the new Jewish society of Judea was torn by fierce internal strife that delayed the work of reconstruction. The Second Temple was inaugurated only around 515 BCE.

19. Robert Alter and Frank Kermode, eds., *The Literary Guide to the Bible* (Cambridge, MA: Harvard University Press, 1990), 601.

20. Robert Alter, "Introduction" to *The Five Books of Moses* (New York: Norton, 2004), p. xii.

21. On Leviticus, see, e.g., Mary Douglas, *Leviticus as Literature* (Oxford: Oxford University Press, 1999).

22. Albert de Pury and Thomas Römer, "Le Pentateuque en question. Position du problème et brève histoire de la recherche," in id., eds., *Le Pentateuque en question* (Geneva: Labor et Fides, 1989), 68.

23. Frank Cruseman, "Le Pentateuque, une Tora. Prolégomènes à une interprétation de sa forme finale," ibid., 341–42.

24. Ibid., 347–49.

25. I.e., the books of Joshua, Judges, Samuel, and Kings. See ibid., 357–58.

26. The original Jerusalem Temple perished in 587 BCE at the hands of the Babylonians. The second—a pale copy of the first—opened some seventy years later, around 515 BCE, having been rebuilt by Jews returning to Judea as decreed by Cyrus II. Lavishly restored and enlarged by Herod in the first century BCE, it was eventually destroyed by the Romans in 70 CE during Titus's sack of Jerusalem.

27. Ephraim E. Urbach, *The Sages: Their Concepts and Beliefs* (Cambridge, MA: Harvard University Press, 1987), 287.

28. André Paul, *Le Judaïsme ancien et la Bible* (Paris: Desclée, 1987), 26.

29. Roger Arnaldez, "La Bible de Philon d'Alexandrie," in Claude Mondésert, ed., *Le monde grec ancien et la Bible* (Paris: Beauchesne, 1984), 48.

30. Gilles Dorival, "Exégèse juive et exégèse chrétienne," in Marie-Odile Goulet-Cazé et al., eds., *Le commentaire entre tradition et innovation* (Paris: Vrin, 2000), 179.

31. Rabbi Akiba was a Palestinian Jewish master of the first to second century CE, who began the work of classifying the halakhic traditions that led to the publication of the Mishnah*. Eager to establish the organic unity of the Written and the Oral Law, he sought to incorporate a large number of halakhic provisions into Scripture and developed a "maximalist" exegesis in which there was a meaning behind every word and every sign, however outwardly superfluous or immaterial, in the text of the Bible. He saw Simeon bar Kokhba as a messianic figure and supported the last Jewish revolt against Rome (132–35). He died a martyr's death, tortured and executed by the Romans.

32. Moshe Halbertal, *People of the Book: Canon, Meaning, and Authority* (Cambridge, MA: Harvard University Press, 1997), 27.

33. Jerusalem Talmud, Megilah 1.5. The cited page of the Jerusalem Talmud clearly teaches that one should not stick to the simple narration of events, to the appearance of their chronological succession: "There is no before and after in the Torah."

34. Ibid.

35. Qohelet Rabba 12.12: "Those who bring home more than twenty-four books introduce confusion into their house."

36. Isaiah, Jeremiah, and Ezekiel.

37. The division of Samuel, Kings, and Chronicles into two books each does not feature in Jewish Bibles before the sixteenth-century Bomberg edition.

38. Hosea, Joel, Amos, Obadiah, Jonah, Micah, Nahum, Habakkuk, Zephaniah, Haggai, Zechariah, and Malachi.

39. Josephus took part in the Jewish revolt against Rome that began in 66. Besieged at Jotapata, he "turned traitor" and surrendered to Vespasian, subsequently witnessing the fall of Jerusalem and the destruction of the Temple in 70 from the Roman camp. Faithful to his God and religion as well as to Rome, Josephus was the author of two historical works of exceptional interest: *Antiquities of the Jews* and *The Jewish War*, an autobiography, and a polemical, apologetic text, *Against Apion*. His works, passed down in Greek and well known among Christians, picked their way into Jewish culture only through a Hebrew adaptation, the *Sefer Yosipon* (Book of Joseph), which appeared in southern Italy in the tenth century.

40. Josephus, *Against Apion* 1.8 (London: Heinemann, 1976), 179. Translation modified.

41. The first verse of Ruth actually situates its action in the age of Judges: "In the days when the judges ruled, there was a famine in the land . . ."

42. Two words in Genesis (31.47), a verse in Jeremiah (10.11), and parts of Daniel (2.4b to 7.28) and Ezra (4.8 to 6.18, and 7.12–26) are in Aramaic.

43. Paul, "'Écritures' dans la société juive," 41–42.

44. Josephus relates that they obtained permission from Alexander the Great to build their own temple there.

45. Especially worthy of mention are (1) the Community Rule; (2) the Temple Scroll; (3) the Damascus Document (fragments copied in the tenth and eleventh centuries had previously been found in 1896–97 in the Cairo Geniza), which might be more precisely entitled the "Document on the New Covenant in the Land of Damascus"; (4) the Rule of War of the Sons of Light against the Sons of Darkness; (5) various hymns; and (6) biblical commentaries (*pesharim*).

46. Olivier Millet and Philippe de Robert, *Culture biblique* (Paris: Presses universitaires de France, 2001), 5.

47. Ibid. Emphasis added.

48. Marcel Simon, "La Bible dans les premières controverses entre Juifs et chrétiens," in Mondésert, ed., *Monde grec ancien et la Bible*, 110–14. On Saint Justin Martyr's charges, see 79 in the present book.

49. Amos Funkenstein, *Styles of Medieval Biblical Exegesis* [in Hebrew] (Tel Aviv: Galei Tsahal, 1990), 16.

50. Neh. 8.

51. Deut. 4.2

52. "The Letter of Aristaeus," 121, 302, 311, in *The Apocrypha and Pseudepigrapha of the Old Testament* (Oxford: Clarendon Press, 1913).

53. Philo of Alexandria, *De vita Mosis*, ed. and trans. Roger Arnaldez et al. (Paris: Cerf, 1967), 203–11.

54. Midrash Tanhuma, Va-yera 5.

55. Babylonian Talmud, Megilah 9a. Cf. Jerusalem Talmud, Megilah 71d.

56. Masekhet Sofrim 1.7.

57. According to these traditions, the date of completion was an 8 *tevet* (December–January); 10 *tevet* (the third of these three days of "darkness") is actually a traditional day of fasting that marks the beginning of the siege of Jerusalem by Nebuchadnezzar, which ended with the destruction of the First Temple and the ruin of the kingdom of Judah (2 Kings 25.1). Note also that Ezra is traditionally said to have died on a 9 *tevet*.

58. Sarah Kamin, "The Theological Significance of the Hebraica Veritas in Jerome's Thought," in id., *Jews and Christians Interpret the Bible* (Jerusalem: Magnes, 1991), 1–11.

59. Babylonian Talmud, Yoma 9a.

60. David Stern, "Midrash and Jewish Interpretation," in Adele Berlin et al., eds., *The Jewish Study Bible* (New York: Oxford University Press, 2003), 1870.

61. "You yourselves saw [God says to Israel on Mount Sinai] that I spoke to you from the very heavens" (Exod. 20.19).

62. Note the preamble to the Decalogue: "God spoke all these words . . ." (Exod. 20.1).

63. "All that the Lord has spoken we will faithfully do" (Exod. 24.7).

64. See Exod. 34.1 and 34.28.

65. E.g., in Exod. 17.14: "Then the Lord said to Moses, 'Inscribe this in a document as a reminder, and read it aloud to Joshua: I will utterly blot out the memory of Amalek from under heaven'!"

66. "Then he took the record of the covenant and read it aloud to the people" (Exod. 24.7).

67. On the two episodes recalled here, which illustrate a shift from the authority of the prophet's word to the written text, see esp. Thomas Römer, "Y a-t-il une rédaction deutéronomiste dans le livre de Jérémie?" in Albert de Pury, Thomas Römer, and Jean-Daniel Macchi, eds., *Israël construit son histoire. L'historiographie deutéronomiste à la lumière des recherches récentes* (Geneva: Labor et Fides, 1996), 419–41.

68. Ezek. 2.7–3.3.

69. Zech. 5.1–4.

70. James L. Kugel and Rowan A. Greer, *Early Biblical Interpretation* (Philadelphia: Westminster Press, 1986), 13–25.

71. James L. Kugel, *The Bible As It Was* (Cambridge, MA: Belknap Press of Harvard University Press, 1997), 5–17.

72. On the word *ha-katuv*, see 4–5 above.

73. See 11–14 above.

74. Babylonian Talmud, Eruvin 13a.

75. On these questions, see, e.g., Menahem Kohen, "Textual Criticism and the Idea of the Sanctity of the Letter of the Biblical Text," in Uriel Simon, ed., *The Bible and Us* [in Hebrew] (Tel Aviv: Dvir, 1979), 42–69.

76. On the rabbinical Bible, see 118–20 above.

77. The first printed edition of the complete Hebrew Bible appeared at Soncino, near Milan, in 1488.

78. On Karaism, see also 87–90 above.

79. On the eventful history of the Aleppo Codex, which will be mentioned again later, see Hayim Tawl and Bernard Schneider, *Crown of Aleppo: The Mystery of the Oldest Hebrew Bible Codex* (Philadelphia: Jewish Publication Society, 2010).

80. Mishneh Torah, Hilkhot Sefer Torah 8.4.

81. Tawil and Schneider, *Crown of Aleppo*, 42–45.

82. On all these questions, see esp. Emmanuel Tov, *Textual Criticism of the Hebrew Bible* (Minneapolis: Fortress Press, 1992).

83. The system of dividing the Bible into chapters in general use today is attributed to Stephen Langton, archbishop of Canterbury (d. 1228).

84. Wellhausen identified three textual "strata" in the Pentateuch: the Yahwist (J/E), the Deuteronomist (D), and the Priestly (P—though he himself called it Q). This differentiation was inseparable from a new conception of the history of Israel and the evolution of its religious ideas. Thus, the monarchical period found expression in source J/E, Josiah's reform around 622 BCE in D, and the post-Exile period of reconstruction in P (Q).

85. Pury and Römer, "Pentateuque en question," 30.

86. On these modern developments and the challenges they posed to the Jewish faith and biblical scholarship, see further 123–30 above.

87. Alter and Kermode, eds., *Literary Guide to the Bible*, 12.

88. Ibid., 13.

Chapter Two: Bible Object, Bible in Pieces

1. Quoted in Jean Halpérin, "Essai de conclusion," in Jean Halpérin and Georges Levitte, eds., *La Bible au présent. Actes du XXIIe colloque des intellectuels juifs de langue française* (Paris: Gallimard, 1982), 347.

2. In Hebrew: *Keter Aram Tsova.* "Aram Tsova," the Hebrew name traditionally given to Aleppo, appears three times in the Bible.

3. See 23 above.

4. On the various aspects of this holiness, see Tawil and Schneider, *Crown of Aleppo*, esp. 62–65, 88–89.

5. Indeed, anyone in Aleppo who had to swear "on the Torah" did so on the codex rather than a Scroll of the Law.

6. This "Cave of Elijah" is only one of a type found in various places in the Middle East and associated with miracles (mostly cures) performed by the prophet. The most famous is the cave on Mount Carmel, in the Holy Land, where Elijah took refuge after he had successfully challenged the false prophets (1 Kings 18–19), and where he lived a life of meditation and teaching.

7. That is, aged thirteen or more.

8. If he is right-handed. His right arm if he is left-handed.

9. He can now form part of the ten-person quorum (*minyan*) required for the celebration of a public service.

10. Deut. 6.4–9; Deut. 11.13–21; Exod. 13.1–10; and Exod. 13.11–16.

11. Deut. 6.8; Deut. 11.18; Exod. 13.9; and Exod. 13.15.

12. On the Karaites, see also 87–90 above.

13. This is so despite, e.g., Abraham Ibn Ezra's energetic protests in his commentary on Exod. 13.9: "No verse [*katuv*] of the Pentateuch [*Torah*] is, God forbid, allegorical [*mashal*]; it must be understood literally [*ke-mashma'o*]. This is why we shall not depart from the obvious meaning [*pshuto*] of this verse, especially as its literal meaning [*mashma'o*] in no way contradicts the teachings of reason [*shikul ha-da'at*], as would [for example, a literal interpretation of] "you shall circumcise the foreskin of your heart" [Deut. 10.16]." This position clearly has a polemical intent: to counter the excesses of a certain kind of allegorical exegesis, Christian as well as Jewish, and at the same time to insist, against the Karaites in particular, that the letter of the biblical text is perfectly congruent with—or at least does not contradict—the teachings of the Oral Tradition.

14. The four texts are copied: (1) on a single parchment in the arm box; and (2) on four separate parchments in four separate compartments of the head box.

15. Although, at first sight, a relative uniformity of customs eventually prevailed, they are known to have varied historically and to have bred controversies at quite a late date (e.g., regarding the order in which the texts should be presented). Similarly, practical divergences of varying importance persisted between Ashkenazis and Sephardis, as well as between *hasidim* (followers of Hasidism) and their opponents (*mitnaggdim*); for each group they had significant value as tokens of collective self-assertion (direction in which the strap should be wrapped around the arm, appropriateness of wearing the tefillin on semi-holidays, and so on).

16. Babylonian Talmud, Berakhot 6a.

17. Deut. 6.4–9 and 11.13–21. It will be noted that these two texts are among those contained in the tefillin.

18. Deut. 6.9; see also Deut. 11.20.

19. One of the names of God, alluding to Pss. 91.1: "O you who . . . abide in the protection of Shaddai."

20. See Deut. 6.6–7 and 11.18–19.

21. Leon of Modena, "Cérémonies et coutumes qui s'observent aujourd'hui parmi les Juifs," in *Les Juifs présentés aux chrétiens. Textes de Léon de Modène et de Richard Simon*, ed. Jacques Le Brun and Guy G. Stroumsa (Paris: Les Belles Lettres, 1998), 36.

22. See 9–10 above.

23. In the Hebrew Bibles, manuscript and later printed, the order of the five books was subject to variation, sometimes following the sequence of the five solemn occasions in the year when they were read (Song of Songs, Ruth, Lamentations, Ecclesiastes, and Esther), sometimes the chronology of the historical periods they relate or with which they are associated: Ruth (period of the Judges), Song of Songs and Ecclesiastes (attributed to Solomon), Lamentations (destruction of the First Temple), and Esther (Persian era).

24. Leon of Modena, *Cérémonies et coutumes*, 35.

25. Babylonian Talmud, Gittin 45b.

26. Urbach, *Sages*, 369.

27. Leon of Modena, *Cérémonies et coutumes*, 36.

28. See 30–32 above.

29. In German Jewish communities, the child's swaddling clothes on the day of his circumcision were used to make a long belt (*mapa*) containing his name, his father's name, the date of circumcision, and the customary wishes for his future (that he would reach his religious majority, marry, and perform good works); at the age of two or three, the child took his *mapa* to the synagogue and left it there for safekeeping; and on the Shabbat* of his Bar Mitzvah, he used this belt to tighten the Sefer Torah from which he was called upon to read.

30. The weekly pericope is actually divided into seven sections. Those called in turn to read it are: one *kohen* (descendant of the priests who once officiated in the Jerusalem Temple), one *levi* (from the tribe of the Levites, assistants to priests), and five ordinary believers.

31. Ezra Suleiman spoke of this in a speech of October 17, 1999, on the occasion of the arrival at the Babylonian Jewish Center of Great Neck, NY of one of the two Scrolls of the Law, or *sifrei Torah*, that his grandfather had ordered from his own brother-in-law in the 1940s, which had reached the Basra synagogue in Iraq in 1948 ("A Religious and Emotional Journey," document provided by its author).

32. Chaim Aron Kaplan, *Scroll of Agony: The Warsaw Diary of Chaim A. Kaplan* (Bloomington: Indiana University Press, 1999), 87, 217.

33. This inner sanctum of the Temple was accessible only once a year, on Yom Kippur*, and only to the high priest.

34. This curtain or "veil," separating the Holy Place from the Holy of Holies, was half drawn on pilgrimage days so that worshipers could see the two cherubim guarding the Ark of the Covenant inside the Holy of Holies (Exod. 26.31–33; 2 Chron. 3.14; Babylonian Talmud, Yoma 54a).

35. Leviticus Rabba 22, 3.

36. Babylonian Talmud, Avodah Zarah 18b.

37. According to some late midrashic sources, it was during the reign of Hadrian (117–36) that Rome inflicted martyrdom on ten eminent figures of ancient Judaism (*asarah harugei malkhut*, lit., "ten victims of the kingdom"), including Rabbi Akiba.

38. According to some traditions (Babylonian Talmud, Megilah 26b), a Sefer Torah should preferably be interred near the tomb of an eminent rabbi.

39. Rabbi Meir was one of the architects of the Mishnah in which he is named some 330 times.

40. Elisha ben Abuya was one of the most renowned sages of his generation in the first and second centuries, before he suddenly went over to the reviled camp of Rome. He is traditionally given the highly significant cognomen Aher ("the Other").

41. Even if the bookcase also contains money. See Mishnah, Shabbat 16.1.

42. Jerusalem Talmud, Hagigah 2.1.

43. A passage in the Babylonian Talmud (Shabbat 105b) teaches that he who attends the death of a Jew may be compared to someone who sees a Sefer Torah burn. He must tear his clothing, Rashi's commentary specifies, even if the dead man is the humblest of Jews. For no Jew is totally lacking in Torah and commandments.

44. In addition to this regular cycle, days of fasting, festival, and neomenia (the beginning of the lunar month) are the occasion of special readings.

45. See Exod. 25.10–22.

46. 1 Kings 8.6–9.

47. Josh. 3–4.

48. Josh. 6.

49. 2 Sam. 6.

50. Mishnah, Avot 5.6.

51. Exodus Rabba 46.1.

52. Babylonian Talmud, Bava Batra 14a.

53. See 170, n. 34, above.

54. Heinrich Heine, *The Rabbi of Bacharach* (New York: Mondial, 2008), 50.

55. Albert Cohen, *Carnets: 1978* (Paris: Gallimard, 1979), 131–32.

56. Heine, *Rabbi of Bacharach*, 54.

57. Similarly, it was an honor for rich people to donate a Sefer to the community. See, e.g., Umberto Piperno, "L'étude de la Bible chez les Juifs italiens," in Yvon Belaval and Dominique Bourel, eds., *Le Siècle des Lumières et la Bible* (Paris: Beauchesne, 1986), 96.

58. *The Wisdom of the Zohar: An Anthology of Texts*, ed. Isaiah Tishby, trans. David Goldstein (Oxford: Oxford University Press, 1989), 3: 1037–39 (*Zohar* II, 206a–206b).

59. Rashi: acronym for the name of the biblical and talmudic commentator Rabbi *Sh*elomo *Y*itshaki (1040–1105). Born in Troyes in the reign of Henri I and

educated in the great academies of the day, he returned to his native city and devoted himself to teaching. He produced a near complete commentary on the Bible
and a commentary on the Babylonian Talmud. These were a milestone in the history of traditional Jewish exegesis and are still part of the basic education received
by believers. The influence of his biblical commentaries extended far beyond the
limits of the Jewish world via the Franciscan Nicholas of Lyra (c. 1270–1349), who
cites them in his *Postillae perpetuae*, as well as various Reformation figures and the
first modern translators of Scripture.

60. The phrase "cognitive comprehension" is used in relation to the Catholic
liturgy in Latin in Millet and de Robert, *Culture biblique*, 267.

61. The content of the chosen *haftarah* always has some connection with the
text of the Pentateuch or the significance of the festival or day of fasting when it is
read. Thus the *Be-shalah* pericope (Exod. 13.17–17.16), which comprises the hymn
sung by Moses and the children of Israel after the crossing of the Red Sea, has a
corresponding *haftarah* (Judg. 4.4–5.31) that contains the hymn sung by Deborah
and Barak after their victory over the Canaanites. Similarly, at the afternoon service on Yom Kippur, the day of mortification when the Jews ask for pardon, a
reading from the Book of Jonas tells of repentance that cancelled out the punishment decreed against a sinful city.

62. See esp. Halbertal, *People of the Book*, 100ff.

63. Sirat, *Hebrew Manuscripts*, 46f.

64. Especially in funeral rites, the recitation of which had the virtue of keeping
away evil spirits that laid siege to the dead person's home (Sylvie-Anne Goldberg,
"La Bible dans les attitudes juives face à la mort," in Belaval and Bourel, eds., *Siècle
des Lumières et la Bible*, 410).

65. Geographical dispersion and migratory movements contributed to a growing diversity of ritual. The ancient Palestinian liturgical tradition gave rise to Ro-
maniot (Byzantine), Italian, and Ashkenazi rites, the latter developing in turn a
Polish variant. The Babylonian tradition, compiled by Amram Gaon (c. 810–74),
inspired Provençal, Sephardi*, Oriental, and Yemenite rituals. As to Hassidism*, it
adopted a modified version of the Sephardi rite, based on the ritual of the Kabbalist Isaac Luria (1534–72).

66. On the Karaites, see also 87–90 above.

67. 1 Sam. 2.1–10.

68. Gen. 22.1–19.

69. Num. 28.1–8.

70. Exod. 30.34–36 and Exod. 30.7.

71. Exod. 13.1–16.

72. Exod. 14.30–15.19.

73. A fine example of this type of composition is the *tsidduk ha-din*, a ritual
formula "justifying the divine verdict" and pronounced after death (Goldberg,
"Bible dans les attitudes juives face à la mort," 410–11).

74. "Order" or "arrangement" of the celebration at every family table, around a plate containing symbolic objects and foods, held on the first and second evenings of Passover in the Diaspora, and only on the first in the Holy Land.

75. Exod. 13.8.

76. See Israel Jacob Yuval, *Two Nations in Your Womb: Perceptions of Jews and Christians in Late Antiquity and the Middle Ages*, trans. from the Hebrew by Barbara Harshav and Jonathan Chipman (Berkeley: University of California Press, 2006), esp. 56–67, and id., "La croisée des chemins: La *Hagadah* de la Pâque juive et les Pâques chrétiennes," in Florence Heymann and Michel Abitbol, eds., *L'Historiographie israélienne aujourd'hui* (Paris: CNRS Éditions, 1998), 64–74.

77. Exod. 20.2–14; Deut. 5.6–18.

78. Jerusalem Talmud, Berakhot 1.5. See also Babylonian Talmud, Berakhot 12a. On this passage from the Jerusalem Talmud, and the ban on including the Decalogue among the tefillin texts (a ban seemingly unknown at Qumran, however), see Urbach, *Sages*, 401 and 860, n. 12.

79. Of the few rare exceptions, Isa. 6.3 and Ezek. 3.12 are praise of God spoken by his Heavenly Court and intoned by believers at the moment of the *kedushah* ("benediction of holiness," no. 3 of the 19), when the cantor repeats the *amidah* aloud; Num. 6.22–16, the "priestly benediction," is intoned by the *kohanim* at the end of this repetition.

80. By way of an introduction on all these questions, see Stefan C. Reif, "The Bible in the Liturgy," in Berlin et al., eds., *Jewish Study Bible*, 1937–48. Also of value here is Reif, *Judaism and Hebrew Prayer: New Perspectives on Jewish Liturgical History* (Cambridge: Cambridge University Press, 1993).

81. See Babylonian Talmud, Megilah 3a. And see also Rashi on Neh. 8.7, who argues that making the Torah "understandable" to the people here means "translating" it for them.

82. Marc Saperstein, *Jewish Preaching, 1200–1800. An Anthology* (New Haven, CT: Yale University Press, 1989), 28.

83. Also known as *Ethics of the Fathers*, this Mishnah tractate consisting of maxims by masters of the Oral Tradition is the only example of ethical literature in the corpus. In Sephardi communities, it is the tradition to read it chapter by chapter from the Shabbat following Passover* to the one preceding Shavuot*.

84. Quoted in Saperstein, *Jewish Preaching*, 63.

85. On all these matters, see Saperstein, *Jewish Preaching*.

86. See Neusner, *Formative Judaism*, 71–121. More generally, in terms of content and the structuring of discourse, Neusner argues (p. 72) that the relationship between a Mishnah tractate and Scripture may be constructed in one of three ways: (1) the Bible furnishes the subject and dictates the program for its analytical treatment; (2) the Bible furnishes only the subject; and (3) even the subject of the treatment is unknown in the Bible.

87. See Moshe Greenberg, "Bible Interpretation as Exhibited in the First Book of Maïmonides" Code," in id., *Studies in the Bible and Jewish Thought* (Philadelphia: Jewish Publication Society, 1995), 421–45.

88. Jacob Neusner, *Judaism and Scripture: The Evidence of Leviticus Rabbah* (Chicago: University of Chicago Press, 1986), 123.

89. The words of the Kabbalist Moses de León, quoted in Gershom Scholem, *On the Kabballah and Its Symbolism*, new ed. (New York: Schocken Books, 1996), 46.

90. Quoted in (and translated from) Charles Mopsik, *Cabale et cabalistes* (Paris: Albin Michel, 2003), 169.

91. Bahya ben Asher (c. 1260–1340) on Num. 11.29, quoted in (and translated from) Mopsik, *Cabale et cabalistes*, p. 168.

92. To quote again the anonymous Kabbalist cited in n. 90 above.

93. René-Samuel Sirat, quoted in Halpérin, "Essai de conclusion," in id. and Levitte, eds., *Bible au présent*, 347.

94. Sirat, *Hebrew Manuscripts of the Middle Ages*, 27.

95. Benedict de Spinoza, *A Theological-Political Treatise*, chap. XII.3 (New York: Dover, 1951), 166.

Chapter Three: The Improbable Locus of an Identity

1. Menahem Kohen, "The Idea of the Holiness of Biblical Literature and Textual Criticism," in Uriel Simon, ed., *The Scriptures and Us* [in Hebrew] (Tel Aviv: Dvir, 1979), 44.

2. John 8.18. All English translations from the New Testament are taken from *Holy Bible: New Revised Standard Version* (Oxford: Oxford University Press, 1995).

3. Gal. 3.16.

4. John 8.33.

5. John 8.39.

6. John 8.41. Cf. Mishnah, Avot 3.14. On certain aspects of this "genealogical" conflict, see my "Enfants sans pères: Jésus et 'le fils de la femme israélite,'" in Jean-Christophe Attias, *Penser le judaïsme* (2010; rev. ed, Paris: CNRS Éditions, 2013), 241–54.

7. See 48 above.

8. A. B. Yehoshua, "From Myth to History," *AJS Review* 28, 1 (2004): 205.

9. Classical rabbinical sources present Hillel as being of Babylonian origin and Davidic ancestry. President (*nasi*) of the Sanhedrin, he and Shammai (its vice-president, or *av beit din*) were the last of the five learned "pairs" (*zugot*) who ensured transmission of the Oral Law. They were behind the formation of two competing schools: *beit Shammai* ("the house of Shammai") and *beit Hillel* ("the house of Hillel"), the former tending to be stricter, the latter suppler, in interpretation of the Law. Consequently, the Babylonian Talmud tells us (Sanhedrin 88b), "conflicts became more numerous in Israel." The debate was finally settled only after 70 at Yavne in favor of the Hillel school.

10. Babylonian Talmud, Shabbat 31a. The first candidate initially claimed to re-

ject the Oral Law and to believe only in the Written Law; the second wanted to be taught the whole Torah while standing on one foot; the third wanted to become a Jew so that he could be appointed high priest.

11. Babylonian Talmud, Yevamot 47a–b.

12. On all these questions, see Attias, *Penser le judaïsme*, 38–41, 205–40.

13. Carsten Lorenz Wilke, "Un judaïsme clandestin dans la France du XVIIe siècle. Un rite au rythme de l'imprimerie," in Esther Benbassa, ed., *Transmission et passages en monde juif* (Paris: Publisud, 1997), 286–87.

14. Jean-Pierre Osier, *D'Uriel da Costa à Spinoza* (Paris: Berg International, 1983), 29.

15. Uriel da Costa, "Sur l'immortalité de l'âme," ibid., 123.

16. Ibid., 117.

17. Bernard J. Bamberger, *The Bible: A Modern Jewish Approach* (New York: B'nai B'rith Hillel Foundations, 1955), 10.

18. James Darmesteter, *Les Prophètes d'Israël*, Paris: Calmann-Lévy, 1892, 244–45.

19. Moshe Greenberg and Shmuel Ahituv, eds., *Mikra Le-Israel Commentary (Bible for Israel): Prospectus* [in Hebrew and English] (Tel Aviv: Am Oved, n.d.). The quoted words have been translated from the Hebrew version of this bilingual document.

20. See 141–49 above.

21. See, e.g., Arlette Elkaïm-Sartre's account of the first steps in her rediscovery of Judaism. In an interview with Shmuel Trigano, she said: "Several times I planned to get closer to some fundamental texts of Judaism; once, a long time ago, I even tried to learn Hebrew. But it was a solitary project that never really took shape. When I met Benny Lévy and some of his friends, both Jewish and non-Jewish, and when the question came up of forming a group with you to learn Hebrew and introduce ourselves to biblical commentary, I leapt at the idea—as you know. The fact is that your lessons gave me a taste for the language. I found it beguiling how your commentaries stuck so close to the words, as if it were they that inspired you; how so many meanings could be derived from the same root; how you opened up to the Bible as a wealth of meanings that I had not suspected" (*L'Arche*, February 1983).

22. Moshe Greenberg, "Biblical Research and the Reality of Eretz Israel" [in Hebrew], in Simon, ed., *Scriptures and Us*, 84.

23. S[olomon] Schechter, "Higher Criticism—Higher Antisemitism," in *Seminary Addresses and Other Papers* (Cincinnati: Ark, 1915), 37–38. Conversely, Schechter explains, the attacks of "higher criticism" against the text of the Bible are nothing more than the expression of a "higher anti-Semitism." On the reaction of Judaism to modern biblical criticism, see 130–36 above.

24. Franz Rosenzweig was a German Jewish philosopher, once tempted to convert to Christianity, who translated the Bible into German together with Martin Buber. He was very reticent toward Zionism.

25. Eliezer Schweid, "The Teaching of the Bible as Torah in Government Schools" [in Hebrew], in Simon, ed., *Scriptures and Us*, 192.

26. Hava Tirosh-Samuelson, "The Bible in the Jewish Philosophical Tradition," in Berlin et al., eds., *Jewish Study Bible*, 1973–74.

27. The testimony of Arlette Elkaïm-Sartre (see n. 21 above) is revealing in this respect.

28. Quoted in Sophie Nordmann, "Hermann Cohen et le sionisme," *Études germaniques* 59, 2 (2004): 330. Emphasis added.

29. What Arlette Elkaïm-Sartre went on to translate was, not the Bible, but a collection of extracts from the Babylonian Talmud compiled by Jacob ben Salomon Ibn Habib (1445?–1515/1516): *Aggadoth du Talmud de Babylone. La Source de Jacob* (Lagrasse: Verdier, 1983).

30. Leo Strauss, "Why We Remain Jews: Can Jewish Faith and History Still Speak To Us?" (1962), in id., *Jewish Philosophy and the Crisis of Modernity* (Albany: State University of New York Press, 1997), 319–20.

31. André Neher, *L'identité juive*, repr. (Paris: Payot, 1994), 15–16.

32. Celsus's attack on the Christians, *The True Word*, has been lost; all that can be done today is to reconstitute sections of it from various quotations and refutations. See Celsus, *On the True Doctrine: A Discourse Against the Christians*, ed. and trans. R. Joseph Hoffman (New York: Oxford University Press, 1987).

33. Quoted in Michel-Yves Perrin, "Christianiser la culture," in Jean-Robert Armogathe et al., eds., *Histoire générale du christianisme*, vol. 1: *Des origines au XVe siècle* (Paris: Presses universitaires de France, 2010), 484.

34. Augustine, *Confessions*, trans. R.S. Pine-Coffin (London: Penguin Books, 1961), 12.

35. Quoted in Perrin, "Christianiser la culture," 485.

36. On these questions, see esp. James Kugel, "The 'Bible as Literature' in Late Antiquity and the Middle Ages," *Hebrew University Studies in Literature and the Arts* 11 (1983): 31–45.

37. Millet and de Robert, *Culture biblique*, 353.

38. Josephus, "Against Apion," in *The New Complete Works of Josephus*, trans. William Whiston (rev. ed., Grand Rapids, MI: Kregel, 1999).

39. On Philo and the Alexandrian Jewish tradition, see chap. 1 above, 12–16.

40. Kugel, "Bible as Literature," 20–30.

41. Josephus, "Against Apion," 939.

42. Ibid.

43. See Pss. 119.54 and Babylonian Talmud, Sota 35a.

44. In Hebrew, *divrei piyutin*.

45. Genesis Rabba 85.2.

46. The capacity of "sacred writings" to make one's hands unclean is related to their holiness, their importance, and the value that people attach to them. If it is said that direct contact with them has a sullying effect, the reason is precisely to

protect them from frivolous or unworthy treatment. See Tosefta, Yadayim 2.19, and Babylonian Talmud, Shabbat 14a.

47. Mishnah Yadayim 4.6. The text here plays on the homophony between "Homer" and *hamor* (= "donkey" in Hebrew).

48. *Zohar* III, 152a.

49. Quoted by Tishby in *Wisdom of the Zohar*, 3: 1082.

50. Abraham Heschel, *God in Search of Man: A Philosophy of Judaism* (New York: Farrar, Straus & Cudahy, 1955), 237.

51. Schweid, "Teaching of the Bible as Torah," 203.

52. James Kugel, "On the Bible and Literary Criticism," *Prooftexts* 1, 3 (September 1981): 219.

53. I readily accept that there is something absurdly reductionist about making "decorativeness" the prime feature of "the literary." What is at stake in this context is the element of literature that gives pleasure before it makes sense, or perhaps even without making sense. The pure seductiveness of literature, the enjoyment of pure form, or, in short, pleasure detached from any real concern for the true and the good, poses a problem. For the Bible, being divinely inspired is not supposed to offer anything like that.

54. Exod. 20.2–14; Deut. 5.6–18.

55. Babylonian Talmud, Shevu'ot 20b.

56. Exod. 20.8. In Hebrew, *zakhor*.

57. Deut. 5.12. In Hebrew, *shamor*.

58. See Jer. 23.29: "Behold, My word is like fire—declares the Lord—and like a hammer that shatters rock!" Cf. Babylonian Talmud, Sanhedrin 34a.

59. James Kugel, *The Idea of Biblical Poetry: Parallelism and Its History* (New Haven, CT: Yale University Press, 1981), 97–8.

60. In Hebrew, *mishpateikha*, literally, "Your judgments."

61. In Hebrew, *toratkha*, literally, "Your Torah."

62. *Sifrei Devarim* [in Hebrew], ed. Louis Finkelstein (repr., New York: Jewish Theological Seminary of America, 1969), §251, p. 408.

63. The term "omnisignificance" is borrowed from the work of James Kugel.

64. See an example of this kind of debate in *Sifrei Be-midbar* [in Hebrew], ed. H. S. Horovitz (repr., Jerusalem: Shalem Books, 1992), §112, p. 121.

65. Adele Berlin, "On the Bible as Literature," *Prooftexts* 2, 3 (September 1982): 324.

66. Kugel, *Idea of Biblical Poetry*, 104. It covers parallelism all the less because the more complex *te'amim* system, by introducing minor or secondary pauses within verses, ends up obscuring their fundamentally binary construction (ibid., 113).

67. On these questions, see Hava Lazarus-Yafeh's articles "Tahrif" and "Tawrat" in P. J. Bearman et al., eds., *The Encyclopaedia of Islam*, new ed. (Leiden: Brill, 2000), 10: 111a–112b and 393b–395a. See also the same author's "Muslim Medieval Attitudes towards the Qur'an and the Bible," in Évelyne Patlagean and

Alain Le Boulluec, eds., *Les retours aux Écritures. Fondamentalismes présents et passés* (Louvain: Peeters, 1993), 253–67.

68. See 77–86 above.

69. Born in Egypt, Saadia Gaon was appointed *gaon* (head) of the Academy of Sura in 928, but a conflict with the exilarch David ben Zakkai soon led to his removal—although he was later reinstated, in 936 or 937. Saadia translated almost the whole Bible into Arabic; he was himself a liturgical poet and compiled a book of prayers; and he was also a prolific halakhist and formidable polemicist (against Karaism). His main work is a defense and illustration of the principles of Judaism, *The Book of Doctrines and Beliefs*, originally written in Arabic, and eventually translated into Hebrew in 1186.

70. Daniel J. Lasker, "Saadya Gaon on Christianity and Islam," in Daniel Frank, ed., *The Jews of Medieval Islam: Community, Society and Identity* (Leiden: Brill, 1995), 176.

71. Adele Berlin, *Biblical Poetry through Medieval Jewish Eyes* (Bloomington: Indiana University Press, 1991), 17.

72. This observation only applies to poetry, since Jews themselves generally preferred Arabic—transcribed in Hebrew characters—for the composition of their scientific or theological-philosophical works.

73. Men like Abraham Ibn Ezra or Rashbam; see Berlin, *Biblical Poetry*, 10.

74. After the Almoravid conquest (post-1090) led to a worsening of the situation for Jews in Muslim Spain, Judah Halevi crossed over to Toledo in the Christian-ruled part of the peninsula. He subsequently left for Palestine, arriving in Alexandria in September 1140, but he evidently died before he reached his destination. His best-known poetic work is the *Songs of Zion*, in which he voices a powerful nostalgia for the Holy Land. Along with various secular compositions, he also left religious poems that are still today part of the synagogue liturgy. Halevi is also the author of one of the masterpieces of medieval Jewish thought, *The Book of Refutation and Proof on Behalf of the Most Despised Religion*, better known as *Kuzari*. Critical of philosophy, his thinking centers on Israel's unique vocation and the singular bond of its people and God with the Holy Land.

75. Berlin, *Biblical Poetry*, 39.

76. See 9 above.

77. See Moses Ibn Ezra, *Sefer ha-iyyunim ve-ha-diyyunim*, Hebrew trans. by A. S. Halkin (Jerusalem: Mekitsei Nirdamim, 1975), 47–49, 117, 221, and Berlin, *Biblical Poetry*, 47.

78. Originally from Catalonia and present in Spain during the great persecutions of 1391, Isaac ben Moses ha-Levi (also called Profiat Duran) was obliged to convert to Christianity and lived as a Christian in Perpignan, while pursuing literary activity in Hebrew. By the time he wrote his grammar, in 1403, he had converted back to Judaism.

79. In Hebrew, *holi*.

80. Profiat Duran [Isaac ben Moses ha-Levi], *Maase Efod*, ed. Jonathan Friedländer and Jakob Kohn (Vienna, 1865), 41.

81. On these questions, see esp. Yosef Hayim Yerushalmi, *Zakhor: Jewish History and Jewish Memory* (rev. ed., Seattle: University of Washington Press, 1996), 27–76; see also the introductory essay to *Isaac Abravanel, La mémoire et l'espérance*, trans. and ed. Jean-Christophe Attias (Paris: Cerf, 1992), 9–50.

82. See 62–63 above.

83. Adolf Harnack, *Marcion: The Gospel of the Alien God*, trans. John E. Steely and Lyle D. Bierma (Eugene, OR: Wipf & Stock, 1990), 23.

84. Ibid., 22.

85. This is not an absolute contrast, though, since the law/grace opposition partly transcends the distinction between the Old and the New Testament, as Bernard Lauret shows in "L'Idée d'un christianisme pur," in the French edition of Harnack's magnum opus, *Marcion. L'Évangile du Dieu étranger. Une monographie sur l'histoire de la fondation de l'Église catholique* (Paris: Cerf, 2003), 340–41. In his 1523 Preface to the Old Testament, Luther wrote: "Know, then, that the Old Testament is a book of laws, which teaches what men are to do and not to do, and gives, besides, examples and stories of how these laws are kept or broken; just as the New Testament is a Gospelbook, or book of grace, and teaches where one is to get the power to fulfill the law. But in the New Testament there are given, along with the teaching about grace, many other teachings that are laws and commandments for the ruling of the flesh, since in this life the spirit is not perfected and grace alone cannot rule. Just so in the Old Testament there are, beside the laws, certain promises and offers of grace, by which the holy fathers and prophets, under the law, were kept, like us, under the faith of Christ" (Martin Luther, "Prefaces to the Books of the Bible—1522–1545," www.godrules.net/library/luther/NEW1luther_f8.htm).

86. Harnack, *Marcion*, trans. Steely and Bierma, 134.

87. Rolf Rendtorff, "The Jewish Bible and its Anti-Jewish Interpretation," *Christian Jewish Relations* 16, 1 (March 1983): 1–20.

88. Guy Lobrichon, *La Bible au Moyen Âge* (Paris: Picard, 2003), 38–40.

89. Ibid., 28.

90. Justin Martyr, *Dialogue with Trypho*, chap. 71, www.earlychristianwritings. com/text/justinmartyr-dialoguetrypho.html.

91. On all these questions, see esp. Bernhard Blumenkranz, "Augustin et les Juifs, Augustin et le judaïsme," *Recherches augustiniennes* 1 (1958): 225–41; and Jeremy Cohen, *Living Letters of the Law: Ideas of the Jew in Medieval Christianity* (Berkeley: University of California Press, 1999), 27–65.

92. Augustine, *Sermons sur l'Écriture 1–15A*, trans. André Bouissou, ed. Goulven Madec (Paris: Institut d'Études augustiniennes, 1994), sermon 5, "Sur la lutte de Jacob avec l'Ange," 128.

93. Rupert de Deutz quoted in Dahan, *Exégèse chrétienne de la Bible*, 365.

94. Uriah was the husband of Bathsheba, whom David coveted. David recalled him from the front, then sent him back with a letter to the commander of his

troops, Joab, containing secret instructions to place Uriah at the thick of the fighting, so that he would die in battle. Naturally this was what happened. See 2 Sam. 21.

95. Dahan, *Exégèse chrétienne de la Bible*, 359–60.

96. Justin Martyr, *Dialogue with Trypho*, chap. 29, www.earlychristianwritings .com/text/justinmartyr-dialoguetrypho.html. The Epistle of Barnabas (4.6–7) enjoins its readers "not to liken yourselves to certain persons who pile up sin upon sin, saying that our covenant remains to them also. Ours it is; but they lost it in this way for ever, when Moses had just received it," Marcel Simon notes ("La Bible dans les premières controverses entre Juifs et chrétiens," in Claude Mondésert, ed., *Le Monde grec ancien et la Bible* [Paris: Beauchesne, 1984], 107–8).

97. Cohen, *Living Letters*, esp. chap. 8.

98. Dahan, *Exégèse chrétienne de la Bible*, 67.

99. Jeremy Cohen, *The Friars and the Jews: The Evolution of Medieval Anti-Judaism* (Ithaca, NY: Cornell University Press, 1982), 140–52; id., *Living Letters*, 321.

100. These "shy away from decency and are an object of horror for those who hear them" (Dahan, *Exégèse chrétienne de la Bible*, 46).

101. Cohen, *Friars and the Jews*, 140–52.

102. Moses ben Nahman, also known by the acronym RaMBaN (*Ra*bbi *M*oshe *b*en *N*ahman), was an eminent representative of the kabbalist circle of Gerona and a noteworthy halakhist, at the crossroads of the French and Spanish traditions. In 1263, he was forced to participate in a public debate organized in Barcelona by a converted Jew named Pablo Christiani in the presence of King James I of Aragon; he subsequently wrote an account of it entitled "The Book of the Disputation." He eventually departed for the Holy Land, where he completed a commentary on the Pentateuch combining philosophical, aggadic, and mystical elements.

103. Moses Nahmanides, *La dispute de Barcelone*, trans. from the Hebrew by Éric Smilévitch, archival text translated from the Latin by Luc Ferrier (Lagrasse: Verdier, 1984), 37. Cf. "The Disputation of Barcelona (1263): The Hebrew Report of Moshe Ben Nachman [Nahmanides]," www.israel613.com/books/ramban_ dispute_e.pdf. See also Cohen, *Friars and the Jews*, 117–18.

104. Exodus Rabba 46.1 (on Exod. 34.1).

105. See 16 above.

106. Pss. 25.14.

107. Midrash Tanhuma, Va-yera 5.

108. Halbertal, *People of the Book*, 124.

109. See the teaching of Rabbi Abin in Jerusalem Talmud, Peah 2.4.

110. See Exodus Rabba 47.1. In Hebrew, "hem mavdilim bein Yisra'el le-vein ha-ovdei kokhavim" ("they [Mishnah and Talmud] distinguish Israel from the idolators").

111. Ibid. In Hebrew: "she-im yavo'u ovdei kokhavim ve-yishta'bdu bahem yihyu muvdalim me-hem" ("if the idolators came to subjugate them, they would [thereby] remain distinct").

112. See the teaching of Rabbi Samuel bar Nahman, as transmitted by Rabbi Haggai, interpreting Exod. 34.27, in Jerusalem Talmud, Peah 2.4.

113. Rabbi Yechiel quoted in Gilbert Dahan, *La polémique chrétienne contre le judaïsme au Moyen Âge* (Paris: A. Michel, 1991), 47–48. Cf. Cohen, *Friars and the Jews*, 69–70.

114. According to Deut. 30.12.

115. According to Exod. 23.2.

116. Babylonian Talmud, Bava Metsia 59b.

117. The secular (Zionist) appropriation of the Bible has evidently strengthened this line. See Uriel Simon, "The Status of the Bible in Israeli Society: From National Midrash to Existential *Pshat*" [in Hebrew], *Yeri'ot* 1 (1999): 26.

118. Leon of Modena, *Le Bouclier et la Targe. Une polémique sur l'identité juive au XVIIe siècle*, trans. and ed. Jean-Pierre Osier (Paris: Centre d'études Don Isaac Abravanel & UISF, 1980), 45–46.

119. Richard Simon, "Comparaison des cérémonies des Juifs et de la discipline de l'Église," in *Juifs présentés aux chrétiens*, ed. Le Brun and Stroumsa, 144.

120. Ibid., 145.

121. Ibid., 202.

122. Ibid., 201.

123. Richard Simon, "Supplément touchant les karaïtes," in *Juifs présentés aux chrétiens*, ed. Le Brun and Stroumsa, 111.

124. Ibid., 113.

125. Ibid., 114.

126. Ibid., 116.

127. Abbé Henri Grégoire, *Essai sur la régénération physique, morale et politique des Juifs* (1788), reissued with a preface by Rita Hermon-Belot (Paris: Flammarion, 1988), 185. Translated as *An Essay on the Physical, Moral, and Political Reformation of the Jews* (London: C. Forster, 1790).

128. Grégoire, *Essai sur la regeneration*, 165; *Essay*, 220.

129. See Attias, *Penser le judaïsme*, chap. 4, 61–78, for a general introduction to Karaism.

130. Aaron ben Joseph the Physician, *Sefer ha-Mivhar* (Kozlov, 1834), "Introduction," f° 9 r°. On this late Karaite revaluation of the rabbinical heritage, see Jean-Christophe Attias, *Le commentaire biblique. Mordekhai Komtino ou l'herméneutique du dialogue* (Paris: Cerf, 1990), 42–43. However, while it is true that for normative Judaism, the Oral Law derives its holiness from its ultimately divine (and Sinaitic) origin, for Karaism the holiness of the "burden of inheritance" derives from that of the human beings who have borne it. See Michael Corinaldi, "Karaite Halakhah," in N. S. Hecht, B. S. Jackson, S. M. Passamaneck, D. Rattelli, and A. M. Rabello, eds., *An Introduction to the History and Sources of Jewish Law* (Oxford: Oxford University Press, 1996), 254.

131. Yosef Kaplan, "Karaites in the Early Eighteenth Century," in id., *An Al-*

ternative Path to Modernity: The Spanish Diaspora in Western Europe (Leiden: Brill Academic, 2000), 238.

132. See 62–63.

133. André Paul, *Le Judaïsme ancien et la Bible* (Paris: Desclée, 1987), 53.

134. Judah M. Rosenthal, "The Talmud on Trial. The Disputation at Paris in the Year 1240," *Jewish Quarterly Review* 47 (1956): 70.

135. The reader will have understood that it matters little here whether—as J. M. Rosenthal suggests—the thirteenth-century attacks on the Talmud by various apostates of Jewish origin testify to actual Karaite influence.

136. Commentary on Deut. 4.2 by the Karaite Aaron ben Elijah of Nicomedia in his *Keter Torah* (repr. of the 1870 Odessa ed. [Ramla]: Ha-mo'atsa ha-artsit shel ha-yehudim ha-kara'im be-Yisra'el, 1966).

137. Reported by Alain Finkielkraut in "Réflexion sur l'ignorance," an intervention at the 22nd colloquium of French-speaking Jewish intellectuals: Halpérin and Levitte, eds., *Bible au présent*, 210.

138. See 85 above.

139. Emmanuel Lévinas, *Outside the Subject* (Stanford, CA: Stanford University Press, 1994), 127.

Chapter Four: Reading the Bible at the Risk of Heresy

1. Babylonian Talmud, Berakhot 8a.

2. If there is no Aramaic version for a given verse, it should be read in Hebrew three times (Mishneh Torah, Hilkhot Tefillah, 13.25).

3. The Shulhan Arukh was printed for the first time in Venice in 1565. With the addition of glosses by the Ashkenazi* Moses ben Israel Isserles (c. 1525–72), it established itself throughout the Jewish world as the halakhic code par excellence. It remains authoritative today in Orthodox milieux.

4. Shulhan Arukh, Orah Hayyim, Hilkhot Shabbat, 285.2.

5. Babylonian Talmud, Berakhot 28b.

6. Pss. 9.17, 19.15, 92.4; Lam. 3.62.

7. Ultimately, however, the two answers are congruent; see 97–98 above.

8. In his commentary on the Babylonian Talmud, Berakhot 28b, Rashi suggests another interpretation: *higgayon* might simply denote the (evidently idle) "talk of children." This proximity of the Bible and the idle talk of children in the same commentary, as alternative interpretations of the same term, is eloquent in itself.

9. On the ancient and medieval interpretations of Rabbi Eliezer's teaching, see Frank Talmage, "Keep Your Sons from Scripture: The Bible in Medieval Jewish Scholarship and Spirituality," in id., *Apples of Gold in Settings of Silver* (Toronto: Pontifical Institute of Mediaeval Studies, 1999), 151–71; and Mordekhai Breuer, "Stop Your Children Indulging in *Higgayon*," in Yitzhak D. Gilat and Eliezer Stern, eds., *Mikhtam le-David: Homage to the Memory of Rabbi David Ochs* [in Hebrew] (Ramat Gan: University of Bar Ilan, 1977), 242–61.

10. Mishnah, Avot 5.21.

11. Leviticus Rabba 7.3.

12. "The childhood of a young Jew . . . does not unfold in this world and in this life, but rather in the biblical pages with which it is imbued from his earliest years. He builds his childhood dreams in the prairies where his forebears pastured their herds of sheep and dug their wells. The birds and animals of the Bible are the only ones with which he is in contact. And the real storm is not the one howling on the plain but the one that rose up when God concluded his pact with Abraham." Shalom Asch, quoted in Finkielkraut, "Réflexions sur l'ignorance," in Halpérin and Levitte, eds., *Bible au présent*, 199.

13. Mary Douglas, *Leviticus as Literature* (Oxford: Oxford University Press, 1999), 14.

14. Babylonian Talmud, Kiddushin 30a and Avodah Zarah 19b.

15. See, e.g., Babylonian Talmud, Bava Metsia 33a.

16. See esp. Halbertal, *People of the Book*, 100ff.

17. Talmage, "Keep Your Sons from Scripture," 154.

18. See 92–93 above and Breuer, "Stop Your Children," 251.

19. See 82 above.

20. The school of Talmudists founded by Rashi continued under his grandchildren and their disciples for several generations, from the twelfth to the fourteenth century. This prestigious line of scholars produced "supplements" (*tosafot*) to Rashi's talmudic commentaries—hence their name *baalei ha-tosafot* ("supplement masters"), or in English "Tosafists." The origin of these supplements is inseparable from the activity of the talmudic schools, where students' questions drew responses from the masters and gave rise to discussions. In the thirteenth century, attempts were made to compile these with a view to publication, and only a part of them figures in current editions of the Talmud. In these today, one finds on the same page the text of the Talmud itself in the central column, Rashi's commentary in the inside column, and the "supplements" (*tosafot*) in the outside column. The authors of the latter studied the text of the Talmud to try to restore its supposedly perfect coherence, noting apparent contradictions between different passages on the same matter, contrasting the probable meaning of a text with interpretations of it given by various commentators, especially that of Rashi (which they even went so far as to criticize), comparing the talmudic sources, adding new remarks, and drawing practical conclusions for daily life.

21. The *Sefer Hasidim* (Book of the Pious Ones), mostly written by Judah ben Samuel of Regensburg (c. 1146–1217), is one of the main literary monuments of the pietist current that developed between 1150 and 1250 in the Jewish communities of southern Germany and the Rhine Valley. See Judah ben Samuel of Regensburg, *Sefer Chasidim: The Book of the Pious*, trans. and ed. Avraham Yaakov Finkel (Northvale, NJ: Jason Aronson, 1997); French ed., Jehudah ben Chemouel le Hassid, *Sefer Hassidim. Le Guide des Hassidim*, trans. Édouard Gourévitch (Paris: Cerf, 1988).

22. According to a formulation in Babylonian Talmud, Bava Metsia 33a: "To

occupy oneself with Scripture is a virtue [in Hebrew, *middah*] and is not a virtue; [to occupy oneself] with the Mishnah, a virtue for which one receives a salary; [to occupy oneself] with the Gemara, a virtue than which none other is higher."

23. See the extract from the *Sefer Hasidim* (§748 of the Parma ms.), quoted in [and here translated from] Breuer, "Stop Your Children . . . ," p. 245. On *pshat* and the issues it involves, see 107–9 above.

24. Moses Maimonides, *The Guide of the Perplexed*, trans. and ed. Shlomo Pines (Chicago: University of Chicago Press, 1963), 2: 619 [3.51].

25. On Ibn Kaspi, see Isadore Twersky, "Joseph Ibn Kaspi: Portrait d'un intellectuel juif medieval," in Marie-Humbert Vicaire and Bernhard Blumenkranz, eds., *Juifs et judaïsme de Languedoc. XIIIe siècle–début XIVe siècle* (Paris: Privat, 1977), 185–204.

26. This general decline prompted a Jewish return to Scripture, as typified in the fourteenth century by Isaac ben Moses ha-Levi (Profiat Duran). See 76 above.

27. Talmage, "Keep Your Sons from Scripture," 163–64.

28. Babylonian Talmud, Sotah 20a.

29. Judah ben Samuel of Regensburg [Jehudah ben Chemouel le Hassid], *Sefer Hassidim*, trans. Gourévitch, 273–75 (§445 of the French translation, §835 of the Parma ms.).

30. See Mishneh Torah, Hilkhot Talmud Torah 1.1 and 1.13.

31. Of course, "popular" here refers to literature produced not by the people but *for* the people, by scholars representing the Jewish cultural elite.

32. Jean Baumgarten, "Une traduction de la Bible en yiddish," in Belaval and Bourel, eds., *Siècle des Lumières et la Bible*, 238.

33. ". . . Go forth / And gaze upon King Solomon / Wearing the crown that his mother / Gave him on his wedding day, / On his day of bliss." See, in French, Jacob ben Isaac Achkenazi de Janow, *Le commentaire sur la Torah*, trans. from the Yiddish by Jean Baumgarten (Paris: Verdier, 1994).

34. The title *Me'am Lo'ez* is drawn from Pss. 114.1: "When Israel went forth from Egypt, the house of Jacob from *a people of strange speech* [*am lo'ez*]."

35. On the *Me'am Lo'ez*, see esp. Alisa Meyuhas Ginio, "La Bible populaire sépharade comme mémoire de la vie juive," in Esther Benbassa, ed., *Les Sépharades. Histoire et culture du Moyen Âge à nos jours* (Paris: Presses de l'université Paris-Sorbonne, 2011), 183–200.

36. *Me'am Lo'ez. El gran comentario bíblico sefardí*, vol. 1, pt. 2 [Gen. 25.16 to 50.26], ed. and transliterated by David Gonzalo Maeso and Pascual Pascual Recuero (Madrid: Editorial Gredos, 1970), 902 (on Gen. 34.1).

37. Jacob ben Isaac Achkenazi de Janow, *Commentaire sur la Torah*, 238 (also on Gen. 34. 1).

38. Halbertal, *People of the Book*, 3.

39. See ibid., 45–89.

40. See 87–90 above.

41. Jeremy Cohen, *"Be Fertile and Increase, Fill the Earth and Master It": The*

Ancient and Medieval Career of a Biblical Text (Ithaca, NY: Cornell University Press, 1989), 180–81.

42. See 9 above.

43. Kugel, *Bible As It Was*, xiii–xv.

44. The term "narrative expansions" is from James L. Kugel, *In Potiphar's House: The Interpretive Life of Biblical Texts* (Cambridge, MA: Harvard University Press, 1990), 6.

45. See, e.g., Howard Schwartz, *Reimagining the Bible: The Storytelling of the Rabbis* (New York: Oxford University Press, 1998).

46. E.g., ibid., 10.

47. Louis Ginzberg, *The Legends of the Jews*, 7 vols. (Philadelphia: Jewish Publication Society, 1909–38; 2nd ed., 2 vols., 2003). James Kugel, however, argues that Ginzberg mistakenly saw the midrashic legacy as a corpus of "legends," a kind of peribiblical or parabiblical "folklore," and that this made him lose sight of their primarily exegetic intent (Kugel, *Bible As It Was*, 46).

48. Jonathan Magonet, "The Biblical Roots of Jewish Identity: Exploring the Relativity of Exegesis," *Journal for the Study of the Old Testament* 54 (June 1992): 20.

49. See 93–95 above.

50. Rashi, commenting on this verse, writes: "All *higgayon* in the Bible is [a matter] of the heart."

51. 2 Chron. 13.22 and 24.27.

52. This formula, already present in ancient rabbinical literature, also occurs among medieval writers. See, e.g., what Rashi says of the opening words of Genesis ("In the beginning God created . . ."): "This scriptural text says nothing other than 'interpret me' [*Ein ha-mikra ha-ze omer ela darsheni*]." This does not prevent a literal reading of it, as Rashi makes clear shortly afterwards: "And if you intend to explain it in accordance with its obvious meaning . . . [*ve-im bata lefarsho ki-fshuto*]." On Rashi's interpretation of Gen. 1.1, see xi–xii above.

53. Marcel-Jacques Dubois, *Rencontres avec le judaïsme en Israël* (Jerusalem: Éditions de l'Olivier, 1983), 62.

54. Compare what Geza Vermes says concerning the four requirements of "pure exegesis" in "Bible and Midrash: Early Old Testament Exegesis," in id., *Post-Biblical Jewish Studies* (Leiden: Brill, 1975), 63–80.

55. Babylonian Talmud, Pesahim 6b. In his commentary, Rashi explains: "The Torah did not unfailingly respect a strictly chronological order [*lo hikpidah Torah al seder mukdam u-me'uhar*], and some later sections were placed before others that are said to be earlier." This means that each statement in the Pentateuch can and should be interpreted independently of its context, and that its commentator must not let himself be constrained by which came first.

56. This supposition is shared by Christian exegesis, as Gilbert Dahan notes in "Le commentaire médiéval de la Bible: Le passage au sens spirituel," in Goulet-Cazé et al., eds., *Commentaire*, 224.

57. In the view of Moses Nahmanides, for instance, the Torah in its original

form was written without any kind of break between the words and was thus one long divine name manifesting the essence of God. For more on the hermeneutic implications of such a conception of the biblical text, see Halbertal, *People of the Book*, 37ff. See also *Zohar* II, 60a: "The Holy One, Blessed be He is called Torah. . . . And the Torah is nothing other than the Holy One, Blessed be He" (*Wisdom of the Zohar*, 3: 1086).

58. James L. Kugel, "Early Interpretation: The Common Background of Late Forms of Biblical Exegesis," in id. and Rowan A. Greer, *Early Biblical Interpretation* (Philadelphia: Westminster Press, 1986), 101–2.

59. "The text is at once perfect and perpetually incomplete, [and . . .] like the universe itself, it was created to be a process rather than a system, a method of inquiry rather than a codified collection of answers." Louis Finkelstein, quoted in Avraham J. Tannenbaum, "Jewish Texts, Education and Identity: Inseparable," *Journal of Jewish Education* 57, 2–4 (Summer–Winter 1989): 10.

60. Michael Fishbane, *The Exegetical Imagination: On Jewish Thought and Theology* (Cambridge, MA: Harvard University Press, 1998), 12.

61. See Rabbi Akiba's interpretation of Deut. 32.47 ("For this is not a trifling thing [or word] for you [*mikkem*]") in Genesis Rabba 1.14: "And if it seems trifling, it is because of you [*mikkem*], because you know not how to interpret [it] [*lidrosh*]."

62. André LaCocque and Paul Ricœur, *Thinking Biblically: Exegetical and Hermeneutical Studies* (Chicago: University of Chicago Press, 2003), xiii, xvi.

63. "I heard and did not understand, so I [Daniel] said, 'My lord, what will be the outcome of these things?' He said, 'Go, Daniel, for these words are secret and sealed to the time of the end'" (Dan. 12.9). See Funkenstein, *Styles of Medieval Hebrew Exegesis* [in Hebrew], 12–13.

64. Moshe Sokolow, "The Bible and Religious Education: A Multi-Dimensional Approach," *Studies in Jewish Education* 4 (1989): 52 (evoking the way in which Sandra Schneiders makes faith play a role in the reading of biblical texts comparable to that of talent and training in the appreciation of music); cf. Dubois, *Rencontres*, 64 (concerning Augustine). Moshe Greenberg calls this a "theological" approach, in which the message of the Bible cannot be understood without the special insight afforded by belief in its divine origin, so that faith is rewarded with a grace that illuminates the meaning of Scripture ("Reflections on Interpretation," in Greenberg, *Studies in the Bible and Jewish Thought*, 227).

65. *Avot de-Rabbi Nathan*, version B, chap. xiii. This transfiguration of Rabbi Eliezer repeats the transfiguration of Moses in Exod. 34.29–35 (on the transfiguration of Moses, see my "Moïse ignorait que la peau de son visage était cornue. Lectures d'Exode 34, 29–35," in Attias, *Penser le judaïsme*, 157–83). It is evidently not without similarities to the transfiguration of Jesus recorded in the Gospels: "Six days later, Jesus took with him Peter and James and his brother John and led them up a high mountain, by themselves. And he was transfigured before them, and his face shone like the sun, and his clothes became dazzling white.

Suddenly there appeared to them Moses and Elijah, talking with him" (Matt. 17.1–3).

66. Sokolow, "Bible and Religious Education," 46.

67. See Vermes, "Bible and Midrash," 80–82.

68. The *tana'im* (lit., "teachers") were teachers of the Oral Tradition active in the first and second centuries.

69. See 53 above.

70. For example, the seven *middot* attributed to Hillel (second half of the first century BCE to early first century CE), or the thirteen attributed to Rabbi Ismael (first half of the second century), which were essentially an enlarged version of the former. The thirteen *middot* of Rabbi Ismael were integrated into the liturgy of the synagogue morning service.

71. Babylonian Talmud, Yevamot 11b and 24a, Shabbat 63a.

72. Funkenstein, *Styles of Medieval Biblical Exegesis*, 21–22.

73. Around the age of fifty, Abraham Ibn Ezra left his Spanish homeland to lead an errant life in Italy, France, and England. A close friend of the secular and religious poet Judah Halevi, he produced a varied and abundant oeuvre in Hebrew and was a key link in the transmission of the Judeo-Arab cultural heritage to Jewish communities in Christian lands. His philosophy, which drew on Neoplatonism and was heavily influenced by Salomon Ibn Gabirol, is expressed above all in his commentaries. Indeed, after Rashi, he made his mark on posterity mainly as a biblical exegete of exceptional rigor and fecundity. His commentaries are difficult to interpret because of their dense, often enigmatic style, but they were widely read, quoted, and imitated, and themselves became the object of numerous secondary commentaries. His method, in particular, established a new landmark, while his independence of mind earned him many attacks—but also the esteem of a Spinoza.

74. *Asmakhta*: that is, use of the scriptural text to "support" a teaching of the Oral Law. On this notion, see *Encyclopaedia Judaica*, 2nd ed. (Detroit: Macmillan, 2007), 3: 590, and *Talmudic Encyclopedia* [in Hebrew] (Jerusalem, 1973–84), 2: 105–8.

75. On these complex issues, see, e.g., Attias, *Commentaire biblique*, 56–65.

76. Cohen, "*Be Fertile and Increase*," 190.

77. Raphael Jospe, "Biblical Exegesis as a Philosophic Literary Genre: Abraham Ibn Ezra and Moses Mendelssohn," in Emil L. Fackenheim and Jospe, eds., *Jewish Philosophy and the Academy* (Madison, WI: Fairleigh Dickinson University Press; London: Associated University Presses, 1996), 64–66.

78. Irene Lancaster, *Deconstructing the Bible: Abraham Ibn Ezra's Introduction to the Torah* (London: Routledge-Curzon, 2003), 172, 175.

79. This long and rich history cannot be even outlined here, so I would refer the reader to the brief survey in Jean-Christophe Attias, "Exégèse. Une reconquête toujours inachevée du sens," in Attias and Esther Benbassa, *Dictionnaire des mondes juifs* (Paris: Larousse, 2008), 245–52, and to its complementary bibliogra-

phy of works in French and English (ibid., 617). See also Maurice-Ruben Hayoun, *L'Exégèse juive. Exégèse et philosophie dans le judaïsme* (Paris: Presses universitaires de France, 2000).

80. Dorival, "Exégèse," in Goulet-Cazé et al., eds., *Commentaire*, 169–81.

81. "After the literal interpretation," Philo wrote, "one should go on to examine the figurative sense, because all texts, or nearly all, in the expression of the Law have an allegorical value." Quoted in Roger Arnaldez, "La Bible de Philon d'Alexandrie," in Claude Mondésert, ed., *Le Monde grec ancien et la Bible* (Paris: Beauchesne, 1984), 40.

82. Although Philo drew out the spiritual and philosophical meanings of the Law, he always stressed that "it is necessary to observe its material provisions to the letter, not to conjure them away behind the allegorical interpretation" (ibid., 41).

83. There were exceptions like Song of Songs, which, for reasons given above, 9, could only support a strictly allegorical exegesis.

84. Millet and de Robert, *Culture biblique*, 240–41.

85. See also Dahan, "Commentaire médiéval de la Bible," 221.

86. On this point, see Dahan, *Exégèse chrétienne de la Bible*, 375–76.

87. Millet and Robert, *Culture biblique*, 244–46.

88. In Hebrew, *sekhel*.

89. In Hebrew, *sod*.

90. Thus, Creation prefigures the history of the world and ancestral actions not only foretell but predetermine the course of world history. This Christian tone of Nahmanides's typological exegesis doubtless explains why it had a limited posterity among the Jews. See Funkenstein, *Styles of Medieval Hebrew Exegesis*, 56–62.

91. See esp. Halbertal, *People of the Book*, 32–37.

92. Prov. 25.11; see Maimonides, "Introduction," in *Guide of the Perplexed*, 1: 11.

93. *Wisdom of the Zohar*, 3: 1083–85, and Elliot R. Wolfson, "The Bible in the Jewish Mystical Tradition," in Berlin et al., eds., *Jewish Study Bible*, 1983.

94. Michael Fishbane, "The Book of Zohar and Exegetical Spirituality," in id., *Exegetical Imagination*, 105–7.

95. Quoted in Dahan, *Exégèse chrétienne de la Bible*, 362.

96. The expression "The Torah has seventy faces [*Shiv'im panim la-Torah*]" occurs regularly in the writings of medieval exegetes.

97. Millet and de Robert, *Culture biblique*, 244.

98. Besides, strictly speaking, *pshat* simply does not exist "in itself."

99. Erwin I. J. Rosenthal, "The Study of the Bible in Medieval Judaism," in *The Cambridge History of the Bible*, vol. 2: *The West from the Fathers to the Reformation* (Cambridge: Cambridge University Press, 1969), 254–55, 268.

100. Ibn Ezra's opponents are explicitly referred to as Christian ("uncircumcised scholars") only in the introduction to his second commentary on the Pentateuch: Abraham Ibn Ezra, *Commentaries on the Pentateuch* [in Hebrew], ed. Asher Weiser (Jerusalem: Mossad Harav Kook, 1977), 1: 137.

101. Ibid., 6 ("Introduction"). Cf. Lancaster, *Deconstructing the Bible*, 158–62.

102. See Colette Sirat, *La philosophie juive au Moyen Âge selon les textes manuscrits et imprimés* (Paris: CNRS Éditions, 1983), 315–16.

103. Dahan, "Commentaire médiéval de la Bible," 214.

104. I am here borrowing phrases from Spinoza's *Theologico-Political Treatise*, trans. R. H. M. Elwes (New York: Dover, 1951), 17 [1.14] and 140 [9.13], where the author, following on directly from a typically medieval tradition, makes free use of an acerbic, sarcastic rhetoric.

105. To be more precise, it applies to male, adult, free Jews—which simultaneously excludes Gentiles, Jewish women, and slaves.

106. See Cohen, *"Be Fertile and Increase,"* passim.

107. Marcel Simon, *Verus Israel: A Study of the Relations between Christians and Jews in the Roman Empire (AD 135–425)* (New York: Littman Library, 1986), 213.

108. For Abraham Ibn Ezra, while the Bible is not in contradiction with science, it is not itself a book of science but is content, at that level, to provide the minimum necessary information for its very different purpose: to define the place and role of man in the world in which he lives (Funkenstein, *Styles of Medieval Hebrew Exegesis*, 43).

109. Hillel II, for example, in the mid-fourth century, stated that "there is no messiah for Israel, because it was already granted him in the age of Hezekiah"—which implies that all the messianic promises were fulfilled in a remote past (early seventh century BCE), that they were therefore not fulfilled in Jesus's time, and that they did not concern the future. For Rashi, the suffering servant in the Book of Isaiah is definitely not Jesus, or even the foretold messiah, but rather a collective entity, Israel; he sometimes presents its suffering as punishment for its sins in Exile, sometimes—in an ultimately very Christian sense—as atonement for the sins of the nations (see Funkenstein, *Styles of Medieval Hebrew Exegesis*, 25–27).

110. Jospe, "Biblical Exegesis," 62–63.

111. Mordekhai Komtino, *Commentary on the Pentateuch*, Hebrew ms. 265 of the Bibliothèque nationale de France, fol. 1 v°, quoted in Attias, *Commentaire biblique*, 137.

112. See Jean-Christophe Attias, "Pour une histoire de la culture rabbinique," in Attias, *Penser le judaïsme*, 31–34.

113. On all these questions, see Jean-Christophe Attias, "'Un livre sans introduction est comme un corps sans âme.' De l'introduction comme genre littéraire dans la production exégétique du judaïsme medieval," in Attias, *Penser le judaïsme*, 121–45.

114. As Greenberg points out in "Reflections on Interpretation," 364.

115. This is almost word for word what Ibn Ezra declares at the end of the introduction to his *Commentary on the Pentateuch* (1: 10).

116. For further details and more precise references, see Attias, *Commentaire biblique*, 93.

117. Ibn Ezra was "a man of enlightened intelligence, and no small learning," Spinoza writes (*Theologico-Political Treatise*, 121 [8.3]).

118. The earliest version of the Mikra'ot Gedolot was printed in Venice in 1516–17 by Daniel Bomberg, a Christian. A second, improved edition appeared in 1524–25.

119. The so-called Rashi script is actually a semicursive Sephardi system employed for the first time in 1485 for the printing of Rashi's glosses; it is still used today in religious works to differentiate commentaries from their object text (Bible or Talmud*), which for its part is printed in square characters.

120. On the "poverty" of the seventeenth-century rabbinical Bibles, see Moshe Goshen-Gottstein, "Bible et judaïsme," in Jean-Robert Armogathe, ed., *Le Grand Siècle et la Bible* (Paris: Beauchesne, 1989), 38.

121. Acronym for Samuel ben Meir (*Rabbi Shmuel Ben Me'ir*), biblical commentator and Tosafist, grandson of Rashi (1085–1158).

122. Acronym for Abraham Ibn Ezra (*Rabbi Avraham Ben 'Ezra*).

123. Acronym for David Kimhi (*Rabbi David Kimhi*), biblical exegete, grammarian, preacher, and teacher; member of a family of scholars of Spanish origin active in Provence in the twelfth century; he defended the philosophical work of Maimonides during the controversy of 1230–33.

124. Acronym for Moses Nahmanides (*Rabbi Moshe Ben Nahman*).

125. Yosef Hayim Yerushalmi, *Zakhor: Jewish History and Jewish Memory* (New York: Schocken Books, 1989).

126. As James L. Kugel rightly points out (*Bible As It Was*, 255), the basic unit for the ancient biblical exegete was the verse or an expression or word in a verse; he did not deal in larger units (pericopes or chapters) at one go. We should therefore not be misled by the appearance of the midrashic collections that have come down to us; far from being continuous commentaries, they are actually nothing but anthologies.

127. I borrow the phrase "immense ocean" from Emmanuel Lévinas, partly deviating from his intended sense: "the vessel of Scripture, afloat in the immense ocean of rabbinical dialectic" (Lévinas, "The Strings and the Wood: On the Jewish Reading of the Bible," in id., *Outside the Subject*, 130).

128. Significantly, the *Toldot Aharon* by the Italian Aaron of Pesaro (d. 1563), which lists the biblical passages quoted in the Babylonian Talmud, is incorporated in abridged form in the *Mikra'ot Gedolot*.

129. Lévinas, "Strings and the Wood," in id., *Outside the Subject*, 130.

Chapter Five: The Bible of the Moderns

1. This pre-Zionist movement originated in late nineteenth-century eastern Europe in the wake of the pogroms following the assassination of Tsar Alexander II, and took institutional form between 1884 and 1889. Its aim was the rebirth of Jewish national life in Palestine, in pursuit of which it helped to set up some twenty settlements in the Holy Land. These would be saved from bankruptcy only through the support of Baron Edmond de Rothschild.

2. A point made in Dahan, *Exégèse chrétienne de la Bible*, 161.

3. See ibid., chap. 4, "La critique textuelle."

4. See 23–25 above.

5. On *pshat*, see 109–14 above.

6. Judah of Regensburg (twelfth–thirteenth centuries) went so far as to attribute a passage from the Torah to the post-Exile period: see Nahum M. Sarna, "The Modern Study of the Bible in the Framework of Jewish Studies," in *Proceedings of the Eighth World Congress of Jewish Studies, Panel Sessions, Bible Studies and Hebrew Language* (Jerusalem: World Union of Jewish Studies and Perry Foundation for Biblical Research, 1983), 24.

7. See Spinoza, *Theologico-Political Treatise*, 121 [8.3].

8. On these complex questions, see inter alia Jospe, "Biblical Exegesis," in Fackenheim and Jospe, eds., *Jewish Philosophy*, 53–63.

9. See Jon D. Levenson, "Response," in Shaye J. D. Cohen and Edward L. Greenstein, eds., *The State of Jewish Studies* (Detroit: Wayne State University Press, 1990), 48–49.

10. See Greenberg, "Reflections on Interpretation," 231–32.

11. This is the position argued by James Kugel in "The Bible in the University," in William Henry Propp, Baruch Halpern, and David Noel Freedman, eds., *The Hebrew Bible and Its Interpreters* (Winona Lake, IN: Eisenbrauns, 1990), 43–165.

12. Kugel, *Bible As It Was*, 553–54.

13. Edward L. Greenstein, "Biblical Studies in a State," in Cohen and Greenstein, eds., *State of Jewish Studies*, 28.

14. Monolatry or monolatrism does not deny the existence of other gods, but insists that only the exclusive worship of one god (e.g., a local or national god) is legitimate for the community of believers.

15. Henotheism is a form of polytheism that recognizes the dominant role of one god among others.

16. See 22 above.

17. Kugel, "Bible in the University," 161.

18. The principle formulated by Benjamin Jowett in *On the Interpretation of Scripture* (1860), quoted here from Levenson, "Response," 49.

19. Greenberg, "Reflections on Interpretation," 232.

20. De Pury and Römer, "Pentateuque en question," 20.

21. See 19 above.

22. De Pury and Römer, "Pentateuque en question," 23–28.

23. Spinoza, *Theologico-Political Treatise*, 121 [8.3].

24. Ibid., 135 [9.5].

25. Ibid., 132 [8.12].

26. Funkenstein, *Styles of Medieval Biblical Exegesis*, 74.

27. Ibid., 77.

28. Spinoza, *Theologico-Political Treatise*, 101 [7.5].

29. Ibid., 99 [7.2].

30. Ibid., 118 [7. 22].

31. Ibid., 98 [7.1].

32. Ibid., 139 [9.11].

33. Ibid., 107 [7.9].

34. Ibid., 91 [6.15].

35. Ibid., 39 [2.15].

36. Ibid., 47 [3.6] and 48 [3.8].

37. Ibid., 165 [12.2].

38. Ibid., 79 [5.19].

39. Acronym for *Meir Loeb ben Yehiel Mikhael* Weisser.

40. Naftali Tsvi Yehuda Berlin is also known as Ha-Netsiv (from the initials of his name).

41. Jonathan Magonet, "How Do Jews Interpret the Bible Today?" *Journal for the Study of the Old Testament* 66 (June 1995): 7–9.

42. See 142–43 above.

43. See inter alia "La religion comme science. La *Wissenschaft des Judentums,*" special issue of *Pardès*, 19–20 (1994), and—on the French equivalent of this movement—Perrine Simon-Nahum, *La Cité investie. La "science du judaïsme" français et la République* (Paris: Cerf, 1991).

44. Sokolow, "Bible and Religious Education," 48–49.

45. As a biblicist, Graetz remained highly traditional in his approach to the Pentateuch, but distinctly less so with regard to the books of the Prophets and the Hagiographa.

46. Born in Slovakia, educated in Hungarian yeshivot* and the universities of Vienna, Berlin, and Tübingen, David Tsvi Hoffmann became the rector of the Berlin rabbinical seminary in 1889 and was recognized as a major halakhic* authority by German Orthodox Judaism. Though a Zionist, he was a member of the executive of Agudat Israel. In his commentaries on Leviticus and Deuteronomy, he directly opposed the documentary theory and aimed to base himself on rabbinical tradition to understand these books.

47. Following studies at the rabbinical seminary and the University of Breslau, Benno Jacob was rabbi in Göttingen and Dortmund. In 1929, he settled in Hamburg, then moved to Britain in 1939. He worked to refute modern biblical criticism and denounced the anti-Semitism that, in his view, drove advocates of "higher criticism" of the Bible.

48. Umberto Cassuto was a rabbi and academic, active first in Italy and after 1939 at the Hebrew University of Jerusalem. Opposing the documentary theory, Cassuto argued that an ancient oral tradition and ancient epic poetry were eventually integrated into single texts. He was also one of the first scholars to weigh the importance of the archeological discoveries made at Ugarit.

49. Born in the Podolia region of Ukraine, Yehezkel Kaufmann received a doctorate from the University of Berne and settled in Palestine in 1928. In 1948, Kaufmann was appointed Bible professor at the Hebrew University of Jerusalem, where he remained until his death.

50. On these questions, see David Banon, "Kritik und Tradition. Jüdische und christliche Lektüre der Bibel," *Judaica* 52, 1 (March 1996): 23–39.

51. Lévinas, "Strings and the Wood," in id., *Outside the Subject*, 130.

52. S[olomon] Schechter, "Higher Criticism—Higher Antisemitism," in *Seminary Addresses and Other Papers* (Cincinnati: Ark, 1915), 35–39.

53. Céline Trautmann-Waller, *Philologie allemande et tradition juive. Le parcours intellectuel de Leopold Zunz* (Paris: Cerf, 1998), 143. On the question of comparativism, see Jean-Christophe Attias, "Comparatisme et religions du Livre: La voie étroite," in Mohammad-Ali Amir-Moezzi, Jean-Daniel Dubois, Christelle Jullien, and Florence Jullien, eds., *Pensée grecque et sagesse d'Orient. Hommage à Michel Tardieu* (Turnhout: Brepols, 2009), 77–87.

54. David S. Sperling, "Modern Jewish Interpretation," in Berlin et al., eds., *Jewish Study Bible*, 1909.

55. Edward Breuer, "Post-medieval Jewish Interpretation," in Berlin et al., eds., *Jewish Study Bible*, 1904.

56. Greenstein, "Biblical Studies in a State," 37.

57. These are some of the reproaches that James Kugel levels against Protestant biblical studies: see Jon D. Levenson, "Theological Consensus or Historicist Evasion? Jews and Christians in Biblical Studies," in Roger Brooks and John J. Collins, eds., *Hebrew Bible or Old Testament? Studying the Bible in Judaism and Christianity* (Notre Dame, IN: University of Notre Dame Press, 1990), 112–15.

58. See 141–49 above.

59. Greenstein, "Biblical Studies in a State,"37. The writings of James Kugel, in particular, testify to this reintegration of the field into "Jewish studies."

60. Marc Zvi Brettler, "A Bible Commentary for Israel (Review of Zakovitch, Ruth)," *Prooftexts* 13 (1993): 175–81; here 177. Robert Alter is one of the main representatives of this tendency.

61. Magonet, "How Do Jews Interpret the Bible Today?" 16–17.

62. One of the best expressions of this postcritical stance is the way in which Franz Rosenzweig in 1927 described a literary enterprise if ever there was one: the German translation of the Bible that he began with Martin Buber: "We two translate the Torah in one piece—as the book of books. We both consider it the work of one mind. We do not know who he was; that it was Moses we cannot believe. Among ourselves we identify him by the siglum used by critical scholarship for its assumed final Redactor: R. But we fill out this R not as redactor but as *rabbenu* [our teacher]. For, whoever he may be, and whatever may be the provenance and composition of the text, he is Our Teacher, and his theology is our teaching" (quoted in Banon, "Kritik und Tradition," 35).

63. See 69 above.

64. On Auerbach's importance in the revaluation of a literary approach to the biblical texts "as they actually exist," see Alter and Kermode, *Literary Guide to the Bible* (1990), 4.

65. Erich Auerbach, *Mimesis: The Representation of Reality in Western Literature* (1946; Princeton, NJ: Princeton University Press, 1968), 17.

66. Ibid., 12.

67. Ibid., 15.

68. Ibid., 14.

69. Ibid., 20.

70. Elias Canetti, *The Human Province* (New York: Seabury Press, 1978), 51.

71. For a slightly different reading of the same text of Canetti's, see Jean-Christophe Attias, "Dieu, le Juif et le poète," the conclusion to Attias and Pierre Gisel, eds., *De la Bible à la littérature* (Geneva: Labor et Fides, 2003), 319.

72. On Mendelssohn, see Dominique Bourel, *Moses Mendelssohn. La naissance du judaïsme moderne* (Paris: Gallimard, 2004), and David Sorkin, *Moses Mendelssohn and the Religious Enlightenment* (Berkeley: University of California Press, 1996).

73. Werner Weinberg, "Les traductions et commentaires de Mendelssohn," in Belaval and Bourel, eds., *Siècle des Lumières et la Bible*, 608.

74. The project was continued after Mendelssohn's death by his colleagues and successors, and the Pentateuch appeared in 1783.

75. See Jean Baumgarten, "Deux bibles en yiddish éditées à Amsterdam (1676 et 1679)," in Armogathe, ed., *Le Grand Siècle et la Bible*, 297–313.

76. One thinks, of course, of the famous "Ferrara Bible" (1553) published in Latin script.

77. On these first translations and commentaries in Yiddish, see 99–100 above.

78. Weinberg, "Traductions et commentaires de Mendelssohn," 601.

79. August von Hennings (1746–1826) was a politician, publicist, and writer of Danish German extraction.

80. Weinberg, "Traductions et commentaires de Mendelssohn," 599. Emphasis added.

81. Martin Buber finally completed the translation in 1961. See esp. Maren Ruth Niehoff, "The Buber-Rosenzweig Translation of the Bible within Jewish-German Tradition," *Journal of Jewish Studies* 44 (1993): 258–79. On Buber and Rosenzweig's resolutely "postcritical" stance, see n. 62 above.

82. Berr Isaac Berr translated the work on educational reform of the German *maskil** Naphtali Herz Wessely (1725–1805), which appeared in Paris in 1790 under the title *Instructions salutaires adressées aux communautés juives de l'Empire de Joseph II*.

83. Quoted in Perrine Simon-Nahum, "Samuel Cahen entre Lumières et science du judaïsme," *Romantisme* 3, 125 (2004): 40.

84. On this Hebrew scholar, who founded the review *Les Archives israélites* in 1840, see Simon-Nahum, "Samuel Cahen."

85. Ibid., 40.

86. Cahen's translation was also severely criticized by Lazare Wogue (1817–97), professor at the Jewish Seminary, who himself published a translation of the Pentateuch, as well as a *Histoire de la Bible et de l'exégèse biblique jusqu'à nos jours* (1881).

87. Danielle Delmaire, "Les traductions de la Bible au XIXe siècle et la Bible du rabbinat," in Jean-Claude Kuperminc and Jean-Philippe Chaumont, eds., *Zadoc Kahn. Un grand rabbin entre culture juive, affaire Dreyfus et laïcité* (Paris: L'Éclat, 2007), 92.

88. See Kuperminc and Chaumont, eds., *Zadoc Kahn*t.

89. Delmaire, "Traductions de la Bible," 101–2.

90. See 93–101 above.

91. "It is unquestionably superior to its predecessors by virtue of its rigorous closeness to the text, the solidity of its language, and the *charming quality* of its style," the *Revue des études juives* 38 (1899): 140–41 stressed in its review of the translation (emphasis added).

92. Simon-Nahum, "Samuel Cahen," 41.

93. The biblical translations into Yiddish by Menahem Mendel Lefin of Satanov (1749–1826), a *maskil* who knew Mendelssohn and the Be'urists, testify to the same evolution. They transmute the Holy Scriptures into poetic text, making them a locus of research on language, literature, and aesthetics that clearly takes precedence over religion. See Baumgarten, "Une traduction de la Bible en yiddish," in Belaval and Bourel, eds., *Siècle des Lumières et la Bible*, 237–52.

94. The first two pages of Lazare Wogue's preface to his French translation of the Pentateuch (1860) summarize things rather well. The Bible is a book "enjoying universal respect," the "doyen of all literatures," but it is also, "for the Israelite race in particular," "the first of all treasures." Without it, "no synagogue, no church, and therefore no civilization" (*Le Pentateuque, ou les Cinq Livres de Moïse*, reprinted with a new preface by René Gutman and a biography of the author by Philippe Touitou [Jerusalem: Ohr Hamaarav Publishers, 2007], 1: v–vi).

95. Halbertal, *People of the Book*, 131.

96. Perrine Simon-Nahum, "Continuité ou rupture? Des précurseurs aux fondateurs de l'Union libérale israélite," *Archives juives* 2, 40 (2007): 25.

97. Darmesteter, *Prophètes d'Israël*, 244–45.

98. Simon-Nahum, "Continuité ou rupture?" 33.

99. Aron Rodrigue, "Rearticulations of French Jewish Identities after the Dreyfus Affair," *Jewish Social Studies*, n.s., 2, 3 (Spring–Summer 1996): 12.

100. See Jean-Christophe Attias and Esther Benbassa, *Israel, the Impossible Land* (Stanford: Stanford University Press, 2003), 134–37.

101. Bezalel was the name of the artisan who, in the biblical story, had the task of building the desert tabernacle.

102. Dalia Manor, "Biblical Zionism in Bezalel Art," *Israel Studies* 6, 1 (Spring 2001): 67.

103. On this point, see Ismar Schorsch, "The Myth of Sephardic Supremacy," *Leo Baeck Institute Yearbook* 34 (1989): 47–66; and Shmuel Feiner, "*Sefarad* dans les représentations historiques de la *Haskalah*. Entre modernisme et conservatisme," in Esther Benbassa, ed., *Mémoires juives d'Espagne et du Portugal* (Paris: Publisud, 1996), 239–59.

104. In fact, the *maskilim* did not hesitate to support reforms by the Austrian or Russian government that seemed likely to advance their cause.

105. Manor, "Biblical Zionism in Bezalel Art," 57.

106. *Archives israélites* 19 (1858): 287–88.

107. See Eliezer Ben Yehuda, *A Dream Come True*, trans. from the Hebrew by T. Muraoka (Boulder, CO: Westview Press, 1993).

108. On the nature and roots of this illusory proximity to the Bible, see, e.g., Yair Zakovitz, "A Secular-Humanist View," *Jewish Bible Quarterly* 21, 4 (1993): 218–21. According to Zakovitz, Israelis would precisely have to recognize the unfamiliarity of the Bible in order to have a chance of understanding it; the Bible is a religious text, and most Israelis are not religious; much of what the Bible speaks about has no direct relationship to their lives, and its language is not fundamentally their language. See also Chaim Rabin, "Bible Study and Hebrew Language Research" [in Hebrew], *Ha-Universita* 14, 1 (May 1968): 13–16.

109. See, e.g., David Ben-Gurion, *Ben-Gurion Looks at the Bible* (London: W.H. Allen, 1972), 53–54.

110. Quoted in [and translated from] R. J. Zwi Werblowsky, "Israël et Eretz Israel," *Les Temps modernes* 253 bis (1967): 372.

111. Attias and Benbassa, *Israel, the Impossible Land*, 25–26.

112. Anita Shapira, "The Bible and Israeli Identity," *AJS Review* 28, 1 (2004): 19.

113. Simon, "Status of the Bible" [in Hebrew], 14.

114. Through the identification of the nomadic biblical Patriarchs with contemporary bedouin.

115. According to S. D. Goiten, cited in Simon, "Status of the Bible in Israeli Society," 40.

116. Manor, "Biblical Zionism in Bezalel Art," 61–62. In fact, this Zionist-biblical tendency had only qualified success. It did not persuade artists or audiences other than those close to the Bezalel school, which therefore remained rather an exception in this respect. The new artists who arrived in Palestine in the 1920s did not recognize themselves in this political-aesthetic ideal and rejected the Bible as a thematic source (ibid., 69).

117. Simon, "Status of the Bible in Israeli Society," 13–14.

118. Hayyim M. Y. Gevariahu, "Recollections of the Bible Circle That Met at David Ben-Gurion's," in Mordekhai Kogan, ed., *Ben-Gurion and the Bible: A People and Its Land* [in Hebrew] (Beer-Sheva: Ben-Gurion University of the Negev Press, 1989), 70–74. Ben-Gurion took this reading of the Bible even farther: he limited the historical scope of the Book of Joshua's tales of conquest and claimed that an overwhelming majority of the people of Israel actually remained in the Land of Canaan, only the family of Jacob emigrating to Egypt (Binyamin Oppenheimer, "Ben-Gourion and the Bible" [in Hebrew], ibid., 54–69).

119. Born into a Hassidic family in Ukraine, Asher Zvi Ginsberg initially received a traditional education, but was attracted early on by the Haskalah*. He urged a renewal of secular Hebrew Jewish culture prior to emigration to Palestine

and the creation of a political entity there, since the country was destined to become a spiritual beacon for the whole of the Jewish world. He himself emigrated to Palestine in 1922. He was one of the rare Zionists of the time to be aware of such a thing as the Arab question.

120. Shapira, "Bible and Israeli Identity," 17 and 31.

121. Yaacov Shavit and Mordechai Eran, *The Hebrew Bible Reborn: From Holy Scripture to the Book of Books* (Berlin: Walter de Gruyter, 2007), 42–43; Uriel Simon, "Status of the Bible in Israeli Society," 13.

122. These are the last two lines of the poem "In Endor" (1893) by Saul Tchernichovsky (1875–1943); Harry H. Fein's English version is in *A Harvest of Hebrew Verse* (Boston: Bruce Humphries, 1934), 115. See 1 Sam. 23. On the role of King Saul in the Zionist ethos, see Anita Shapira, *Land and Power: The Zionist Resort to Force, 1881–1948* (1992; repr., Stanford, CA: Stanford University Press, 1999), 23, 31, 337.

123. The "Canaanite" group of young writers, students, and journalists, active from 1942 on, expressed radical views on a new Hebrew identity. As they saw it, this was shared with all the inhabitants of the Middle East by virtue of their common past and local roots; it differed fundamentally from Jewish identity, which they held to be essentially religious and unconnected to the land and its history.

124. Alan T. Levenson, *The Making of the Modern Jewish Bible: How Scholars in Germany, Israel, and America Transformed an Ancient Text* (Lanham, MD: Rowman & Littlefield, 2011), 131.

125. Ruth Kark, "Historical Sites—Perceptions and Land Purchase: The Case of Modin, 1882–1931," *Studies in Zionism* 9, 1 (1988): 1–17.

126. Mireille Hadas-Lebel, *Massada. Histoire et symbole* (Paris: Albin Michel, 1995).

127. Attias and Benbassa, *Israel, the Impossible Land*, 177. The last armed uprising against Roman occupation, in 132, was led by Simon Bar Kosiva, also known in various sources as Bar Kokhba ("Son of the Star") or Bar Koziva ("Son of the Lie"). The war was fought in southern Judea and crushed by Julius Severus in 135.

128. On the Codex of Aleppo, see 28–30 above.

129. On the biblocentrism of the Gush Emunim, see inter alia Gideon Aran, "Return to the Scripture in Modern Israel," in Évelyne Patlagean and Alain Le Boulluec, eds., *Les retours aux Écritures. Fondamentalismes présents et passés* (Louvain: Peeters, 1993), 101–31.

130. Moshe Greenberg, "To Whom and for What Should a Bible Commentator Be Responsible?" in id., *Studies in the Bible and Jewish Thought*, 231.

131. Simon, "Status of the Bible in Israeli Society," 32.

132. Emphasis added, of course.

133. On post-Zionism, see inter alia Attias and Benbassa, *Israel, the Impossible Land*, 212–23.

134. Simon, "Status of the Bible in Israeli Society," 24. I use "galutic" to translate the Hebrew *galuti*—which has negative connotations in Zionist rhetoric—rather than the overly neutral "exilic."

135. Shapira, "Bible and Israeli Identity," 41.

136. See Esther Benbassa, *Suffering as Identity: The Jewish Paradigm* (London: Verso, 2010), 129–37.

137. In Hebrew, "Tanakh. Ein mimtza'im ba-shetah." An English translation, from which this quotation is adapted, is available at http://mideastfacts.org/facts/?option=com_content&task=view&id=32&Itemid=34.

138. The term "Book of the Site" is from Zali Gurevitch and Gideon Aran, "On the Site (Israeli Anthropology)" [in Hebrew], *Alpayim* 4 (1991): 14.

139. Attias and Benbassa, *Israel, the Impossible Land*, 4.

140. See Shlomo Sand, *The Invention of the Jewish People* (London: Verso, 2009), and the numerous debates to which it gave rise. See also the contributions by Esther Benbassa, Denis Charbit, Maurice-Ruben Hayoun, Tony Judt, and Maurice Sartre, and the response by Shlomo Sand, in *Le Débat* 158 (January–February 2010): 147–92.

141. See 135–36 above.

142. Orly Castel-Bloom, *Halakim enoshiyim* (Tel Aviv: Kineret, 2002), trans. Dalya Bilu as *Human Parts* (Boston: David R. Godine, 2003), 125–26.

143. In fact, Kati decides to become a makeup artist and to brighten her life with stars and studio lights. She finds the address of a special school in the Yellow Pages, but does not quite know how she will be able to pay for training. But she goes there. I have already commented on this passage from the novel, though in a markedly different way, in "Le judaïsme: Une religion du Livre?" in Attias, *Penser le judaïsme*, 44–59.

144. Greenstein, "Biblical Studies in a State,"37. In French, the reader may usefully consult "Quand les femmes lisent la Bible," ed. Janine Elkouby and Sonia Sarah Lipsyc, *Pardès* 43 (2007).

145. See, e.g., Ilana Pardes, *Countertraditions in the Bible: A Feminist Approach* (1992; repr., Cambridge, MA: Harvard University Press, 1993).

146. Tannenbaum, "Jewish Texts, Education and Identity," 8.

147. Simon, "Status of the Bible in Israeli Society," 33.

148. This has been pointed out a number of times in this work.

149. When ordered by God, Abraham did not hesitate for a moment to sacrifice his only "son, [his] favored one, Isaac" (Gen. 22.2). Only man's firstborn, who belongs to God, escapes the sacrifice that God is entitled to demand: he will have to be redeemed by his father (Num. 18.15–18).

Epilogue

1. Yosef Hayim Yerushalmi, *Freud's Moses: Judaism Terminable and Interminable* (New Haven, CT: Yale University Press, 1991), 71.

2. Ludwig Philippsohn (1811–1889), founder of the *Allgemeine Zeitung des Judenthums*, tried to steer a middle course between Reform Judaism and Orthodox Judaism. His Bible—which was republished several times, including in an illustrated edition—presents the original Hebrew text together with a translation

and commentaries in German. Its tenor is rather conservative: it never doubts the integrity of the Massoretic text, rejects the insights of "higher criticism," and roundly asserts its loyalty to the postbiblical Jewish tradition.

3. See the Hebrew text, together with a translation and a list of the biblical and rabbinical sources, in Yerushalmi, *Freud's Moses*, 104–6.

4. Freud's father himself drew this analogy when he pointed out in his inscription that, between his two gifts, the Book "has been stored like the fragments of the Tablets in an ark with me" (ibid., 105).

5. Sigmund Freud, *Moses and Monotheism* (New York: Knopf, 1939), 17.

6. Ibid., 131.

7. Yerushalmi, *Freud's Moses*, 124.

8. Freud, *Moses and Monotheism*, 36. "Some fragments of sound tradition," Freud writes, "which had found no place in the Pentateuch may lie scattered in that material" (ibid.). But see, farther on, an interesting discussion of the relations between written and oral tradition. Here is a short sample: ". . . a difference began to develop between the written version and the oral report—that is, the tradition—of the same subject-matter. That which has been deleted or altered in the written version might quite well have been preserved uninjured in the tradition. Tradition was the complement and at the same time the contradiction of the written history" (ibid., 85).

9. Martin Buber, "The Man of Today and the Jewish Bible," in id., *On the Bible: Eighteen Studies*, ed. Nahum N. Glatzer (Syracuse, NY: Syracuse University Press, 2000), 1–2.

10. Emil L. Fackenheim, *The Jewish Bible after the Holocaust: A Re-reading* (Manchester: Manchester University Press, 1990), 26.

11. On all these questions, see Esther Benbassa, *Suffering as Identity*, 93–106.

12. A chronicler of the events, quoted in [and translated from] Joseph R. Hacker, "Superbe et désespoir. L'existence sociale et spirituelle des Juifs ibériques dans l'Empire ottoman," *Revue historique* 578 (April–June 1991): 262.

13. Anonymous elegy for the Ninth of Av, ibid., 263.

14. See 9 above.

15. See Deut. 28.15–68.

16. Deut. 28.63.

17. George Steiner, "A Preface to the Hebrew Bible," in id., *No Passion Spent: Essays 1978–1995* (New Haven, CT: Yale University Press, 1996), 78.

18. For Israeli literature too, the Bible features as "the father of all texts." To emancipate oneself from it is always a difficult, unequal combat—perhaps already lost in advance. See Nehama Aschkenasy, "Introduction: Recreating the Canon," *AJS Review* 28, 1 (2004): 3–10.

19. See 71 above.

20. Midrash Mishlei, Salomon Buber ed. (Vilna [Vilnius], 1893), 1.8.

21. Literally "[divine] Presence." Not found in the body of Scripture, the term designates in classical rabbinical literature God as He is immanent in this world.

Medieval Judaism tended to separate God from His *Shekhinah*. For some philosophers, such as Saadia Gaon and Maimonides, the *Shekhinah* is a *created* light identical with the "glory" of God (*kavod*): it, not God, appears to the prophet. In the Kabbalah*, it is identified with *Malkhut* (royalty), the tenth and last of the *sefirot*, those emanations and first manifestations of the divine (in relation to the created world) that are contrasted with *Ein-Sof*, the "Infinite" or "Boundless," which is the hidden, unknowable, and absolutely transcendent God. *Malkhut* is the female principle and the closest hypostasis to the created world; for this reason it is the main target for the forces of Evil. But adherence to the Torah, observance of the commandments, and prayer can bring redemptive action to bear on it and help to restore the union of the male and female principles in God.

22. See, e.g., Lamentations Rabba, Petihta 25.

23. See Attias and Benbassa, *Israel, the Impossible Land*, 39, and Moshe Weinfeld, "Inherit the Earth—Right and Duty: The Idea of the Promise in the Sources of the First and Second Temple Period" [in Hebrew] *Zion* 49, 2 (1984): 115–37.

24. Aviezer Ravitzky, "Peace: Historical Versus Utopian Models in Jewish Thought," in Aviezer Ravitzky, *History and Faith: Studies in Jewish Philosophy* (Amsterdam: J. C. Gieben, 1996), 31.

25. See what Rabbi Kahana says in Babylonian Talmud, Shabbat 63a: "Does that not refer to the words of the Torah?"

26. This is the complete translation of Rashi's commentary: "*Gird your sword upon your thigh*: to fight the Torah's fight, and that is your splendor and glory." The psalm continues (verse 5): "ride on in the cause of truth and meekness and right."

27. This is the complete translation of Rashi's commentary: "*He who finds a wife has found happiness*. He who finds the Torah. But also, in the primary sense: [He who finds] a suitable wife." Compare Midrash Mishlei on Prov. 31.10, which identifies with the Torah the "capable wife" who gives happiness to the man who finds her.

28. Babylonian Talmud, Menahot 29b.

29. See 85 above.

30. See, e.g., Cohen, *"Be Fertile and Increase,"* 214, and *Wisdom of the Zohar*, 3: 1103.

Glossary

Aggadah, the (fem. n., pl. **aggadot**; adj. **aggadic**): "tale" in Hebrew. The Aggadah includes everything in classical rabbinical literature that does not belong to the Halakhah* and is therefore not invested with binding legal authority. It is not easy to define it as a literary genre, since it includes both actual tales and theological or ethical treatments and scriptural exegeses based on seemingly immaterial peculiarities or insignificant details of the text, or offering a new elaboration or treatment roughly compatible with its context.

amidah: "standing position" in Hebrew. The prayer recited at each of the daily services. The *amidah* originally consisted of eighteen benedictions—hence the name *shemoneh esreh*, literally, "eighteen," which is still given to it even though a nineteenth benediction (against heretics) was later added. It undergoes changes (additions, cuts, etc.) on Shabbat*, new moons, and feast days.

Ashkenazi: Ashkenaz is the son of Gomer in the Bible (Gen. 10.1–3). Talmudic sources already identify Gomer (the son of Japheth and grandson of Noah) with Germania, and from the eleventh century, *Ashkenaz* denotes Lotharingia (the medieval Carolinigian kingdom). So-called Ashkenazi Jewish communities were initially present in northeastern France, Flanders, and the Rhineland. Persecution and migration extended the limits of the Ashkenazi cultural area, to include England, Germany, Switzerland, northern Italy, and later all of central Europe, eastern Europe, and the Americas. Ashkenazi Judaism, which was itself diverse and always maintained contact with Sephardi* communities, developed a culture that was distinctive in both literature and language (Yiddish) as well as in its ritual and religious, intellectual, and legal dimensions.

Av, Ninth of the Month of: Jews commemorate with strict fasting two catastrophes of national and religious significance on this day (in July–August), the destruction of the First Temple of Jerusalem by the Babylonians (586 BCE) and of the Second Temple (70 CE—or 68 CE according to rabbinical tradition) by the Romans.

Decalogue, the: "the ten commandments" in Greek. In Hebrew, *aseret ha-devarim* or *aseret ha-dibrot* (lit., "the ten words"). Spoken by God at the theophany on Mount Sinai and engraved on the stone Tablets of Testimony, the Decalogue is the constitutive text of the Covenant and defines the theological and ethical principles intended to guide the conduct of Israel: (1) exclusive submission to the God who led the Hebrews out of Egypt; (2) prohibition of idolatry; (3) and of blasphemy; (4) observance of Shabbat*; (5) the due honoring of one's parents; (6) prohibition of murder; (7) of adultery; (8) of theft; (9) of false testimony; and (10) of covetousness.

Essenes (adj. **Essene**): a current of ancient Judaism active between the second century BCE and the first century CE, which is known to us from Greek and Roman sources (Philo of Alexandria, Flavius Josephus, and Pliny the Elder). The Greek etymology of the word "Essenes" is controversial, and researchers have suggested many possibilities, including "pious," "silent," and "healers." The Essenes were found in various parts of the Holy Land, with a major concentration on the west bank of the Dead Sea. According to Philo, they were never very numerous (four thousand in the first century). Entry into the sect was preceded by a long probationary period; the initiate declared his vows and was then able to take part in common meals. Organized in semimonastic hierarchical communities, from which women were usually excluded, and subsisting on (mostly agricultural) manual labor, the Essenes refused to own slaves, lived an austere existence, and took great care to ensure ritual purity and scrupulous observance of the Sabbath. They zealously studied the "works of the ancients" (Josephus) and believed in the immortality of the soul and the punishment or reward of human actions. Deeming the worship at the Jerusalem Temple corrupt, they sent offerings there but refused to perform animal sacrifices. The great majority of scholars consider that the documents discovered at Qumran are of Essene origin.

Halakhah, the (fem. n., pl. *halakhot*; adj. **halakhic**): "law, legal rule" in Hebrew, from the root *hlkh*, "to go," or "to walk." Unlike the Aggadah*, which is not invested with binding legal authority, the Halakhah teaches the path Jews should follow, in accordance with the formula used by Jethro to define Moses's task: "You enjoin upon them the laws and the teachings, and make known to them the way they are to go and the practices they are to follow" (Exod. 18.20). Far from confining itself to strictly religious or ritual matters, the Halakhah covers all aspects of life and all branches of law.

Hanukkah (fem. n.): "inauguration" in Hebrew. Celebrated at the beginning of winter, Hanukkah commemorates the victory of the Maccabees in their war against the occupation and forced hellenization that the Seleucid monarch Antiochus IV Epiphanes imposed on the Holy Land (167 BCE).

hasid (masc. n., pl. *hasidim*): "good," "benevolent," "pious," or "pietist" in Hebrew. Applicable to any individual displaying special piety, it has been historically associated with three groups: (1) the *hasidim rishonim* ("early pietists") mentioned in classical rabbinical literature; (2) the *Hasidei Ashkenaz* ("German pietists") of the thirteenth century; and (3) the followers of Israel ben Eliezer (c. 1700–1760), known as Baal Shem Tov ("Master of Good Name"), founder of Hasidism in Podolia, Ukraine. A mystical mass movement, Hasidism encourages fervor in the fulfilment of God's commandments, sometimes emphasizing religious spontaneity to the detriment of study; the key thing is to reach a special state of commitment to God. This path is open to all. But he who reaches the summit and feels the divine breath on him is a being vested with exceptional moral power that he can use for the benefit of others. This is the *tsadik*, the privileged intercessor and thaumaturge. The cult of the *tsadik* and his hereditary responsibilities led to the crystallization of multiple dynasties and schools, each with its specific traditions and sometimes in rivalry with one another.

Hasidism: see *hasid*.

Haskalah, the (fem. n.): "intelligence," "discernment," or "culture" in Hebrew. Specifically refers to the Jewish Enlightenment movement that arose in the late eighteenth century in western and central Europe and spread in the second half of the nineteenth to eastern Europe, the Balkans, and North Africa. The Haskalah, which affected both the Ashkenazi* and Sephardi* worlds, was a key intermediary stage in the redefinition of Jewish identity in the age of modernization.

Kabbalah: "tradition" in Hebrew, referring especially to the mystical tradition in Judaism. It has ancient roots, as we know particularly from the so-called *heikhalot* (lit., palaces) literature, some of which goes back to the third or fourth century. A Jewish pietism influenced by Sufism developed in Spain and Egypt in the eleventh to twelfth centuries, and German pietists active between 1150 and 1250 left behind a dual theological and ethical legacy. But it was in Provence and Languedoc, and later in Spain, that Kabbalah properly so called bore its first fruits. In the second half of the thirteenth century, two Spaniards left a lasting mark on this current: Abraham Abulafia (who developed a mysticism of language leading to ecstatic experience) and Moses of León (the cultivator of a theosophical Kabbalah whose teachings can be found in the *Zohar**). From that time on, but most clearly after the expulsion of the Jews from Spain in 1492, Kabbalah never ceased to accompany, or even dominate, the development of Judaism—in the Holy Land at the flourishing Sephardi* center of Safed in the sixteenth century, but also in eastern Europe, with Hasidism*, from the eighteenth century on.

kaddish: "holy" in Aramaic. A hymn to the glory of God and call for His kingdom on earth to be established, kaddish is recited standing, with head turned to Jerusalem, in the presence of a *minyan* (the quorum of ten Jewish adult males necessary for the holding of a public service). There are four versions: (1) full kaddish, read especially by the officiating minister after the *amidah**; (2) half kaddish, an abbreviated form occurring at various points in the synagogue service; (3) the scholars' kaddish, calling for divine mercy on the teachers of Israel and their disciples, recitation of which concludes study sessions; and (4) the orphan's kaddish, dating from at least the thirteenth century, which, though making no particular allusion to death, is recited by mourners (especially the eldest son) during the first eleven months after a person's death. The form and content of kaddish reflect its antiquity, the recitation having originally been linked to preaching and study. However, it is first mentioned as an integral part of synagogue liturgy only in a text from the sixth century or thereabouts.

Kippur (masc. n.): "atonement" in Hebrew. The great fast of Yom Kippur (Day of Atonement), in early fall, ten days after the New Year (Rosh Hashanah*), lasts for twenty-five hours, from sunset to nightfall on the following day. Believers collectively affirm their repentance by devoting the whole day to mortification and prayer, making atonement and imploring God to pardon them.

kosher: "suitable, fitting" in Hebrew, that is, ritually authorized; especially, compliant with the religious provisions concerning food.

Marranos: a derogatory Spanish and Portuguese term used of Jews or descendants of Jews converted to Christianity (*conversos*). The number of *conversos* grew considerably after the Spanish persecutions of 1391, the expulsion of the Jews from Spain in 1492, and the forced conversion of Portuguese Jews in 1497. Their rapid rise fanned the hostility of original Christians, who rightly or wrongly suspected them of continuing to judaize in secret. Baptism no longer gave them sufficient immunity, and those called "New Christians," whether or not they were sincere in professing the faith, were pitilessly persecuted because of the "impurity" of their blood and driven out of various offices and institutions. Paradoxically, as the pressure of the Inquisition increased, the ferocity of the investigations, trials, and executions favored the emergence and persistence of a distinctively Marrano religion in certain milieux. Strictly speaking, these conversos gave up all visible signs of Judaism and tried to live outwardly as good Christians. Moreover, the religion they practiced secretly varied from normative Judaism: circumcision was rarely observed, funeral practices were kept only in part, while the liturgy, mainly in the vernacular, was learned by heart and communicated orally. Their acts of worship combined Jewish with Christian elements, as well as new practices that they introduced themselves. A distinctive subculture, passed on in the greatest secrecy, took shape and consolidated their group identity. Its two main components were rejection of Christian dogmas and a firm conviction of belonging to the People of Israel that worshiped one God and awaited the coming of a messiah-redeemer in the Holy Land. This strong sense of belonging, and the expectation that sustained it, were expressed in the messianic fevers that shook groups of Marranos from the sixteenth century on. Together with the persecutions, these explain the waves of emigration outside the Iberian Peninsula and the return to Judaism that took place there. Between the sixteenth and seventeenth centuries, thousands of Marranos dispersed in the Spanish and Portuguese colonies, but above all in the Netherlands, southwestern France, Germany, England, North Africa, and the East, where they sought security and the right to think freely even when they remained Catholics. Many joined the existing Sephardi* communities and returned, sometimes with difficulty, to normative Judaism.

maskil (masc. n., pl. *maskilim*): Haskalah*, or Jewish Enlightenment, supporter.

midrash (masc. n., pl. **midrashim**; adj. **midrashic**): "interpretation" in Hebrew. In its current acceptation, *midrash* denotes the classical rabbinical exegesis of Scripture as it developed in (primarily) the Holy Land and as it was preserved in an abundant literature that testifies to high-value teaching and preaching activity. Two varieties are distinguished: halakhic* Midrashim, which are of tannaitic origin and bear upon the legislative sections of the Pentateuch, and aggadic Midrashim, which comprise materials from various sources and periods grouped one after another to form a sustained commentary on the books of Scripture. Their compilation continued from the fifth to the twelfth century, at various places in the Diaspora such as Palestine, Babylonia, Byzantium, and Languedoc. But far from simply designating a well-defined corpus, the term *midrash* also refers to a hermeneutic attitude and a literary genre evident elsewhere than in the midrashic collections proper (particularly the Talmud*).

Mishnah, the (fem. n.; adj. **mishnic**): "teaching" in Hebrew. The codification of the Oral Law published by Judah the Prince around the year 200 CE, completing the work of compilation and classification begun by Rabbi Akiba and continued by Rabbi Meir. Written in a characteristic "mishnic" Hebrew (distinct from biblical Hebrew), in a style both concise and precise, the Mishnah formulates the Halakhah*, without always recording the debates and disagreements that shaped its evolution, and only rarely mentioning the scriptural texts on which it is based. The Mishnah comprises six sections or "orders" (*sedarim*), amounting to a total of sixty-three "tractates."

Passover: See Pesach.

Pesach: "Passover" in Hebrew. Celebrated in March–April, this feast is the spring festival. It was the occasion when new barley was presented as an offering at the Sanctuary. But Passover is also the commemoration of the Exodus, of Israel's deliverance from enslavement in Egypt and its constitution as a free people.

Pharisees (adj. **Pharisaic**): A current in ancient Judaism active during the Second Temple period, out of which rabbinical Judaism emerged after 70 CE. The significance of the term is uncertain. The Hebrew *perushim* could be translated as "separate," in which case it would refer to the Pharisees' concern to avoid any contact that might involve ritual impurity, or to their wish to keep apart from pagans or those within Judaism who seemed compromised with paganism. Seeing themselves as the inheritors of Ezra, affirming the equal authority of the Oral and the Written Tradition, the Pharisees placed study of the Law at the heart of their value system. They managed to get over two events that were fatal to the other currents of ancient Judaism: the definitive loss of political independence and the destruction of the Sanctuary (in 70 CE). Their successors then created a Judaism without a Temple, founding academies at Yavne and then in Galilee; they refined their hermeneutic practice and saw to the transmission and preservation of the teachings of the Oral Tradition. This work reached its peak in the compilation of the Mishnah*.

Purim: "lots" in Hebrew, from the Akkadian *puru* = "stone," used in drawing lots. Celebrated exactly a month before Passover*, Purim recalls the miraculous rescue by Esther and her cousin and tutor Mordecai of the Jews dispersed through the Persian kingdom of Ahasuerus, whose minister Haman "drew by lot" the date of their planned extermination.

pshat or *pshut* (masc. n.): "simple [meaning]" in Hebrew. This term from the technical vocabulary of biblical exegesis usually denotes the primary, obvious, and context-dependent meaning of a word or verse, mainly by contrast to the *drash*, the derivative sense developed for homiletic purposes. It may cover a variety of exegetic realities, depending on the author, period, or context.

Rosh Hashanah (masc. n.): "head of the year" in Hebrew. Denotes the Jewish New Year. This solemn occasion opens a ten-day period of contrition or *yamim nora'im* ("terrible days"), for which believers have already prepared by reciting *selihot* (penitential prayers), early each morning since the previous Sunday (among Ashkenazis*) or a month before (among Sephardis*). This festival, marking the anniversary of the creation of the world, is also known as the "Day of Judgment" and "Day of Remembrance." The hollowed ram's horn (*shofar*) that sounds during the synagogue service urges the faithful to be alert, to turn inward and return to God, to examine their actions, and to repent.

Sadducees: A political and religious current in ancient Judaism, active in Judea between the second century BCE and the first century CE. According to one hostile source, the term *Tzadokim*—the Hebrew original of "Sadducees"—denotes the followers of Zadok, a heretical disciple of Antignos of Sokho (early second century BCE), but it more probably refers back to another Zadok, the high priest under David and Solomon, whose descendants were placed in charge of the Sanctuary by Ezekiel. The Sadducees rallied the wealthiest elements of the population linked to the priestly aristocracy. Being closely tied to the ruler, however, exercising important functions in the Sanhedrin, and placing the Temple and sacrificial worship at the center of Jewish religiosity, they did not withstand the destruction of the Sanctuary in 70 and gave way to their eternal rivals, the Pharisees*. No source stemming directly from the Sadducees has survived, and the testimony on their conception of Judaism is generally hostile and written from outside (Flavius Josephus, New Testament, rabbinical literature). Stressing man's absolute freedom of choice, the Sadducees—unlike the Pharisees—believed in neither the immortality of the soul nor the resurrection of the dead. Scrupulous in applying the provisions of the Bible, they insisted that the teachings of the Oral Tradition handed down by the Pharisees had no authority. Although the original current disappeared, medieval normative Judaism continued to use *tzadokim* as a pejorative term for the Karaites, since it regarded Karaism, apart from a few variants, as no more than a resurgence of the Sadducean heresy.

Samaritans: the Hebrew term *Shomronim* appears only once in a biblical text (2 Kings 17.29), in a passage referring to the fall of the kingdom of Israel (in 722 BCE) and the deportation of a part of its population to Assyria. To repopulate the region, King Sargon brought in settlers from Babylonia to Samaria, who assimilated with the Israelites still living there, but who, though joining in the worship of Yahweh, continued to serve gods of their own (2 Kings 17.29). It was from this mixture that the Samaritans emerged. The Jews who eventually returned from exile in Babylon, in 538 BCE, would not allow them to take part in the rebuilding of the Temple in Jerusalem (Ezra 4.1–5), and an open schism resulted in constant hostility toward them. The Samaritans did not recognize themselves in this account: they called themselves *Bnei Yisrael*, "children of Israel," or *shomrim* ("guardians" or "observers" [of the truth]).

Sephardi: *Sefarad* appears only once in the Bible, in Obadiah 20, and originally refers to Sardis, the capital of Lydia, in Asia Minor. In medieval Hebrew, *Sefarad* denotes the Iberian Peninsula. Sephardi Jewish communities were therefore those living or originating in the Peninsula, before or after the expulsion from Spain in 1492. Today, by extension and by virtue of ancient cultural contacts and a relative similarity of ritual, "Sephardi" is used to refer to all or nearly all non-Ashkenazi Jews, and most especially the Jews of the Maghreb and Middle East. Judeo-Spanish in language, this Peninsular Sephardi Judaism spread after 1492 to the Balkans and, to a lesser extent, western Europe, North Africa, and the New World. Very much a numerical minority today, it has developed a rich and diverse cultural tradition of its own, which has long been held in high regard throughout the Jewish world.

Shabbat: "day of rest," or Sabbath, in Hebrew. The last day of the week in the Jewish calendar, beginning on Friday at sunset and ending at nightfall on Saturday, Shabbat commemorates the completion of the work of Creation. It is also associated with the memory of the deliverance from slavery. Rabbinical law rigorously defined and itemized the tasks that are forbidden on Shabbat. Released from his secular obligations, the observant Jew relaxes his grip on the world and uses the weekly freedom of Shabbat to tighten his links with the community, devoting himself to his family and refocusing his life on its spiritual dimension by means of prayer and study. Impressing as it does a particular rhythm on Jewish time, Shabbat is not only the day when certain activities are forbidden; it is above all the day of joy, of pleasure valued and positively sought after. It prefigures and heralds the redemption to come.

Shavuot: "weeks" in Hebrew. Observed seven weeks after Passover*, Shavuot is the harvest festival and used to be the day when the firstfruits were presented at the Temple. As a national historical festival, it is part of the sequence begun at Pesach*: it calls to mind the theophany on Mount Sinai and the giving of the Torah* to Israel.

Shema: "Hear!" in Hebrew. The first word of Deuteronomy 6.4: "Hear, O Israel! The Lord is our God, the Lord alone." The term usually refers to a set of three scriptural passages beginning with this verse that are recited daily (in application of Deut. 6.7) at the morning and evening services: (1) Deuteronomy 6.4–9; (2) Deuteronomy 11.13–21; and (3) Numbers 15.37–41 (the first two being reproduced also on the parchments of the *tefillin* and the *mezuzah*). The *Shema*, which has acquired the status of a fundamental profession of the Jewish faith, is also recited by the believer before retiring for the night and on his deathbed. The first verse appears at many other places in the liturgy.

Shemini Atzeret: "closing of the eighth day" in Hebrew. A holiday—lasting one day in the Holy Land, two in the Diaspora—immediately following Sukkot* (which lasts a total of seven days). The Diaspora celebrates *Simhat Torah* the next day (that is, the ninth), which is also a holiday. In the Holy Land, the two solemnities are celebrated on the same day (the eighth).

Sukkot: "booths" in Hebrew. Harvest festival five days after Kippur*, beginning with two holidays (one in the Holy Land). Sukkot enjoins believers to live—or at least to take their meals—for a week in a *sukkah*, a makeshift construction without a roof, covered only with tree branches and installed in a garden or on a balcony. Life in the *sukkah* calls to mind the precarious existence that Israel led in camps during the crossing of the desert.

Talmud, the (adj. **talmudic**): "teaching" in Hebrew. The commentary on the Mishnah produced by the *amora'im*, or teachers of the Palestinian and Babylonian academies. Once the Mishnah of Judah the Prince had been recognized as the supreme authority, the Jewish teachers of Palestine and Babylonia made it the principal object of their instruction. One generation of *amora'im* after another elucidated the Mishnah and attempted to identify its sources, searching all the time for an ultimate cohesion that could resolve its visible contradictions, and to develop general principles applicable to the new realities of the day. The Talmud preserves the traces of this searching and debate, and reports the commentaries of later generations of *amora'im* on the rulings of their predecessors. By no means confined to legal matters, it gives considerable space to the Aggadah* and aims to draw lessons from stories recalling the deeds and gestures of the great Jewish teachers.

There are two talmuds. The first, the Jerusalem (or, more precisely, Palestinian) Talmud, hastily compiled in Hebrew and Palestinian Judeo-Aramaic in Tiberias toward the end of the fourth century, in a context of instability and persecution, gives an account of debates in the academies of Lydda, Tiberias, Sephoras, and Caesarea. The Babylonian Talmud, written in Hebrew and Babylonian Judeo-Aramaic, testifies to the activity of the schools of Sura, Nehardea, Pumbedita, and Mahoza. It took shape gradually and acquired its definitive form through the efforts of Rav Ashi (352–427), the head of the Academy of Sura, and one of his successors, Rabina II (d. 499). Afterwards, the *savora'im* added some final touches and supplements to the text; the two major compilations of this material are known as the Franco-Rhenish and the Ibero-African. The Babylonian Talmud imposed its authority in the Jewish world, essentially because of the influence that the heads of the Sura and Pumbedita academies exerted on a large number of Jewish communities between the seventh and eleventh centuries.

targum (masc. n.; pl. **targumim**): "translation" in Hebrew. A term denoting the ancient Aramaic translations of the Bible. When Aramaic became the Jewish vernacular, first in Babylonia, then in Palestine, it became common to translate and interpret in that language the text of the Pentateuch and the passages from the books of the prophets read aloud during the synagogue service. Far from being literal, these translations often took the form of paraphrases and aggadic treatments. This ancient oral use of targum in the liturgy went hand in hand with its gradual commitment to writing. There are targumim for all the biblical books (save those partly written in Aramaic in the first place), and the same book sometimes gave rise to more than one targum. They originated both in Babylonia and in the Holy Land, differing from one another in their language as well as their method (more literal in Babylonia, more paraphrastic in Palestine). The most celebrated targum of the Pentateuch, attributed to Onkelos, is faithful to the letter of the text; it was adopted as the official Aramaic version by the Babylonian academies and underwent a final revision in the third century. The targumim were a constant source of inspiration for the great medieval commentators.

Torah, the: derived from a Hebrew verb meaning "to show, to instruct," this noun—which is often restrictively translated as "Law"—may refer either to a particular legal provision or to the entire divine message handed down to Israel through Moses. Jewish tradition thus denotes what we call the Pentateuch, the first and most venerated of the three components of the Hebrew Bible, as the "Torah of Moses." By extension, the word has come to denote the normative teachings of Judaism taken as a whole, not only the Written Torah but also the Oral Torah. In fact, nothing escapes this denomination: it includes the Bible, the Mishnah*, the Talmud*, all the forms of rabbinical literature, and so on.

yeshivah (fem. n., pl. **yeshivot**): derived from the root *yshv*, meaning "to be seated," this word in postbiblical Hebrew denotes a traditional center of higher learning. From the early nineteenth century, after two hundred years of decline, the world of the Ashkenazi *yeshivot* experienced a spectacular renaissance. Disciples of the Vilna Gaon (1720–97) created a whole network of new-style establishments in Lithuania and Belarus, the most famous being the yeshivah at Volozhyn, opened in 1802 by Hayyim ben Isaac of Volozhyn (1749–1821), which turned out most of the nineteenth-century rabbis and talmudists and became a bastion of resistance to the Haskalah*. In the wake of the *Musar* (lit., "ethics") movement initiated by Israel Lipkin Salanter (1810–83), the yeshivahs of Slobodka, Telz, Mir, and Novardok concentrated on both the intellectual and moral development of their students, and talmudic or halakhic study was associated in them with the reading of ethical works. In Poland, by contrast, the Hassidic model prevailed. At Pressburg, Hungary (now Bratislava, Slovakia), the Yeshiva founded by Moses Sofer (1762–1839) organized the struggle against Reform Judaism.

yishuv (masc. n., pl. *yishuvim*): Jewish communities in Palestine prior to the founding of the State of Israel. Jewish communities dating from before 1882, which lived mainly on charity from the Diaspora and led a strictly religious way of life, were the "old *yishuv.*" Jews who settled in the country from 1882 on, aiming to build a national Jewish society that was productive and provided for its own needs, constituted the "new *yishuv.*"

Zohar, the (adj. **zoharic**): a pseudepigraphic text in Aramaic called the *Sefer ha-Zohar* (Book of Splendor), originally ascribed to Simeon bar Yohai, a Palestinian sage of the second century, but in fact, a mystical midrash* expressing the doctrines of theosophical Kabbalah of Moses of León (1240–1305) and his school. Parts of the *Zohar* began to circulate in manuscript in the late thirteenth century. Though limited at first to Spain and Italy, its influence gradually spread eastward, reaching Byzantium and the Middle East as well as the Ashkenazi* world. Its status as a sacred text and supreme authority reached its peak in the sixteenth and seventeenth centuries. It was first printed in Mantua (1558–60) and Cremona (1559–60), and became the object of a rich exegetical literature.

Select Bibliography

This bibliography is not intended to be exhaustive. Its primary purpose is to guide readers to further discoveries. Editions of the Bible are listed separately from other texts. Entries appear in alphabetical order by author's name, then chronologically. Essays in collected volumes are generally not listed, only the titles of those collections. Also listed here, though not explicitly referenced in citations, are the titles of some books and articles that gave the author food for thought.

Bibles

La Bible. Edited by Édouard Dhorme. 2 vols. Paris: Gallimard, Bibliothèque de la Pléiade, 1959.

————. Translated by members of the French Rabbinate under the direction of Zadoc Kahn. Repr., Paris: Colbo, 1966.

————. Translated by Émile Osty with Joseph Trinquet. Paris: Seuil, 1973.

————. Translated and introduced by André Chouraqui. Repr., Paris: Desclée de Brouwer, 1989.

————. Translated by Samuel Cahen, with an introduction by Marc-Alain Ouaknine, and introduction and appendices by Gilbert Werndorfer. Paris: Les Belles Lettres, 1994.

————. *La Bible TOB*. Ecumenical translation by the Société biblique française. Repr., Paris: Cerf, 2005.

————. New translation edited by Frédéric Boyer. Repr., Paris: Bayard, 2005.

La Bible d'Alexandrie. Translation of the Greek Septuagint. 17 vols. to date. Paris: Cerf, 1986–2011.

La Bible de Jérusalem. 13th rev. expanded ed. Paris: Cerf, 1992.

La Bible. Écrits intertestamentaires. Edited by André Dupont-Sommer and Marc Philonenko. Paris: Gallimard, Bibliothèque de la Pléiade, 1987.

La Bible. Nouveau Testament. Translations, introductions, and notes by Jean Grosjean and Michel Léturmy, with Paul Gros. Paris: Gallimard, Bibliothèque de la Pléiade, 1971.

Book of Exodus. *Les Noms. Traduction de l'Exode*. Translated by Henri Meschonnic. Paris: Desclée de Brouwer, 2003.

Book of Genesis. *Au commencement. Traduction de la Genèse.* Translated by Henri Meschonnic. Paris: Desclée de Brouwer, 2002.

Book of Leviticus. *"Et il a appelé." Traduction du Lévitique.* Translated by Henri Meschonnic. Paris: Desclée de Brouwer, 2005.

Book of Numbers. *Dans le désert. Traduction du Livre des Nombres.* Translated by Henri Meschonnic. Paris: Desclée de Brouwer, 2008.

L'Ecclésiaste et son double araméen. Qohélet et son targoum. Translated from the Hebrew and Aramaic by Charles Mopsik. Lagrasse: Verdier, 1990.

Holy Bible: New Revised Standard Edition. Oxford: Oxford University Press, 1995.

The Jewish Study Bible. The Jewish Publication Society Tanakh Translation. Edited by Adele Berlin, Marc Zvi Brettler, and Michael Fishbane. New York: Oxford University Press, 2003.

Le Pentateuque . . . , accompagné du commentaire de Rachi. Bilingual Hebrew-French ed under the direction of Élie Munk. 5 vols. Repr., Paris: Fondation Samuel et Odette Lévy, 1987.

Le Pentateuque, ou les Cinq Livres de Moïse. Reproduction in full of the 1860–69 Durlacher edition. Translated and annotated by Lazare Wogue, with a preface by René Gutman and a biography of the author by Philippe Touitou. 5 vols. Jerusalem: Ohr Hamaarav, 2007.

Other Works

Aaron Ben Elijah of Nicomedia. *Keter Torah.* Repr. of the 1870 Odessa edition. [Ramla]: Ha-mo'atsa ha-artsit shel ha-yehudim ha-kara'im be-Yisra'el, 1966.

Aaron ben Joseph the Physician. *Sefer ha-Mivhar.* Kozlov, 1834.

Abramson, Glenda. "Israeli Drama and the Bible: The Stage." *AJS Review* 28, 1 (2004): 63–82.

Abravanel, Isaac. *Commentaire du récit de la Création. Genèse 1:1 à 6:8.* Translated from the Hebrew. Lagrasse: Verdier, 1999.

Aggadoth du Talmud de Babylone. La Source de Jacob. An anthology by Jacob ben Salomon Ibn Habib. Translated and annotated by Arlette Elkaïm-Sartre. Lagrasse: Verdier, 1983.

Ahad Ha-Am. *Complete Works.* 8th impression. Tel Aviv: Dvir; Jerusalem: Hotsa'ah Ivrit, 1964–65. In Hebrew.

Alter, Robert. *The Five Books of Moses.* New York: Norton, 2004.

Alter, Robert, and Frank Kermode, eds. *The Literary Guide to the Bible.* Cambridge, MA: Harvard University Press, 1987, 1990.

Armogathe, Jean-Robert, ed. *Le Grand Siècle et la Bible.* Paris: Beauchesne, 1989.

Aschkenasy, Nehama. "Introduction: Recreating the Canon." *AJS Review* 28, 1 (2004): 3–10.

Attias, Jean-Christophe. *Le commentaire biblique. Mordekhai Komtino ou l'herméneutique du dialogue.* Paris: Cerf, 1990.

———. *Isaac Abravanel, la mémoire et l'espérance.* Paris: Cerf, 1992.

———. "Traduction et commentaire." *Les Cahiers de l'Alliance israélite univer-selle*, n.s., 2 (April 1992): 10–12.

———. "Politiques du livre saint. Les usages politiques de la Bible et du Coran." In Philippe Barnet and Jean-Marie Génard, eds., *L'historien et la religion. Réflexions et ressources pour la recherche et l'enseignement en histoire du fait reli-gieux*, 21–22. Orléans: Académie d'Orléans-Tours, 2005.

———. "Comparatisme et religions du Livre: La voie étroite." In Mohammad-Ali Amir-Moezzi, Jean-Daniel Dubois, Christelle Jullien, and Florence Jullien, eds., *Pensée grecque et sagesse d'Orient. Hommage à Michel Tardieu*, 77–87. Turnhout: Brepols, 2009.

———. "Lire la Torah: La Bible dans le judaïsme." In Patrice Decormeille, Isabelle Saint-Martin, and Céline Béraud, eds., *Comprendre les faits religieux. Approches historiques et perspectives contemporaines*, 30–40. Dijon: SCÉRÉN-CRDP Bour-gogne, 2009.

———. "Des Juifs et du tragique." In Thierry Fabre, ed., *La Méditerranée. Figures du tragique*, 51–57. Rencontres d'Averroès 16. Marseilles: Éditions Parenthèses, 2010.

———. "Qu'est-ce qu'un penseur sépharade?" In Esther Benbassa, ed., *Itinérai-res sépharades. Complexité et diversité des identités*, 223–33. Paris: Presses de l'université Paris-Sorbonne, Cahiers Alberto-Benveniste, 2010.

———. *Penser le judaïsme*. 2010. Rev. ed. Paris: CNRS Éditions, 2013.

———, ed. *Les Sépharades et l'Europe. De Maïmonide à Spinoza*. Paris: Presses de l'université Paris-Sorbonne, Cahiers Alberto-Benveniste, 2012.

Attias, Jean-Christophe, and Esther Benbassa. *Israel, the Impossible Land*. Stan-ford, CA: Stanford University Press, 2003.

———. *The Jew and the Other*. Ithaca, NY: Cornell University Press, 2004.

———. *Dictionnaire des mondes juifs*. Paris: Larousse, 2008.

———. "Parcours biblique en dix tableaux." In Mark Alizart, ed., *Traces du sacré. Visitations*, 8–35. Paris: Éditions du Centre Georges-Pompidou, 2008.

Attias, Jean-Christophe, and Pierre Gisel, eds. *De la Bible à la littérature*. Geneva: Labor et Fides, 2003.

Attias, Jean-Christophe, Pierre Gisel, and Lucie Kaennel, eds. *Messianismes. Varia-tions autour d'une figure juive*. Geneva: Labor et Fides, 2000.

Auerbach, Erich. *Mimesis: The Representation of Reality in Western Literature*. Princeton, NJ: Princeton University Press, 1968.

Augustine, Saint. *Confessions*. Translated by R. S. Pine-Coffin. London: Penguin Books, 1961.

———. *Sermons sur l'Écriture 1–15A*. Translated by André Bouissou Introduction and notes by Goulven Madec. Paris: Institut d'Études augustiniennes, 1994.

———. *Sermons 1–19*. New York: New City Press, 2009.

Bach, Alice. *Women, Seduction, and Betrayal in Biblical Narrative*. Cambridge: Cambridge University Press, 1997.

———, ed. *Women in the Hebrew Bible: A Reader*. London: Routledge, 1999.

Bahya ben Asher. *Commentary on the Pentateuch.* Hebrew text edited by Hayyim Dov Shevel. 3 vols. Jerusalem: Mosad Ha-Rav Kook, [1966–68]. In Hebrew.

Bamberger, Bernard J. *The Bible: A Modern Jewish Approach.* New York: B'nai B'rith Hillel Foundations, 1955.

Banon, David. *La lecture infinie. Les voies de l'interprétation midrachique.* Paris: Seuil, 1987.

———. *Le Midrach.* Que sais-je? Paris: Presses universitaires de France, 1995.

———. "Kritik und Tradition. Jüdische und christliche Lektüre der Bibel." *Judaica* 52, 1 (March 1996): 23–39.

Barthes R., F. Bovon, F. J. Leenhardt, R. Martin-Achard, and J. Starobinski. *Analyse structurale et exégèse biblique. Essais d'interprétation.* Neuchâtel: Delachaux & Niestlé, 1971.

Baumgarten, Albert, "Knowledge of Reading and Writing, and the Polemic Surrounding Biblical Exegesis in the Second Temple Period." In Rivka Feldhai and Immanuel Etkes, eds., *Education and History: Cultural and Political Contexts,* 33–45. Jerusalem: Zalman Shazar, 5759 [1998–99]. In Hebrew.

Baumgarten, Jean. *Récits hagiographiques juifs.* Paris: Cerf, 2001.

———. *Le peuple des livres. Les ouvrages populaires dans la société ashkénaze, XVIe–XVIIIe siècle.* Paris: Albin Michel, 2010.

Beal, Timothy K., and David M. Gunn, eds. *Reading Bibles, Writing Bodies: Identity and the Book.* London: Routledge, 1997.

Bedouelle, Guy, and Bernard Roussel. *Le temps des Réformes et la Bible.* Paris: Beauchesne, 1989.

Belaval, Yvon, and Dominique Bourel, eds. *Le Siècle des Lumières et la Bible.* Paris: Beauchesne, 1986.

Benbassa, Esther. *The Jews of France: A History from Antiquity to the Present.* Princeton, NJ: Princeton University Press, 1999.

———. *Suffering as Identity: The Jewish Paradigm.* London: Verso, 2010.

Benbassa, Esther, and Aron Rodrigue. *Sephardi Jewry: A History of the Judeo-Spanish Community, 14th–20th Centuries.* Berkeley: University of California Press, 2000.

Ben-Gurion, David. *Ben-Gurion Looks at the Bible.* London: W. H. Allen, 1972.

Bensussan, Gérard. *Qu'est-ce que la philosophie juive?* Paris: Desclée de Brouwer, 2004.

Ben-Yehouda, Eliezer. *A Dream Come True.* Boulder, CO: Westview Press, 1993.

Berlin, Adele. *Biblical Poetry through Medieval Jewish Eyes.* Bloomington: Indiana University Press, 1991.

Berlin, Adele, and James Kugel. "On the Bible as Literature." *Prooftexts* 2, 3 (September 1982): 323–32.

Biale, David, ed. *Cultures of the Jews: A New History.* New York: Schocken Books, 2002.

Blumenkranz, Bernhard. "Augustin et les juifs, Augustin et le judaïsme." *Recherches augustiniennes* 1 (1958): 225–41.

Bordreuil, Pierre, and Françoise Briquel-Chatonnet. *Le temps de la Bible*. Repr., Paris: Gallimard, 2003.

Bourel, Dominique. *Moses Mendelssohn. La naissance du judaïsme moderne*. Paris: Gallimard, 2004.

Boyarin, Daniel. *Intertextuality and the Reading of Midrash*. Bloomington: Indiana University Press, 1990.

Brettler, Marc Zvi. "A Bible Commentary for Israel. Yair Zakovitch, *Ruth: Introduction and Commentary*, Mikra Leyisra'el—A Bible Commentary for Israel, Moshe Greenberg and Shmuel Ahituv, dir., Tel Aviv and Jerusalem: Am Oved and Magnes, 1990. 124 pages [Hebrew]." *Prooftexts* 13 (1993): 175–81.

Breuer, Mordekhai. "Stop Your Sons Indulging in *Higgayon*." In Yitzhak D. Gilat and Eliezer Stern, eds., *Mikhtam le-David: Homage to the Memory of Rabbi David Ochs*, 242–61. Ramat-Gan: University of Bar-Ilan, 1977. In Hebrew.

Brooks, Roger, and John J. Collins, eds. *Hebrew Bible or Old Testament*. Notre Dame, IN: University of Notre Dame Press, 1990.

Buber, Martin. *Zu einer neuen Verdeutschung der Schrift*. Cologne: Hegner, 1954. Translated by Marc de Launay, with an introduction, as *Une nouvelle traduction de la Bible* (Paris: Bayard, 2004).

———. *On the Bible: Eighteen Studies*. Edited by Nahum N. Glatzer, with an introduction by Harold Bloom. Syracuse, NY: Syracuse University Press, 2000.

Büttgen, Philippe, Alain de Libera, Irène Rozier, and Marwan Rashed, eds. *Les Grecs, les Arabes et nous. Enquête sur l'islamophobie savante*. Paris: Fayard, 2009.

Canetti, Elias. *The Human Province*. New York: Seabury Press, 1978.

Cassuto, Philippe. *Spinoza et les commentateurs juifs. Commentaire biblique au premier chapitre du* Tractatus Theologico-Politicus *de Spinoza*. Aix-en-Provence: Publications de l'université de Provence, 1998.

Castel-Bloom, Orly. *Halakim enoshiyim*. Tel Aviv: Kineret, 2002.

———. *Human Parts*. Translated by Dalya Bilu. Boston: David R. Godine, 2003.

Celsus. *On the True Doctrine: A Discourse against the Christians*. Edited and translated by R. Joseph Hoffmann. New York: Oxford University Press, 1987.

———. *Discours vrai contre les chrétiens*. Paris: Phébus, 1999.

"Le christianisme au miroir du judaïsme." Edited by Shmuel Trigano. *Pardès* 43 (2007).

Cohen, Albert. *Carnets: 1978*. Paris: Gallimard, 1979.

Cohen, Jeremy. *The Friars and the Jews: The Evolution of Medieval Anti-Judaism*. Ithaca, NY: Cornell University Press, 1982.

———. *"Be Fertile and Increase, Fill the Earth and Master It": The Ancient and Medieval Career of a Biblical Text*. Ithaca, NY: Cornell University Press, 1989.

———. *Living Letters of the Law: Ideas of the Jew in Medieval Christianity*. Berkeley: University of California Press, 1999.

———, ed. *Essential Papers on Judaism and Christianity in Conflict from Late Antiquity to the Reformation*. New York: New York University Press, 1991.

Cohen, Shaye D., and Edward L. Greenstein, eds. *The State of Jewish Studies*. Detroit: Wayne State University Press, 1990.

Costa, José. *La Bible racontée par le Midrash*. Paris: Bayard, 2004.

Dahan, Gilbert. *Les intellectuels chrétiens et les juifs au Moyen Âge*. Paris: Cerf, 1990.

———. *La polémique chrétienne contre le judaïsme au Moyen âge*. Paris: A. Michel, 1991.

———. *The Christian Polemic against the Jews in the Middle Ages*. Notre Dame, IN: University of Notre Dame Press, 1992.

———. *L'exégèse chrétienne de la Bible en Occident médiéval, XIIe–XIVe siècle*. Paris: Cerf, 1999.

Dahan, Gilbert, Gérard Nahon, and Élie Nicolas, eds. *Rashi et la culture juive en France du Nord au Moyen Âge*. Louvain: Peeters, 1997.

Darmesteter, James. *Les prophètes d'Israël*. Paris: Calmann-Lévy, 1892.

Deitcher, Howard. "Between Angels and Mere Mortals: Nechama Leibowitz's Approach to the Study of Biblical Characters." *Journal of Jewish Education* 66, 1–2 (Spring–Summer 2000): 8–22.

Delmaire, Danielle. "Les traductions de la Bible au XIXe siècle et la Bible du Rabbinat." In Jean-Claude Kuperminc and Jean-Philippe Chaumont, eds., *Zadoc Kahn. Un grand rabbin entre culture juive, affaire Dreyfus et laïcité*, 89–108. Paris: L'Éclat, 2007.

Delmaire, Jean-Marie. *De Hibbat-Zion au sionisme politique*. 2 vols. Lille: ANRT, 1990.

Díaz Esteban, Fernando, ed. *Abraham Ibn Ezra y su tiempo*. Madrid: Asociación española de orientalistas, 1990.

Douglas, Mary. *Leviticus as Literature*. Oxford: Oxford University Press, 1999.

Dubois, Marcel-Jacques. *Rencontres avec le judaïsme en Israël*. Jerusalem: Éditions de l'Olivier, 1983.

Edelman, Diana V., Philip R. Davies, Christophe Nihan, et al., eds. *Clés pour le Pentateuque. État de la recherche et thèmes fondamentaux*. Geneva: Labor et Fides, 2013.

Encyclopaedia Judaica. 2nd ed. Edited by Fred Skolnik and Michael Berenbaum. 22 vols. Detroit: Macmillan, 2007.

Eslin, Jean-Claude, and Catherine Cornu, eds. *La Bible. 2000 ans de lectures*. Paris: Desclée de Brouwer, 2003.

Fackenheim, Emil L. *The Jewish Bible after the Holocaust. A Re-reading*. Manchester: Manchester University Press, 1990.

Feiner, Shmuel. "*Sefarad* dans les représentations historiques de la *Haskalah*. Entre modernisme et conservatisme." In Esther Benbassa, ed., *Mémoires juives d'Espagne et du Portugal*, 239–59. Paris: Publisud, 1996.

———. *The Jewish Enlightenment*. Philadelphia: University of Pennsylvania Press, 2004.

Feldman, Yael S. "'A People That Dwells Alone?' Toward Subversion of the Fathers' Tongue in Israeli Women's Fiction." *AJS Review* 28, 1 (2004): 83–104.

Fellous, Sonia. *Histoire de la Bible de Moïse Arragel, Tolède, 1422–1433. Quand un rabbin interprète la Bible pour les chrétiens.* Preface by Gérard Nahon. Paris: Somogy, 2001.

Fenton, Paul B. *Philosophie et exégèse dans* Le Jardin de la métaphore *de Moïse Ibn ʿEzra, philosophe et poète andalou du XIIe siècle.* Leiden: Brill, 1997.

Finkelstein, Israel, and Neil Asher Silberman. *The Bible Unearthed: Archaeology's New Vision of Ancient Israel and the Origin of Its Sacred Texts.* New York: Free Press, 2001.

Fishbane, Michael. *The Exegetical Imagination: On Jewish Thought and Theology.* Cambridge, MA: Harvard University Press, 1998.

Fredriksen, Paula. "*Excaecati Occulta Justitia Dei*: Augustine on Jews and Judaism." *Journal of Early Christian Studies* 3, 3 (1995): 299–324.

Freud, Sigmund. *Moses and Monotheism.* New York: Knopf, 1939.

Funkenstein, Amos. *Styles of Medieval Biblical Exegesis.* Tel Aviv: Galei Tsahal, 1990. In Hebrew.

Genot-Bismuth, Jacqueline. "De l'idée juive du sens." In Gérard Nahon and Charles Touati, eds., *Hommage à Georges Vajda. Études d'histoire et de pensée juives,* 105–16. Louvain: Peeters, 1980.

Gibert, Pierre. *L'invention critique de la Bible, XVe–XVIIIe siècle.* Paris: Gallimard, 2010.

Ginzberg, Louis. *The Legends of the Jews.* 7 vols. Philadelphia: Jewish Publication Society, 1909–38; 2nd ed., 2 vols., 2003.

Gouguenheim, Sylvain, *Aristote au mont Saint-Michel. Les racines grecques de l'Europe chrétienne.* Paris: Seuil, 2008.

Goulet-Cazé, Marie-Odile, Tiziano Dorandi, Richard Goulet, and Henri Hugonnard-Roche, eds. *Le commentaire entre tradition et innovation: Actes du colloque international de l'Institut des traditions textuelles, Paris et Villejuif, 22–25 septembre 1999.* Paris: Vrin, 2000.

Graetz, Heinrich. *The Structure of Jewish History, and Other Essays.* New York: Jewish Theological Seminary of America, 1975.

Grégoire, Henri. *Essai sur la régénération physique, morale et politique des Juifs.* 1788. Paris: Flammarion, 1988. Translated as *An Essay on the Physical, Moral, and Political Reformation of the Jews* (London: C. Forster, 1790).

Greenberg, Moshe. *Studies in the Bible and Jewish Thought.* Philadelphia: Jewish Publication Society, 1995.

———, ed. *Jewish Biblical Exegesis: An Introduction.* Jerusalem: Mosad Bialik, 1983. In Hebrew.

Greenberg, Moshe, and Shmuel Ahituv, eds. *Mikra Le-Israel Commentary (Bible for Israel): Prospectus.* Tel Aviv: Am Oved, 1990. In Hebrew and English.

Gurevitch, Zali, and Gideon Aran. "On the Site (Israeli Anthropology)." *Alpayim* 4 (1991): 9–44. In Hebrew.

Guttmann, Julius. *Philosophies of Judaism: The History of Jewish Philosophy from Biblical Times to Franz Rosenzweig.* New York: Holt, Rinehart & Winston, 1964.

Hacker, Joseph R. "Superbe et désespoir. L'existence sociale et spirituelle des Juifs ibériques dans l'Empire ottoman." *Revue historique* 578 (April–June 1991): 261–93.

Hadas-Lebel, Mireille. *Massada. Histoire et symbole.* Paris: Albin Michel, 1995.

———. *Philo of Alexandria: A Thinker in the Jewish Diaspora.* Boston: Brill, 2012.

Haddad, Hassan, and Donald Wagner, eds. *All in the Name of the Bible.* Brattleboro, VT: Amana Books, 1986.

Halbertal, Moshe. *People of the Book: Canon, Meaning, and Authority.* Cambridge, MA: Harvard University Press, 1997.

Hallévi, Juda. *Le Kuzari. Apologie de la religion méprisée.* Translated and annotated by Charles Touati. Lagrasse: Verdier, n.d.

Halpérin, Jean, and Georges Levitte, eds. *La Bible au présent. Actes du XXIIᵉ colloque des intellectuels juifs de langue française.* Paris: Gallimard, 1982.

Haran, Menahem. *The Biblical Canon: Its Consolidation in the Late Second Temple Period and Form Changes in the Late Middle Ages.* Jerusalem: Mosad Bialik & Magnes, 1996. In Hebrew.

Harnack, Adolf von. *Marcion: The Gospel of the Alien God.* Translated by John E. Steely and Lyle D. Bierma. Eugene, OR: Wipf & Stock, 1990.

———. *Marcion. L'Évangile du Dieu étranger. Une monographie sur l'histoire de la fondation de l'Église catholique.* Translated by Bernard Lauret, with essays by Bernard Lauret, Guy Monnot, and Émile Poulat, and by Michel Tardieu, "Marcion depuis Harnack." Paris: Cerf, 2003.

Hartman, Geoffrey H., and Sanford Budick, eds. *Midrash and Literature.* New Haven, CT: Yale University Press, 1986.

A Harvest of Hebrew Verse. Translated by Harry S. Fein. Boston: Bruce Humphries, 1934.

Hasan-Rokem, Galit. "The Biblical Verse as Proverb and as Quotation." *Jerusalem Studies in Hebrew Literature* 1 (1981): 155–66. In Hebrew.

Hassán, Jacob M., ed. *Introducción a la Biblia de Ferrara. Actas del Simposio internacional sobre la Biblia de Ferrara (25–28 de noviembre de 1991).* Seville: Universidad de Sevilla, Sefarad 92 Comisión nacional quinto centenario & CSIC, 1994.

Hayoun, Maurice-Ruben. *L'Exégèse juive. Exégèse et philosophie dans le judaïsme.* 1992. Repr., Paris: Presses universitaires de France, Que sais-je?, 2000.

Hecht N. S., et al., eds. *An Introduction to the History and Sources of Jewish Law.* New York: Oxford University Press, 1996.

Heine, Heinrich. *The Rabbi of Bacharach.* New York: Mondial, 2008.

Heineman, Yitshak. *Paths of Haggadah.* Jerusalem: Magnes, 1970. In Hebrew.

Heschel, Abraham Joshua. *God in Search of Man: A Philosophy of Judaism.* New York: Farrar, Straus & Cudahy, 1955. Repr., New York: Octagon, 1972.

Hizkia ben Manoah. *Commentary on the Pentateuch.* Edited by Hayyim Dov Shevel. Jerusalem: Mosad Ha-Rav Kook, 1981. In Hebrew.

Holtz, Barry W. *Back to Sources: Reading the Classic Jewish Texts.* New York: Simon & Schuster, 1984.

Ibn Ezra, Abraham. *Commentaries on the Pentateuch*. Published, introduced, and annotated by Asher Weiser. 3 vols. Jerusalem: Mosad Ha-Rav Kook, 1977. In Hebrew.

Ibn Ezra, Moses. *Sefer ha-iyunim ve-ha-diyunim*. Edited and translated into Hebrew by A. S. Halkin. Jerusalem: Mekitsei Nirdamim, 1975.

Israel, Jonathan I. *A Revolution of the Mind: Radical Enlightenment and the Intellectual Origins of Modern Democracy*. Princeton, NJ: Princeton University Press, 2010.

Jacob ben Isaac Achkenazi de Janow. *Le Commentaire sur la Torah*. Translated from the Yiddish by Jean Baumgarten. Paris: Verdier, 1994.

Jacobs, Louis. *Beyond Reasonable Doubt*. Portland, OR: Littman Library of Jewish Civilization, 1999.

Japhet, Sarah, ed. *The Bible in the Mirror of Its Interpreters*. Jerusalem: Magnes, 1994. In Hebrew.

Joseph de Hamadan. *Fragment d'un commentaire sur la Genèse*. Translated from the Hebrew by Charles Mopsik. Bilingual ed. Lagrasse: Verdier, 1998.

Josephus, Flavius. *Against Apion*. Loeb Classical Library. London: Heinemann, 1976.

Jospe, Raphael. "Biblical Exegesis as a Philosophic Literary Genre: Abraham Ibn Ezra and Moses Mendelssohn." In Emil L. Fackenheim and Raphael Jospe, eds., *Jewish Philosophy and the Academy*, 48–92. Madison, WI: Fairleigh Dickinson University Press; London: Associated University Presses, 1996.

Judah ben Samuel of Regensburg. *Sefer Chasidim: The Book of the Pious*. Translated and edited by Avraham Yaakov Finkel. Northvale, NJ: Jason Aronson, 1997. French ed., *Jehudah ben Chemouel le Hassid, Sefer Hassidim. Le Guide des Hassidim*, trans. Édouard Gourévitch (Paris: Cerf, 1988).

Les Juifs présentés aux chrétiens. Textes de Léon de Modène et de Richard Simon. Edited, introduced, and annotated by Jacques Le Brun and Guy G. Stroumsa. Paris: Les Belles Lettres, 1998.

Justin Martyr, Saint. *Dialogue avec Tryphon*. Critical edition with translation and commentary by Philippe Bobichon. 2 vols. Fribourg: Academic Press, 2003.

———. *Dialogue with Trypho*. Translated by Thomas B. Falls, revised by Thomas P. Halton, and edited by Michael Slusser. Washington, DC: Catholic University of America Press, 2003.

Kamin, Sarah. *Rashi's Exegetical Categorization in Respect to the Distinction between Peshat and Derash*. Jerusalem: Magnes, 1986. In Hebrew.

Kamin, Sarah. *Jews and Christians Interpret the Bible*. Jerusalem: Magnes, 1991. In English and Hebrew.

Kaplan, Chaim A. *Scroll of Agony: The Warsaw Diary of Chaim A. Kaplan*. Repr., Bloomington: Indiana University Press, 1999.

Kaplan, Yosef. *Les nouveaux-juifs d'Amsterdam. Essais sur l'histoire sociale et intellectuelle du judaïsme séfarade au XVIIe siècle*. Translated from Spanish and English. Paris: Chandeigne, 1999.

Kark, Ruth. "Historical Sites—Perceptions and Land Purchase: The Case of Modiin, 1882–1931." *Studies in Zionism* 9, 1 (1988): 1–17.

Kaufmann, Yehezkel. *Connaître la Bible*. Paris: Presses universitaires de France, 1970.

———. *The Religion of Israel from Its Beginnings to the Babylonian Exile*. Translated and abridged by Moseh Greenberg. New York: Schocken Books, 1972.

Kessler, Edward. *Bound by the Bible: Jews, Christians and the Sacrifice of Isaac*. Cambridge: Cambridge University Press, 2004.

Knight, Douglas A., and Gene M. Tucker. *The Hebrew Bible and Its Modern Interpreters*. Chico, CA: Scholars Press, 1985.

Kogan, Mordekhai, ed. *Ben-Gurion and the Bible: A People and Its Land*. Beer-Sheva: Ben-Gurion University of the Negev Press, 1989. In Hebrew.

Kravitz, Leonard S. "Reading In and Reading Out: The Identity Symbol of Our People." *CCAR Journal*, Winter 1974: 27–46.

Kugel, James L. *The Idea of Biblical Poetry: Parallelism and Its History*. New Haven, CT: Yale University Press, 1981.

———. "On the Bible and Literary Criticism." *Prooftexts* 1, 3 (September 1981): 217–36.

———. "The 'Bible as Literature' in Late Antiquity and the Middle Ages." *Hebrew University Studies in Literature and the Arts* 11 (1983): 31–45.

———. *In Potiphar's House: The Interpretive Life of Biblical Texts*. Cambridge, MA: Harvard University Press, 1990.

———. *The Bible As It Was*, Cambridge, MA: Harvard University Press, 1997.

———. *How to Read the Bible: A Guide to Scripture, Then and Now*. New York: Free Press, 2007.

Kugel, James L., and Rowan A. Greer. *Early Biblical Interpretation*. Philadelphia: Westminster Press, 1986.

Kuperminc, Jean-Claude, and Jean-Philippe Chaumont, eds. *Zadoc Kahn. Un grand rabbin entre culture juive, affaire Dreyfus et laïcité*. Paris: L'Éclat, 2007.

LaCocque, André, and Paul Ricœur. *Thinking Biblically: Exegetical and Hermeneutical Studies*. Chicago: University of Chicago Press, 1998.

Lancaster, Irene. *Deconstructing the Bible: Abraham Ibn Ezra's Introduction to the Torah*. London: Routledge-Curzon, 2003.

Lasker, Daniel J. "Saadya Gaon on Christianity and Islam." In Daniel Frank, ed., *The Jews of Medieval Islam: Community, Society, and Identity*, 165–77. Leiden: Brill, 1995.

Lazarus-Yafeh, Hava. "Tahrif" and "Tawrat." In P. J. Bearman et al., eds., *The Encyclopaedia of Islam*, new ed. (Leiden: Brill, 2000), 10: 111a–112b and 393b–395a.

Le Boulluec, Alain. "Le problème de l'extension du canon des Écritures aux premiers siècles." *Recherches de science religieuse* 92, 1 (2004): 45–87.

Leçons des Pères du monde. Pirké Avot et Avot de Rabbi Nathan Versions A et B. Translated from the Hebrew by Éric Smilévitch. Lagrasse: Verdier, 1983. For an earlier English translation, see *Sayings of the Jewish Fathers*, trans. Joseph I. Gorfunkle (New York: Bloch, 1923).

Legendre, Pierre, ed. *"Ils seront deux en une seule chair."* *Scénographie du couple humain dans le texte occidental.* Brussels: Émile van Balberghe, 2004.

"The Letter of Aristaeus." In *The Apocrypha and Pseudepigrapha of the Old Testament.* Oxford: Clarendon Press, 1913.

Levenson, Alan T. *The Making of the Modern Jewish Bible: How Scholars in Germany, Israel and America Transformed an Ancient Text.* Lanham, MD: Rowman & Littlefield, 2011.

Lévinas, Emmanuel. *Difficult Freedom: Essays on Judaism.* Baltimore, MD: Johns Hopkins University Press, 1990.

———. *Outside the Subject.* Stanford, CA: Stanford University Press, 1994.

Libera, Alain de. *La philosophie médiévale.* Paris: Presses universitaires de France, 1993.

Libera, Alain de, and Émilie Zum Blum, eds. *Celui qui est—Interprétations juives et chrétiennes d'Exode 3,14.* Paris: Cerf, 1986.

Lobrichon, Guy. *La Bible au Moyen Âge.* Paris: Picard, 2003.

Loeb, Isidore. "La controverse de 1240 sur le Talmud." *Revue des études juives* 1 (1880): 247–61; 2 (1881): 248–70; 3 (1881): 39–57.

Macchi, Jean-Daniel, et al., eds. *Les recueils prophétiques de la Bible. Origines, milieux, et contexte proche-oriental.* Geneva: Labor et Fides, 2012.

Magonet, Jonathan. "The Biblical Roots of Jewish Identity: Exploring the Relativity of Exegesis." *Journal for the Study of the Old Testament* 54 (June 1992): 3–24.

———. "How Do Jews Interpret the Bible Today?" *Journal for the Study of the Old Testament* 66 (June 1995): 3–27.

Maimonides, Moses. *Le Livre de la connaissance.* Translated from the Hebrew and annotated by Valentin Nikiprowetzky and André Zaoui. Introductory Essay by Salomon Pinès. Paris: Presses universitaires de France, 1961.

———. *The Guide of the Perplexed.* Translated with an introduction and notes by Shlomo Pines. Introductory Essay by Leo Strauss. 2 vols. Chicago: Chicago University Press, 1963.

———. *The Book of Knowledge.* Translated from the Hebrew by H. M. Russell and J. Weinberg. Edinburgh: Royal College of Physicians of Edinburgh, 1981.

Manor, Dalia. "Biblical Zionism in Bezalel Art." *Israel Studies* 6, 1 (Spring 2001): 55–75.

Martin, Hervé. *Le métier de prédicateur à la fin du Moyen Âge (1350–1520).* Paris: Cerf, 1988.

Masalha, Nur. *The Bible and Zionism: Invented Traditions, Archaeology and Post-Colonialism in Palestine-Israel.* London: Zed Books, 2007.

Me'am Lo'ez. El gran comentario bíblico sefardí. Vol. 1, pt. 2 [Genesis 25. 16 to 50.26]. Edited and transliterated by David Gonzalo Maeso and Pascual Pascual Recuero. Madrid: Editorial Gredos, 1970.

Méchoulan, Henry. *Être juif à Amsterdam au temps de Spinoza.* Paris: Albin Michel, 1991.

Melammed, Ezra-Zion. *The Commentators on the Bible*. Rev. ed. 2 vols. Jerusalem: Magnes and Hebrew University of Jerusalem, 1978. In Hebrew.

Merklein, Helmut, et al., eds. *Bibel in jüdischer und christlicher Tradition. Festschrift für Johann Maier zum 60. Geburtstag*. Frankfurt a/M: Anton Hain, 1993.

Meschonnic, Henri. *Un coup de Bible dans la philosophie*. Paris: Bayard, 2004.

Meyuhas Ginio, Alisa. "La Bible populaire sépharade comme mémoire de la vie juive." In Esther Benbassa, ed., *Les Sépharades. Histoire et culture du Moyen Âge à nos jours*, 183–200. Paris: Presses de l'université Paris-Sorbonne, Cahiers Alberto-Benveniste, 2011.

Millet, Olivier, and Philippe Robert. *Culture biblique*. Paris: Presses universitaires de France, 2001.

Modena, Leon of [Yehudah Aryeh Mi-Modena]. *Magen wa-hereb* [Shield and Sword]. Translated by Allen Howard Podet. Lewiston, NY: E. Mellen Press, 1983, 2001.

———. *Le Bouclier et la targe. Une polémique sur l'identité juive au XVIIe siècle*. Introduced, translated, and annotated by Jean-Pierre Osier. Paris: Centre d'études Don Isaac Abravanel & UISF, 1980.

Mondésert, Claude, ed. *Le monde grec ancien et la Bible*. Paris: Beauchesne, 1984.

Mopsik, Charles. *Cabale et cabalistes*. Repr., Paris: Albin Michel, 2003.

Mulder, Martin Jan, and Harry Sysling, eds. *Mikra: Text, Translation, Reading and Interpretation of the Hebrew Bible in Ancient Judaism and Early Christianity*. Philadelphia: Fortress Press, 1988.

Munk, Salomon. *Mélanges de philosophie juive et arabe*. Repr., Paris: Vrin, 1955.

Nahmanides, Rabbi Moses (Ramban). *Commentary on the Pentateuch*. Edited by Hayyim Dov Shevel. 2 vols. Jerusalem: Mosad Ha-Rav Kook, [1959 or 1960]. In Hebrew.

———. *La dispute de Barcelone*. Translated from the Hebrew by Éric Smilévitch. Lagrasse: Verdier, 1984.

Neher, André. *Moses and the Vocation of the Jewish People*. New York: Harper Torchbooks, 1959.

———. *The Exile of the Word: From the Silence of the Bible to the Silence of Auschwitz*. Philadelphia: Jewish Publication Society of America, 1981.

———. *L'identité juive*. Repr., Paris: Payot, 1994.

Nemoy, Leon. *Karaite Anthology*. New Haven, CT: Yale University Press, 1952.

Neusner, Jacob. *Judaism and Scripture: The Evidence of Leviticus Rabbah*. Chicago: University of Chicago Press, 1986.

———. *Formative Judaism: Religious, Historical, and Literary Studies*. Atlanta: Scholars Press, 1989.

Niehoff, Maren Ruth. "The Buber-Rosenzweig Translation of the Bible within Jewish-German Tradition." *Journal of Jewish Studies* 44 (1993): 258–79.

Nordmann, Sophie. "Hermann Cohen et le sionisme." *Études germaniques* 59, 2 (2004): 327–42.

Oshry, Ephraim. *The Annihilation of Lithuanian Jewry*. New York: Judaica Press, 1995.

Osier, Jean-Pierre. *D'Uriel da Costa à Spinoza*. Paris: Berg International, 1983.

Pagis, Dan. *Secular Poetry and Poetic Art in Moses Ibn Ezra and His Contemporaries*. Jerusalem: Mossad Bialik, 1970. In Hebrew.

Pardes, Ilana. *Countertraditions in the Bible: A Feminist Approach*. 1992. Repr., Cambridge, MA: Harvard University Press, 1993.

Patlagean, Évelyne and Alain Le Boulluec, eds. *Les retours aux Écritures. Fondamentalismes présents et passés*. Louvain: Peeters, 1993.

Paul, André. *Le Judaïsme ancien et la Bible*. Paris: Desclée, 1987.

———. "Les 'Écritures' dans la société juive au temps de Jésus." *Recherches de science religieuse* 89, 1 (January–March 2001): 13–42.

Pelikan, Jaroslav. *Whose Bible Is It? A History of the Scriptures through the Ages*. New York: Viking, 2004. Translated by Denis-Armand Canal as *À qui appartient la Bible? Le Livre des livres à travers les âges* (Paris: CNRS Éditions, 2010).

Perrin, Michel-Yves. "Christianiser la culture." In Jean-Robert Armogathe, Pascal Montaubin, and Michel-Yves Perrin, eds., *Histoire générale du christianisme*, vol. 1: *Des origines au XVe siècle*, 479–515. Paris: Presses universitaires de France, 2010.

Philo of Alexandria. *De vita Mosis*. Greek text with French translation by Roger Arnaldez, Claude Mondésert, Jean Pouilloux, and Pierre Savinel. Paris: Cerf, 1967.

Polliack, Meira, ed. *Karaite Judaism: A Guide to Its History and Literary Sources*. Leiden: Brill, 2003.

Pontrémoli, Rafael Hiya. *Me'am Lo'ez, Livre d'Esther*. Translated from the Ladino by Albert Benveniste. Lagrasse: Verdier, 1997.

Profiat, Duran. *Maase Efod*. Edited by Jonathan Friedländer and Jakob Kohn. Vienna, 1865. In Hebrew.

Propp, William Henry, et al., eds. *The Hebrew Bible and Its Interpreters*. Winona Lake, IN: Eisenbrauns, 1990.

Pury, Albert de, and Thomas Römer, eds. *Le Pentateuque en question*. Geneva: Labor et Fides, 1989.

Pury, Albert de, Thomas Römer, and Jean-Daniel Macchi, eds. *Israël construit son histoire. L'historiographie deutéronomiste à la lumière des recherches récentes*. Geneva: Labor et Fides, 1996.

"Quand les femmes lisent la Bible." Edited by Janine Elkouby and Sonia Sarah Lipsyc. *Pardès* 35 (2003).

Rabin, Hayyim. "Bible Study and Hebrew Language Research." *Ha-Universita* 14, 1 (May 1968): 13–16. In Hebrew.

Rashi [Shlomo Yitzchaki]. *Der Kommentar des Solomo b. Isak über den Pentateuch*. Critical edition of the Hebrew text by Abraham Berliner. Frankfurt a/M: J. Kauffmann, 1905. In Hebrew.

———. *Commentaries on the Pentateuch*. New York: Norton, 1970.

Ravitzky, Aviezer. *History and Faith. Studies in Jewish Philosophy.* Amsterdam: J. C. Gieben, 1996.

Reif, Stefan C. *Judaism and Hebrew Prayer. New Perspectives on Jewish Liturgical History.* Cambridge: Cambridge University Press, 1993.

"La religion comme science. La *Wissenschaft des Judentums.*" Edited by Jean Baumgarten and Shmuel Trigano. Special issue, *Pardès* (1994): 19–20.

Rendtorff, Rolf. "The Jewish Bible and Its Anti-Jewish Interpretation." *Christian Jewish Relations* 16, 1 (March 1983): 1–20.

Riché, Pierre, and Guy Lobrichon, eds. *Le Moyen Âge et la Bible.* Paris: Beauchesne, 1984.

Rodrigue, Aron. "Rearticulations of French Jewish Identities after the Dreyfus Affair." *Jewish Social Studies*, n.s., 2, 3 (Spring–Summer 1996): 1–24.

Rosenthal, Erwin I. J. "The Study of the Bible in Medieval Judaism." In *The Cambridge History of the Bible*, vol. 2: *The West from the Fathers to the Reformation*, 252–79. Cambridge: Cambridge University Press, 1969.

Rosenthal, Judah M. "The Talmud on Trial. The Disputation at Paris in the Year 1240." *Jewish Quarterly Review*, n.s., 47 (1956): 58–76, 145–69.

Rubin-Dorsky, Jeffrey, and Shelley Fisher Fishkin, eds. *People of the Book. Thirty Scholars Reflect on Their Jewish Identity.* Madison: University of Wisconsin Press, 1996.

Ruth. With an introduction and commentary by Yair Zakovitz. Tel Aviv: Am Oved and Magnes, 1990. In Hebrew.

Sand, Shlomo. *The Invention of the Jewish People.* London: Verso, 2008.

Saperstein, Marc. *Jewish Preaching 1200–1800: An Anthology.* New Haven, CT: Yale University Press, 1989.

Sapir Abulafia, Anna. *Christians and Jews in the Twelfth-Century Renaissance.* London: Routledge, 1995.

Sarna, Nahum M. "The Modern Study of the Bible in the Framework of Jewish Studies." *Proceedings of the Eighth World Congress of Jewish Studies, Panel Sessions, Bible Studies and Hebrew Language*, 19–27. Jerusalem: World Union of Jewish Studies & Perry Foundation for Biblical Research, 1983.

Schechter S[olomon]. "Higher Criticism—Higher Antisemitism." In id., *Seminary Addresses and Other Papers*, 35–39. Cincinnati: Ark, 1915.

Schniedewind, William M. *How the Bible Became a Book: The Textualization of Ancient Israel.* New York: Cambridge University Press, 2004.

Scholem, Gershom. "The Science of Judaism—Then and Now" (1959). In id., *The Messianic Idea in Judaism and Other Essays on Jewish Spirituality*, 304–13. New York: Schocken Books, 1971.

———. *On the Kabbalah and Its Symbolism.* Repr., New York: Schocken Books, 1996.

Schoneveld, Jacobus. *The Bible in Israeli Education: A Study of Approaches to the Hebrew Bible and Its Teaching in Israeli Educational Literature.* Amsterdam: Van Gorcum, 1976.

Schorsch, Ismar. "The Myth of Sephardic Supremacy." *Leo Baeck Institute Year Book* 34 (1989): 47–66.

Schwartz, Howard. *Reimagining the Bible: The Storytelling of the Rabbis.* New York: Oxford University Press, 1998.

Schwarzfuchs, Simon. *Rashi de Troyes.* Paris: Albin Michel, 1991.

Sed-Rajna, Gabrielle, ed. *Rashi, 1040–1990. Hommage à Ephraïm E. Urbach.* Paris: Cerf, 1993.

Segal, Moshe Zvi. *Biblical Exegesis.* Jerusalem: Kiriat Sefer, 1971. In Hebrew.

Sephiha, Haïm Vidal. *Le Ladino, judéo-espagnol calque. Deutéronome, versions de Constantinople, 1547, et de Ferrare, 1553.* Paris: Institut d'études hispaniques, 1973.

Shaked, Gershon. "Modern Midrash: The Biblical Canon and Modern Literature." *AJS Review* 28, 1 (2004): 43–62.

Shapira, Anita. *Land and Power: The Zionist Resort to Force, 1881–1948.* 1992. Repr., Stanford, CA: Stanford University Press, 1999.

———. "The Bible and Israeli Identity." *AJS Review* 28, 1 (2004): 11–42.

———. *The Bible and Israeli Identity.* Jerusalem: Magnes, 2005. In Hebrew.

Shatzmiller, Joseph. *La deuxième controverse de Paris. Un chapitre dans la polémique entre chrétiens et juifs au Moyen Âge.* Louvain: Peeters, 1994.

Shavit, Yaacov, and Erai Mordechai. *The Hebrew Bible Reborn: From Holy Scripture to the Book of Books.* Berlin: Walter de Gruyter, 2007.

Sierra, Sergio J., ed. *La lettura ebraica delle Scritture.* Rev. ed., Bologna: EDB, 1996.

Simon, Marcel. *Verus Israel: A Study of the Relations Between Christians and Jews in the Roman Empire (AD 135–425).* New York: Littman Library, 1986.

Simon, Uriel. *Four Approaches to the Book of Psalms: From Saadia Gaon to Abraham Ibn Ezra.* Albany: State University of New York Press, 1991.

———. "The Status of the Bible in Israeli Society: From National Midrash to Existential *Pshat.*" *Yeri'ot* 1 (1999): 14. In Hebrew.

———, ed. *The Bible and Us.* Tel Aviv: Dvir, 1979. In Hebrew.

Simon-Nahum, Perrine. *La Cité investie. La "science du judaïsme" français et la République.* Paris: Cerf, 1991.

———. "Samuel Cahen entre Lumières et science du judaïsme." *Romantisme* 3, 125 (2004): 27–42.

———. "Continuité ou rupture? Des précurseurs aux fondateurs de l'Union libérale israélite." *Archives juives* 2, 40 (2007): 23–42.

Sirat, Colette. *La philosophie juive médiévale en pays de chrétienté.* Paris: Presses du CNRS, 1988.

———. *La philosophie juive médiévale en terre d'Islam.* Paris: Presses du CNRS, 1988.

———. *Hebrew Manuscripts of the Middle Ages.* New York: Cambridge University Press, 2002.

Sirat, Colette, Michèle Dukan, Claude Heymann, Carsten L. Wilke, and Monique Zerdoun. *La conception du livre chez les piétistes ashkénazes au Moyen Âge.* Geneva: Droz, 1996.

Sirat, René-Samuel, ed. *Héritages de Rachi.* Paris: L'Éclat, 2006.

Sokolow, Moshe. "The Bible and Religious Education: A Multi-Dimensional Approach." *Studies in Jewish Education* 4 (1989): 42–62.

Sorkin, David. *Moses Mendelssohn and the Religious Enlightenment.* Berkeley: University of California Press, 1996.

Spinoza, Benedictus de [Baruch]. *Hebrew Grammar (Compendium grammatices linguae hebraeae).* Edited and translated by Maurice J. Bloom. New York: Philosophical Library, 1962.

———. *A Theologico-Political Treatise.* Translated by R. H. M. Elwes. New York: Dover, 1951.

Steiner, George. "A Preface to the Hebrew Bible." In id., *No Passion Spent: Essays 1978–1995,* 40–87. New Haven, CT: Yale University Press, 1996.

Strauss, Janine. *La Haskalah. Les débuts de la littérature hébraïque moderne.* Nancy: Presses universitaires de Nancy, 1989.

Strauss, Léo. "Jerusalem and Athens: Some Introductory Reflections." In id., *Studies in Platonic Political Philosophy,* ed. Thomas L. Pangle, 147–73. Chicago: University of Chicago Press, 1983.

Sutcliffe, Adam. *Judaism and Enlightenment.* New York: Cambridge University Press, 2003.

Talmage, Frank. *David Kimhi: The Man and the Commentaries.* Cambridge, MA: Harvard University Press, 1975.

———. "Keep Your Sons from Scripture: The Bible in Medieval Jewish Scholarship and Spirituality." In id., *Apples of Gold in Settings of Silver,* 151–71. Toronto: Pontifical Institute of Mediaeval Studies, 1999.

Tannenbaum, Avraham J., "Jewish Texts, Education and Identity: Inseparable." *Jewish Education* 57, 2–4 (Spring–Winter 1989): 7–12, 26.

Tardieu, Michel, ed. *Les règles de l'interprétation.* Paris: Cerf, 1987.

———, ed. *La formation des canons scripturaires.* Paris: Cerf, 1993.

Tawil, Hayim, and Bernard Schneider. *Crown of Aleppo: The Mystery of the Oldest Hebrew Bible Codex.* Philadelphia: Jewish Publication Society, 2010.

Tchernichovsky, Sha'ul. *Poems.* Tel Aviv: Dvir, n.d. In Hebrew.

Touati, Charles. "La controverse de 1303–1306 autour des études philosophiques et scientifiques." *Revue des études juives* 127, 1 (January–March 1968): 21–37.

———. *La pensée philosophique et théologique de Gersonide*: Paris, Minuit, 1973.

———. *Prophètes, talmudistes, philosophes.* Paris: Cerf, 1990.

Tov, Emmanuel. *Textual Criticism of the Hebrew Bible.* Minneapolis: Fortress Press, Van Gorcum, 1992.

Trautmann-Waller, Céline. *Philologie allemande et tradition juive. Le parcours intellectuel de Leopold Zunz.* Paris: Cerf, 1998.

Trevisan-Semi, Emanuela. *Les caraïtes. Un autre judaïsme.* Translated from the Italian by Simone Kauders. Paris: Albin Michel, 1992.

Trigano, Shmuel, ed. *La société juive à travers l'histoire.* 4 vols. Paris: Fayard, 1992–93.

Twersky, Isadore. "Joseph ibn Kaspi: Portrait of a Medieval Jewish Intellectual." In id., ed., *Studies in Medieval Jewish History and Literature,* 1: 239–42. Cambridge, MA: Harvard University Press, 1979.

———. *Introduction to the Code of Maïmonides*. New Haven: Yale University Press, 1980.

———, ed. *Rabbi Moses Nahmanides (Ramban): Explorations in His Religious and Literary Virtuosity*. Cambridge, MA: Harvard University Press, 1983.

Twersky, Isadore, and Jay M. Harris, eds. *Rabbi Abraham Ibn Ezra: Studies in the Writings of a Twelfth-Century Polymath*. Cambridge, MA: Harvard University Center for Jewish Studies, 1993.

Urbach, Ephraim E. *The Sages: Their Concepts and Beliefs*. Translated from the Hebrew by Israel Abrahams. Cambridge, MA: Harvard University Press, 1987.

Vajda, Georges. *Introduction à la pensée juive du Moyen Âge*. Paris: Vrin, 1947.

———. *Sages et penseurs sépharades de Bagdad à Cordoue*. Paris: Cerf, 1989.

Vermes, Geza. "Bible and Midrash: Early Old Testament Exegesis." In id., *Post-Biblical Jewish Studies*, 37–49. Leiden: Brill, 1975.

Weiler, Gershon. *Jewish Theocracy*. Leiden: Brill, 1988.

Weiss, Halivni David. *Pshat and Derash: Plain and Applied Meaning in Rabbinic Exegesis*. New York: Oxford University Press, 1991.

Werblowsky, J. Zwi. "Israël et Eretz Israel." *Les Temps modernes*, 253 bis (1967): 371–93.

Wieseltier, Leon. *Kaddish*. New York: Knopf, 1998.

Wilke, Carsten Lorenz. "Un judaïsme clandestin dans la France du XVIIe siècle. Un rite au rythme de l'imprimerie." In Esther Benbassa, ed., *Transmission et passages en monde juif*, 281–311. Paris: Publisud, 1997.

The Wisdom of the Zohar: An Anthology of Texts. Edited and presented by Isaiah Tishby. Translated into English by David Goldstein. 3 vols. Oxford: Oxford University Press, 1989.

Yardeni, Myriam. *Anti-Jewish Mentalities in Early Modern Europe*. Lanham, MD: University Press of America, 1990.

Yehoshua, A. B. "From Myth to History." *AJS Review* 28, 1 (2004): 205–12.

Yerushalmi, Yosef Hayim. *Freud's Moses: Judaism Terminable and Interminable*. New Haven, CT: Yale University Press, 1991.

———. *Zakhor: Jewish History and Jewish Memory*. 1982. New ed. Seattle: University of Washington Press, 1996.

Yovel, Yirmiyahu. *The Other Within: The Marranos: Split Identity and Emerging Modernity*. Princeton, NJ: Princeton University Press, 2009.

Yuval, Israel Jacob. *Two Nations in Your Womb: Perceptions of Jews and Christians in Late Antiquity and the Middle Ages*. Translated by Barbara Harshav and Jonathan Chipman. Berkeley: University of California Press, 2006.

Yuval, Israël Yaacov. "La croisée des chemins: La *Hagadah* de la Pâque juive et les Pâques chrétiennes." In Florence Heymann and Michel Abitbol, eds., *L'historiographie israélienne aujourd'hui*, 64–74. Paris: CNRS Éditions, 1998.

Zafrani, Haim, and André Caquot. *L'Ecclésiaste et son commentaire. Le livre de l'ascèse: La version arabe de la Bible de Sa'adya Gaon*. Paris: Maisonneuve & Larose, 1989.

Zakovitz, Yair. "A Secular-Humanist View." *Jewish Bible Quarterly* 21, 4 (1993): 218–25.

Zipperstein, Steven J. *Elusive Prophet: Ahad Ha-Am and the Origins of Zionism.* Berkeley: University of California Press, 1993.

The Zohar. Translation and commentary by Daniel C. Matt. Pritzker Edition. 12 vols. Stanford, CA: Stanford University Press, 2003–.

Le Zohar. Genèse. Translated, annotated, and presented by Charles Mopsik. 4 vols. Lagrasse: Verdier, 1981–96.

———. *Livre de Ruth.* translated, annotated, and presented by Charles Mopsik. Lagrasse: Verdier, 1987;

———. *Cantique des cantiques.* Translated, annotated, and presented by Charles Mopsik. Lagrasse: Verdier, 1999,

———. *Lamentations.* Translated, annotated, and presented by Charles Mopsik. Lagrasse: Verdier, 2000.

Index